.T

Kansas City

The Big City Food Biography Series
as part of the Rowman & Littlefield Studies in Food and Gastronomy

General Editor: Ken Albala, Professor of History, University of the Pacific
(kalbala@pacific.edu)
Rowman & Littlefield Executive Editor: Suzanne Staszak-Silva (sstaszak
-silva@rowman.com)

Food helps define the cultural identity of cities in much the same way as the distinctive architecture and famous personalities. Great cities have one-of-a-kind food cultures, offering the essence of the multitudes who have immigrated there and shaped foodways through time. The Big City Food Biography series focuses on those metropolises celebrated as culinary destinations, with their iconic dishes, ethnic neighborhoods, markets, restaurants, and chefs. Guidebooks to cities abound, but these are real biographies that will satisfy readers' desire to know the full food culture of a city. Each narrative volume, devoted to a different city, explains the history, the natural resources, and the people that make that city's food culture unique. Each biography also looks at the markets, historic restaurants, signature dishes, and great cookbooks that are part of the city's gastronomic makeup.

New Orleans: A Food Biography, by Elizabeth M. Williams (2012)

San Francisco: A Food Biography, by Erica J. Peters (2013)

New York City: A Food Biography, by Andrew F. Smith (2013)

Portland: A Food Biography, by Heather Arndt Anderson (2014)

Chicago: A Food Biography, by Daniel Block and Howard B. Rosing (2015)

Kansas City

A Food Biography

Andrea Broomfield

ROWMAN & LITTLEFIELD
Lanham • Boulder • New York • London

Published by Rowman & Littlefield
A wholly owned subsidiary of
The Rowman & Littlefield Publishing Group, Inc.
4501 Forbes Boulevard, Suite 200, Lanham, Maryland 20706
www.rowman.com

Unit A, Whitacre Mews, 26-34 Stannary Street, London SE11 4AB

British Library Cataloguing in Publication Information Available

Library of Congress Cataloging-in-Publication Data

Broomfield, Andrea, author.
Kansas City : a food biography / Andrea L. Broomfield.
pages cm. — (The big city food biography series)
Includes bibliographical references and index.
ISBN 978-1-4422-3288-4 (cloth : alk. paper) — ISBN 978-1-4422-3289-1
(electronic)
1. Food—Missouri—Kansas City—History. 2. Cooking, American—
Midwestern style—History. 3. Food industry and trade—Missouri—Kansas
City—History. 4. Kansas City (Mo.) —History. I. Title.
TX360.U63K364 2016
641.59778'411—dc23   2015029520

Printed in the United States of America

For Charles S. Broomfield, Native Son

Contents

Preface

Kansas City

The Nation's Hospitality Crossroads

Visitors to Kansas City should come ready to be welcomed, and if they are staying with a host, they can bet that their welcome will involve food, and lots of it. An excursion to the Nelson-Atkins Museum of Art, the National World War I Memorial, and the Country Club Plaza might also come into play, but meals in the home and out on the town will most likely take priority. Fall visitors at a Chiefs football game may not remember much about the game, but they won't forget the tailgate party, where the Truman Sports Complex parking lot will be crammed with upwards of 25,000 vehicles that function in some cases as complete kitchens. Charcoal grills sit alongside 560-pound PitBoss smokers, and many fans will also have a three-crock slow cooker featuring the family chili recipe and other decadent cold-weather foods. Roasted green chili and tomato queso, jambalaya loaded with shrimp and Andouille sausage, and gooey Crock-Pot brownies often accompany the barbecued ribs, briskets, and brats. It might take strangers ten minutes of wandering around in that thick hickory haze before they are invited over to partake of what is on offer. Why is this? After all, most cities market hospitality and great food to visitors, and many cities start the football game with a tailgate party, but Kansas City is special. Its very existence was founded on food and hospitality. At no time in the city's past have the two items been separate from one another.

Geography has a lot to do with this fact. Located roughly in the center of the contiguous United States and at the confluence of the Kaw (Kansas) and Missouri Rivers, Kansas City is a crossroads, historically a place that people came through on their way to somewhere else. Prior to the Civil War, Kansas City was a main jumping-off place for the overland journey west, and while here, traders and pioneers stocked up on provisions. They also wanted to rest and eat a couple of final well-prepared meals before setting out.

After the Civil War, Kansas City's location codified its identity as a hospitality crossroads and provisions center, but this time on an industrial scale. Between 1870 and 1890, Kansas City became the nation's second-largest processor of grain and meat after Chicago. As home to twelve rail trunk lines, millions of travelers came through on their way elsewhere, but now they were pouring in by train instead of by steamboat. In the 1920s, a train arrived to Union Station every eight minutes. Meanwhile, the rails brought in livestock and wheat from Kansas's plains and beyond, and they left Kansas City as meat and flour. While Kansas Citians worked in all manner of occupations, unusually high numbers of them worked in provisions and/or catering, and in all respects, their labor forged Kansas City's culinary habit of looking after the needs of others.

However, the same geography that helped to shape Kansas City's culinary identity is also admittedly confusing to nonresidents. There are two Kansas Cities: Kansas City, Missouri, with a population of roughly 460,000, and Kansas City, Kansas, with a population of roughly 146,000. When the area was first settled in the 1820s, there was no "Kansas" at all. The Native American tribe, the Kansa, or Kaw, were the main inhabitants, although their villages were nearby the larger settlements of their allies and linguistic kin, the Osage. When John Calvin McCoy and thirteen investors bought a riverfront farm on the Missouri River in 1837, they organized a company to lay out the Town of Kansas. At this time, the state of Kansas did not exist. On Missouri's western border lay Indian Territory, where Northeast tribes were forcibly relocated by the U.S. government.

In 1853, the Missouri legislature approved a charter for a municipal government for the Town of Kansas and changed its name to the City of Kansas. Shortly thereafter, confusion set in when the U.S. Congress organized what had been Indian Territory into Kansas and Nebraska Territories. When Kansas became the thirty-fourth state of the Union on January 29, 1861, three months before the Civil War erupted, the City of Kansas was already an important crossroads, discussed in numerous emigrant and pioneer guides as the best place to outfit before going west. The idea of changing its name in this time of chaos and uncertainty was likely not on the minds of officials.

In spite of the tragedy that resulted from "Bleeding Kansas" (what residents refer to as the Border War) and the Civil War that followed, Kansas City nonetheless prospered, and the state line in Kansas City itself often served only to annoy the entrepreneurs and planners who were building the industries. This fact is essential when considering Kansas City's food biography. Industrialists might have harbored passionate opinions when it came to slavery, states' rights, and free soil, but repeatedly, ideological concerns were secondary to those of economic opportunity and expediency. As a result, stockyards, rail lines, packinghouses, and mills began to crowd into the bottomland, and Civil War grievances were thrust aside.

The West Bottoms, as this industrial area was called, started on the Kansas side of the line and moved into Missouri, forming a wide crescent that followed the contours of Kawsmouth, or the confluence of the Kaw and Missouri Rivers. Kansas City, Kansas, was platted in 1868, and it was formally incorporated in 1872. It coexisted with Wyandotte, Armourdale, Riverview, Armstrong, and other small communities, most of which were identified with meatpacking, the railroad, and related industries. In 1886, these towns consolidated and became one: Kansas City, Kansas. Meanwhile, on the Missouri side, the City of Kansas name again changed in 1889 to Kansas City, Missouri. Kansas City, Missouri, is the Jackson County seat along with Independence; Kansas City, Kansas, is the Wyandotte County seat. Together, these two counties make up a considerable portion of the Greater Kansas City Metropolitan Area, or the KC Metro, as it is called by locals. This entity subsumes the border and encompasses not only Jackson County on the Missouri side, but also Clay and Platte Counties. On the Kansas side, Johnson and portions of Miami and Leavenworth Counties join with Wyandotte to complete the Metro and put the Metro population at around 2.34 million.

Regarding cuisine, the two Kansas Cities share many affinities, particularly when one takes into account their provisions and crossroads economies. To prosper, the cities had to cooperate and work toward common goals, especially for transportation, labor, and municipal governance. Furthermore, suburban growth spreads far beyond each city's urban core, making the two downtowns actually closer together psychologically and physically than the farthest-flung suburbs that surround them, again irrespective of a state line.

For matters of logistics, "Kansas City" in this book will usually refer to the bigger Kansas City, Missouri; at numerous times, however, it will also take into account the Kansas City Metro; Kansas City, Kansas; and parts of the Metro that were at one time distinct entities, particularly before freeways altered our sense of distance: Independence and Liberty, Missouri; and Overland Park and Olathe, Kansas, for example. In some instances, this study will also make much of how the state line did affect the two cities' culinary identities, and why that distinction matters.

My own understanding of the place I call home is shared by my fellow residents, in that we are aware of borders, but we do not allow them to stop us from the movement that best facilitates our day-to-day living. I grew up in the Northland, that area of Kansas City, Missouri, that lies across the Missouri River from downtown Kansas City, Missouri. I attended, as my father did before me, North Kansas City High School. A music scholarship took me over the state line to the University of Kansas in Lawrence, Kansas, itself just on the edge of the Kansas City Metro. I became, to my father's initial consternation, a Jayhawk, a word that for many Missourians still conjures up smoldering resentments from the bloody Border War. Although my husband (himself a Kansan) and I left the area for graduate school and to begin our careers, we returned and settled in Overland Park, Kansas, in Johnson County, twenty-five minutes via I-35 from downtown Kansas City, Missouri.

To what degree do these various locations affect my culinary identity, let alone my allegiances? Ultimately, little. Most people in this area allow sports teams to become their whipping boys. It is to the Missouri Tigers and the Kansas Jayhawks or Kansas State Wildcats that people consign their rivalries, resentments, and the old scores left unsettled. Doing this allows them to marry, live, work, play, and support one greater Kansas City, the place that they, like me, call home. The explosion of restaurants, coffee houses, supper clubs, barbecue joints, farm-to-fork cafés, CSAs, markets, breweries, distilleries, and wineries testify to Kansas City's robust culinary renaissance, one enjoyed by the majority of us, regardless of where in the Kansas City Metro the business is located. A car, bus, bike, or lately, the growing streetcar line, helps people reach their culinary destination. It is true, however, that when my father tires of an evening at our house in Overland Park, the wrap-up will inevitably include him grimly noting that he had best get going before "they close the bridge," his not-so-subtle reminder that Order Number Eleven still has some resonance with a good ol' Southern boy caught over the line in Jayhawker Territory after dark—although he is married to my lovely stepmother, a Kansas Native.

Certainly in the course of researching and writing this food biography, I have had the pleasure of meeting people from all over the Metro who have graciously shared with me their memories, leads, perspectives, recipes, cookbooks, and artifacts. Many have opened their homes to me so that I could experience firsthand their culinary traditions. Among them are Barb Able, Barbara Bayer, Sandra Czarlinsky, Scott Dalzell, Marcia Dodson, Don Duey, Karen Gaines, Julienne Gehrer, Carla Hanson, Kevin Hanson, Greg Hack, Clif Hall, Sharon Kleban, Birgit Love, Jennifer Phegley, Linda Salvay, and the exuberant, helpful members of the Facebook group *Things and Places We Loved in Greater KC When We Were Much Younger*, most especially Michael Shakespeare, whose Kansas City history posts oftentimes offered me the most important leads, photographs, and stories about our city's foodways.

I am keenly aware that the potential for offense is heightened when the topic is food, because people take food personally. It shapes their identity in ways so profound and integral to their psyche that they are not even aware of that fact until they notice that in a food biography of *their* city, their favorite historic restaurant has been omitted, their favorite barbecue joint seems to have been slighted, too little space has been devoted to their ethnic culinary traditions, or something valuable to them food-wise has not received mention. I can only admit that as the author of Kansas City's first full-length food history, this book is too brief and inevitably superficial at times. Each chapter was once twice its published length, and more chapters could easily have been added, particularly regarding the cities and towns that now make up the Metro. So let this Kansas City food history serve as the impetus and foundation for more to follow, ones that drill deeper and allow us to complicate and enrich an ongoing and overdue conversation.

Along with the home cooks and food enthusiasts I have recognized above, I would like to acknowledge the culinary professionals, scholars, and librarians whose knowledge and resources have allowed me to do as much as I could. They include senior librarian Jeremy Drouin and the staff at the Missouri Valley Special Collections at the Kansas City Public

Library; Denise Morrison, director of collections at Union Station and the Kansas City Museum; and Michael Sweeney, former librarian at the Black Archives of Mid-America. Also, I thank Jay Antle, Jess Barbosa, Roxanne Wyss Bateman, Janet Brooks, Carl J. DiCapo, Tai Edwards, Judith Fertig, Charles Ferruzza, Joseph William Gilbert, James Leiker, William McFarlane, Rick Moehring, Kathy Moore, Aaron Prater, Lindy Robinson, and Jesse Vega. Ken Albala's support has been invaluable, from the inception to the completion of this manuscript; likewise, working with Suzanne Staszak-Silva, Karen Ackermann, Kathryn Knigge, and Kathy Dvorsky at Rowman & Littlefield has made the production of this book a pleasure.

Without the support of my students, colleagues, and administrators at Johnson County Community College, I would not have found the energy and motivation to complete this project. A special thanks to Cathleen O'Neil. It goes without saying that my deepest appreciation and love go to my family, Vince, Clara, and Gavin, for the many hours they have spent listening to me discuss Kansas City history and tooling all around town to peek into countless butcher shops, groceries, chili parlors, barbecue joints, and restaurants.

Chapter One

"Here Stands a City Built o' Bread and Beef"

Kansas City's Natural and Material Resources

Ships made Carthage, gold made Nome,
Grain built Babylon, the wars built Rome,
Hogs made Chicago with their dying squeal,
Up popped Pittsburgh at the birth of steel.
Come Kansas City, make your story brief:
'Here stands a city built o' bread and beef.'

—Charles L. Edson, "Ballad of Kansas City," 1920

But before bread and beef, there was a river, and even better for Kansas City's future, the convergence of two rivers: the Kansas (or Kaw, as it is known locally) and the Missouri. *Chez les Canses*, or "Home of the Kansa Indians," is what French trappers called the area where the Missouri bends and the Kaw empties into it. "Kawsmouth" soon became its more accepted name, however. Most cities grew up near a body of water, but it was how the inhabitants utilized Kawsmouth that made Kansas City distinct and ultimately gave the city its culinary identity and reputation as a provisions center and crossroads. While subsequent chapters in this book will explore the foodways of native peoples, African Americans, Europeans, the "bread and beef" processing industry, and the markets and restaurants that such an industry supplied, this chapter offers an overview of how the area's inhabitants from ancient times until present have utilized the natural and material resources available to assuage their hunger and create a distinctive cuisine.

KAWSMOUTH FLORA AND
FAUNA AND PREHISTORIC SETTLEMENTS

It is helpful to think of Kawsmouth as one would a Venn diagram, where the Eastern Woodland, heavy with its oak-hickory canopy, meets the rolling prairies of the Western Plains, with its tall grasses. An extraordinary diversity resulted from the meeting of these two ecosystems, thus making the area attractive to the various peoples who passed through or decided to make Kawsmouth their home. Certainly the region's earliest inhabitants would have found it easy to sustain themselves here. During droughts that adversely affected woodland flora and fauna, prairie flora and fauna were less affected because they demanded less water. When the climate remained relatively consistent, inhabitants exploited a variety of foods to meet their alimentary needs.

The archaeological record indicates that people were present in the Kawsmouth region approximately twelve thousand years ago, a time when the dominant human culture was referred to as Archaic. These prehistoric people inhabited much of North America, and variations of their culture extended into Kansas and Missouri. However, the first culture at Kawsmouth to leave significant evidence of its foodways and habits are the Kansas City Hopewell, who lived in this region from around 100 BCE to 500–700 CE. After them, variants of what archaeologists call Central Plains Village people resided here, both before and around the time that historic Native Americans, the Kansa and Osage, migrated to this region. These prehistoric peoples lived along the Missouri and Kaw Rivers, using stone, plants, clay, and bone to make tools, cookware, and pottery; over the course of centuries, they domesticated squashes, marsh elder, chenopod, sunflowers, and between 1000 and 1450 CE, maize, the Mother Crop. In all cases, their technologies facilitated their ability to hunt, cultivate, and cook food.

Kawsmouth teemed with fish, including pallid and shovelnose sturgeon, longnose gar, catfish, crappie, paddlefish, white carp, and freshwater drum, along with mussels and crayfish, hard- and soft-shelled terrapins, and giant bullfrogs. Recovered bone fishhooks indicate that people fished the rivers for food, and mussel shells of different sizes suggest that they not only ate mussels, but relied on their shells for dishes and spoons. Quiet backwaters and river tributaries were also replete with fish, including bluegill and black perch, and these areas were obviously important fishing grounds. While water offered food and a transportation route, the bottoms or flood plains offered silt-rich soil that lent itself to crop cultivation.

Kansas City is situated in the glaciated region of the Central Plains, what is more technically called the dissected till plain. During the pre-Illinoian glacial episodes of the Pleistocene era, the region was covered with a thick ice sheet that melted and cut valleys, dissecting the uplands with coursing streams. For centuries, the Kansas City Metropolitan region has been defined by rolling hills and valleys created by the Missouri and Kaw Rivers and their tributaries. The region where Kansas City itself lies was also characterized by bottomland giving way abruptly to towering loess-covered bluffs that resembled mantle rock. Left undisturbed, such bluffs will stand vertical for centuries. Europeans intent on connecting river commerce to a city above those bluffs first had to cut through and gradually level them.

Ample rainfall, around one hundred centimeters annually, resulted in permanently moist subsoil composed of ground-up limestone, shale, sandstone, and fragments of granite, schist, gneiss, and quartz. These minerals, combined with prehistoric animal remains and vegetable matter, have created some of the most fertile topsoil in the United States. Prior to European settlement, the area was covered with deep-rooted grasses, including bluestem, wheat grass, Indian grass, prairie dropseed, and perennial herbs. Thick forests of oak, hickory, walnut, and sycamore grew in long, branching ribbons along the Missouri and the Kaw Rivers and along the valley bottoms of tributary streams. These forests also fringed the bluffs and in some places extended onto the adjacent prairie uplands. Hazelnut, walnut, and hickory nuts provided essential protein for inhabitants, while the wood was important for cooking, heating, and shelter.

Many native trees also provided fruit. Three varieties of plum, along with wild black cherry, crabapple, and persimmon, grew in forest groves, as did pawpaws (*Asimina triloba*). A profusion of berries and ground fruits also sustained the inhabitants; it would have been hard to walk long in early summer without finding grapes, black currants, elderberries, gooseberries, and strawberries. Along with fruits and nuts, many wild greens and fungi were valuable food sources.

For sustenance and flavor, game was the most prized food for early inhabitants. Artifacts at Kansas City Hopewell sites indicate that these

ancient people consumed white-tailed deer and small woodland mammals, perhaps also some bear. Later prehistoric cultures depended
increasingly on bison both for food and material goods, including
clothing, shelter, adornment, and eating utensils, and they also relied on
increased cultivation of maize.

THE KANSA, OSAGE, AND MISSOURIA SETTLEMENTS

Maize also helped sustain the historic tribes, the Kansa and the Osage,
who were living in this area at the time of European contact. These tribes
were semisedentary, situating their livelihoods around seasonal cycles of
planting and harvesting and moving in the summer and winter to hunt
game on the upland prairies.

Along with the Missouria, who lived near the confluence of the Grand
and Missouri Rivers in central present-day Missouri, Kansa and Osage
aligned themselves in the early 1700s with the French, first the itiner-
ant traders or *coureurs de bois* whom William E. Foley described as the
"advance agents of French colonization," and then by the 1720s, with
sanctioned officials, the *marchand* and the *voyageurs*.[1] Prior to the introduction of domesticated European livestock, native people hunted bison
by driving the frightened herds into enclosures where designated men
clubbed the animals to death, or they ran them over cliffs. After Spanish
explorers introduced modern-day horses into the Americas, Osage and
Kansa became renowned equestrians and experts at using the bow and
arrow to exploit game.

EARLY EUROPEAN SETTLEMENT:
COMMERCE AND THE KAWSMOUTH, 1820s–1830s

While the Missouri River had been an essential water and food source as
well as trade route for prehistoric peoples and Native American tribes, Europeans looked on this major waterway as essential to accumulating capital and control of the lands through which it coursed. The first permanent
European settlement within Kansas City's borders began in 1822 when
Francois and Berenice Chouteau expanded the family's St. Louis–based

fur business by building a trading post and home on the north bank of the Missouri River at present-day Randolph Bluff.

Located roughly a half mile from today's Chouteau Bridge (named, of course, after the Chouteaus), the post was not in an ideal location because it was difficult for traders approaching from the west to cross the river to reach Chouteau's post. However, land on the Missouri River's south bank was still part of the Osage Nation. The Chouteau post was nonetheless successful because for some years prior to the 1820s, members of the Chouteau family and their employees had established rapport with the Osage and the Kansa who brought in for trade beaver, raccoon, otter, and muskrat pelts destined for St. Louis and from there, Europe. Joining Francois in 1825 were his brothers, Frederic and Cyprien, who established satellite fur-trading posts farther up the Kaw River, in the vicinity of today's Bonner Springs, Kansas. When a flood in April 1826 destroyed the Chouteau post at Randolph Bluff, the family rebuilt on the more desirable south side of the Missouri River, roughly seven blocks from today's City Market. By then the Osage Nation had ceded their land to the U.S. government.[2]

During the 1820s and 1830s, a small French Creole-Metis community continued to rely primarily on native flora and fauna for sustenance. Travel along the Missouri was done seasonally via slow-moving keel boats and pirogues, making it difficult for early settlers to rely heavily on imported luxuries such as wheat flour, coffee, cane sugar, chocolate, and rice. Instead, they relied on what they could produce by farming, hunting, and fishing. Settlers' farms sat alongside cultivated native and nonnative cereal and vegetable crops as well as newly established orchards and vineyards. The settlement stretched from the West Bottoms (aptly called the French Bottoms) as far east as Chouteau's Landing. Native American foodways thus blended with those of the French Creole, the Metis, and African slaves to create the flavors that became Kansas City's culinary foundation. As would be the case from the 1820s on, Kansas City cuisine is ever-changing; it absorbed the traditions of those who settled here and equally important, it reflected a lot more than the inhabitants' mere will to survive. It continues to celebrate abundant native foods and eagerly borrows the culinary strategies of newcomers, no matter who they are. This liberal approach to food, with its combination of adventurous tastes and pragmatic adaptation to what is available, is essential to understanding Kansas City foodways.

While the Chouteaus were not the first to establish a trading post in the region, their location was simultaneously strategic and serendipitous. The Chouteau Landing was positioned where the Missouri River's current was swift and the water deep enough to allow the first generation of steamboats to dock, collect fur destined for St. Louis, and unload army officials and supplies destined for Fort Leavenworth, Kansas, and traders bound for Santa Fe. In the 1840s, pioneers would likewise disembark from even larger, more powerful steamboats to begin their overland journeys west. As James R. Shortridge has pointed out in *Kansas City and How It Grew, 1822–2011*, the physical and political geography are critical to how Kansas City looked and functioned in the antebellum years. The Missouri River at this particular juncture was "destined to become an emporium" as it abruptly changed its southerly course through Iowa and Nebraska to an easterly one through Missouri to St. Louis. The Chouteaus' success, and ultimately Westport's and the Town of Kansas's success, was intricately bound up in that geography.[3]

WESTPORT AND KANSAS CITY, 1830s–1865

Entrepreneurs were eager to establish new markets and services close to Missouri River steamboat landings, and also close to Indian Territory on Missouri's western border. Independence was one of these early boom towns. Laid out in 1825–1826 when the Osage Nation ceded their land, Independence was four miles from the Missouri River and built along an existing trail that ran west. Its designation as the Santa Fe Trail's eastern terminus was the result of a flood that destroyed the older terminus out of Franklin, Missouri, roughly one hundred miles to the east. Many travelers stayed in Independence to refuel, literally and figuratively. They first needed rest after disembarking from the steamboats that took them on the first leg of their journey, and they oftentimes took in entertainment, drank some whiskey, and if they were wealthy, slept in a (relatively) clean hotel bed and ate some (relatively) well-prepared meals.

Many travelers also purchased livestock, feed, wagons, and provisions: fatback, sorghum molasses, cornmeal, flour, salt, and beans, and if they could afford luxuries out of St. Louis and New Orleans, then also Ben & Co. Coffee, Havana Sugar, and brick tea (compressed into bricks that could be broken up with a hammer and reconstituted in boiling water). Nonetheless, Independence was not ideal, geographically speaking. To continue west from there, travelers had to ford the steeply banked and often flooded Blue River. For Native Americans who had grown accustomed to European goods, their journey from Indian Territory to Independence was equally difficult for the same reason, albeit going east instead of west.

Some twenty miles west of Independence, John Calvin McCoy was eager to go into the provisions business, selling food and supplies to 1,250 Shawnee living in villages in Indian Territory right over the Missouri state line.[4] McCoy, the principal founder of West Port (now Westport) and an organizer of the Town of Kansas Company, was a surveyor who understood how geography facilitated commerce. Partnering with two Independence men, he began a supply line to transport provisions from Independence to his two-story log store that opened one mile away from the Shawnee villages.

The Blue River's frequent flooding hindered McCoy's supply line, too, so he was motivated to seek an alternative. In spite of the forbidding bluffs that separated his store on the upland prairie from the river bottoms at Kawsmouth, and in spite of periodic, treacherous floods on the Missouri River itself, McCoy nonetheless searched out a sturdy rock landing near the foot of today's Grand Boulevard in downtown Kansas City, west of Chouteau's Landing. This rock shelf, soon known as the Westport or

The Levy and Westport Landing in 1842: an artistic rendition of what in reality would have been a crowded, hectic, and muddy area.
Westport, 1812–1912 (Franklin Hudson Publishing Company, Kansas City 1912). Author's personal collection

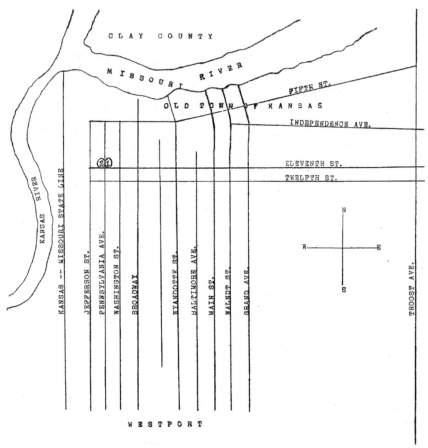

Note that Grand Boulevard (initially Market Street) was the French trace that McCoy widened to move goods from Westport Landing (also called Town of Kansas Landing) to Westport. In actuality, that road would have curved slightly to the southwest to move through a natural break in the bluffs.

Catholic Beginnings in Kansas City, Missouri, by Gilbert J. Garraghan (Loyola University Press, 1920). Author's personal collection

Town of Kansas Landing, allowed a St. Louis steamboat captain to regularly deliver McCoy's supplies, thus cutting his reliance on Independence. With the use of his slaves and hired men, McCoy improved an old French trace to carve a road through a break in the bluffs to his store.

McCoy did not consider Westport a rival of Independence, but it inevitably became one. Wagon masters and traders based in Santa Fe appreciated the convenience of Westport when it came to their own restocking. If they could rely on stores in Westport instead of Independence, it shaved four days off their round-trip journey. Ultimately tens of thousands of pioneers came to appreciate Westport for its rich prairie grasses, natural springs, and streams where they could feed and water livestock. In describing the advantages of this "eastern tract known among the overland travelers to Oregon and California," Jacob Ferris pointed out that the grass "attains to the hight [sic] of three feet, toward the close of summer; but where the land is moist it grows more luxuriantly, and is said to become 'tall enough to hide from view horse and rider.'"[5]

Grass would again become essential to Kansas City's prosperity after the Civil War, but during this era, its abundance fed livestock: a tremendous asset. As Westport's popularity grew, the Westport Landing likewise saw an increase in business, including pioneers who wanted to outfit themselves right on the levy after they disembarked from the steamboats. Hence, the entire area's economy soon centered on provisions and hospitality, facilitating thousands of people passing through. This early crossroads identity would have lasting effects on Kansas City's food history.

THE RAILROADS

Kansas City's growth from provisions outpost on the edge of wilderness to major metropolis was the result of railroads, and most importantly, Kansas City securing the first railroad bridge to span the Missouri River. "Geographical determinism" is how historian Charles Glaab characterized contemporary accounts of Kansas City's good fortune, including one from an early *Kansas City Star* editor, Henry J. Haskell. In the 1920s, Haskell explained Kansas City's destiny this way: "Take a freight car two hundred miles to the northwest, west or southwest of that strategic point [mouth of the Kaw], give it a shove, and it will coast down to Kansas City. That fact determined the location of the future distributing center." It was inevitable, as Haskell understood it, that the natural water-level grades which railroad companies liked to follow would bring trains to Kansas City.[6] To a degree, these early boosters had it correct. Railroad companies were often swayed by the logic that trade and commerce should continue to follow river paths. Kansas City had grown up just below the river's "elbow" where the current direction changed and thus flowed into the Mississippi, close to St. Louis, a large metropolis.

The river in the pre-railroad era was "the only natural north-south line of communication in the area," wrote Glaab.[7]

However, other Missouri river towns were also geographically feasible when it came to a bridge. The difference for Independence, St. Joseph, and Leavenworth, the main contenders, was more entrenched business interests. St. Joseph and Independence had thriving wagon trades, and these businessmen did not welcome rail competition. Leavenworth pork producers and cattlemen did not want cheap meat transported in from the east, nor did they relish the prospect of the rails bringing to town Texas longhorns. Kansas City, on the other hand, was too young to have such entrenched interests.[8]

A group of financiers and officials bolstered Kansas City's chances of securing a bridge because they put Civil War grievances behind them and focused on persuading residents, politicians, and railroad executives that the city was ideally situated for such an investment. A mere fifty-four miles of track could connect Cameron in Northern Missouri, a stop on the Hannibal and St. Joseph line, to Kansas City; from there, Kansas City could be connected to Chicago. New Englander John Murray Forbes and his investors also supported Kansas City as a major rail hub because it would ultimately connect their rail system to the Southwest.[9] Kansas City won the bid, and the Hannibal and St. Joseph Railroad Bridge was completed and opened to great fanfare on July 3, 1869.

With the Civil War disruptions behind them, Americans came to expect more meat on their dinner tables in part because cattlemen were now able to use the railroads to cut the cost of supplying it. Railcars hauled cattle and hogs into Kansas City, and then hauled them out as tinned hams and corned beef (and after refrigerated railcars, also as butcher's meat). The Hannibal Bridge, as it is still called today, facilitated this transportation. Within a matter of years, it augmented Kansas City's reputation as a provisions center, but instead of a preindustrial economy of Conestoga wagons, the city's economy was now an industrial one of stockyards and meatpacking. The railroad also added greatly to Kansas City's reputation for crossroads hospitality. In just the first year after the Hannibal Bridge opened, a quarter-million travelers passed through Kansas City, with seventy thousand of them coming in by train. The city population likewise grew, but many residents worked in industries that supported either catering or provisions, hence perpetuating and enhancing the importance of both.

"IN THE KINGDOM OF THE BIG RED STEER": KANSAS CITY STOCKYARDS AND MEATPACKING

Fifty years after the Hannibal Bridge opened, a farmer placed an advertisement in a New York City newspaper. He was ready to sell his eighty-acre farm located "in the kingdom of the big red steer, in the blue-grass belt of Kansas." With both a fenced hog production unit and cropland, this farm was a short "fifty miles from Kansas City: second largest grain and livestock market in the world."[10] The farmer did not need to explain. By that date, most Americans understood that the lucrativeness of this Kansas farm had to do not only with the grass and steer, but its proximity to Kansas City stockyards and grain elevators, not to mention railroad trunk lines.

Prior to the Civil War, Kansas City butchers and meatpackers supplied the local economy with fresh beef, pork, and mutton. Washington Henry Chick, the son of one of Kansas City's founders, recalled that the first packinghouse was partly owned by his family. Located east of Grand Boulevard near the Missouri River, it processed "several hundred hogs . . . each season."[11] Cowboys (as Leavenworth cattlemen had rightly predicted) began driving Texas cattle north along the Chisholm Trail to the Kansas Pacific Railroad terminus in Abilene, Kansas. Joseph G. McCoy purchased the cattle, held them at his pens, and then sold them to the railroads. In 1867, McCoy sold eighteen thousand head of cattle, and the year later, an extraordinary fifty-three thousand.[12] The most popular cattle during this period were indeed longhorns, one descendant of cattle brought to the Americas by the Spanish. Of the *criollo* cattle, longhorns were hardy and gentle, in spite of their intimidating horns. They were bred to survive arid, extreme temperatures.

While McCoy's operation was designed to hold cattle until transport, Kansas City's stockyard operation and meatpacking plants would have to be huge if they were to encourage more dealers, more railroads, and more financing. Watching these developments closely were two powerful investors: Charles F. Adams Jr., grandson of President John Quincy Adams, and Philip D. Armour, creator of Chicago's meatpacking industry. Both men realized that Kansas City's location in relation to ranchland and rail made it an ideal extension of Chicago's (and Armour's) meatpacking business. The men acted.

In 1871, Armour built a meatpacking plant on a fifteen-acre tract a half mile from a stockyard cofounded by Adams. These operations sat on what geographer James Shortridge described as "a small thumb of bottomland that extends west from the state line between the Kansas and Missouri Rivers" on the Kansas side. This out-of-the-way area was convenient because rivers carried away the animal waste and sewage, and the meat could be shipped by barge or by rail. Somewhat distant from downtown Kansas City, Missouri, this bottomland was also cheap and available in uninterrupted acreages. By 1871, the West Bottoms expanded to accommodate competitors' stockyards and packing plants. By 1890, more than five million head of cattle were moved from the west to eastern markets, with a majority of them fattened, slaughtered, and packaged in Kansas City.

This industry created a wide crescent that wrapped around two-thirds of both Kansas Cities, ending just a few blocks west of Kansas City, Missouri's downtown; however, the longhorns which had originally dominated the beef supply industry fell out of popularity because their meat was tough. The quest for tender beef obsessed area ranchers specializing in animal husbandry. Most important were Charles Gudgell and Thomas A. Simpson, who owned a ranch near Independence. In 1881, the two men imported Anxiety IV from England, a Hereford bull that was an anomaly for his large hindquarters and that is credited with being the "father of American Herefords." Further breeding experimentation produced what is known as the American Polled Hereford, a large breed that surpassed all others in popularity for its tender, flavorful beef.[13] By the 1890s, the majority of the cattle in Kansas City stockyards were raised closer in to Kansas City, including Kansas, Missouri, and Oklahoma ranchland. Jackson County itself sustained large livestock and dairy operations well into the 1960s.

GRAIN: MILLING, DISTILLING, BREWING

The tall-grass prairie that bolstered Kansas City's cattle industry gives way to short-grass prairie that ultimately bolstered its grain and milling industry. By the late 1860s, the government and railway companies were aggressively promoting west-central Kansas farmland to prospective settlers, chief among them German Mennonites. When given an ultimatum by their host country, Russia, to become Russian (and thus eligible for military service), or leave, the Mennonites left, and in the 1870s began immigrating to Kansas. Accustomed to farming the semi-arid Ukrainian steppes, Mennonites brought with them in stone crocks, trunks, and even their coat pockets, a hard winter wheat variety known as "Turkey red" that fared well in harsh, dry climates. By 1875, Kansas farmers harvested twenty-five million bushels of Turkey red. By 1892, that number had soared to nearly seventy-five million bushels, thirty million bushels more than anywhere else in the United States.[14]

Kansas City's proximity to wheat, corn, and rail made it an obvious place to process grain. A journalist for the industry magazine, *Roller Mill*, wrote in 1897 that that year's wheat crop was estimated at five hundred million bushels and would require five hundred thousand rail cars to move it east "to one of the great transfer stations, of which Kansas City and Duluth are perhaps the largest."[15] Prior to the Hannibal Bridge, Kansas City also supported gristmills, some flour mills, and some grain elevators. To handle such an abundance of Turkey red wheat, however, more sophisticated grain elevators had to be constructed. The first such elevator was built by H. J. Latshaw and R. W. Quade in 1871 and stored up to one hundred thousand bushels. Sensing the money to be made from such an enterprise, Burlington, Chicago Great Western, Kansas City Southern, and Pacific Railroads also built elevators and leased them to grain firms.[16] In a chain reaction that mirrored the growth of Kansas City's stockyard industry, the availability of so much grain storage led next to milling companies. Mills attracted regional and national bakers, and the industry continued to grow. At the apex of this industry in 1946, Kansas City had 56 national and regional bakeries that employed roughly 2,175 people.[17]

Grain was also distilled into spirits and brewed into beer. While Kansas City was never the beverage giant that were Milwaukee and St. Louis, alcohol has profoundly shaped Kansas City's culinary culture. Writing in 1857, former Kansas City mayor and editor Robert Van Horn wryly suggested that Kansas City had best establish some of its own distilleries, given that whiskey consumption in 1857 had reached an unprecedented $135,000 in sales for a population at just around 1,500.[18] The same mineral springs that helped sustain John Calvin McCoy's Westport also became essential to the early distilling industry, as did the Southern sensibility of many Kawsmouth settlers. Those arriving from Kentucky, Tennessee, and Virginia treated distilling corn liquor as an art, and serving it was critical to one's show of hospitality.

From the earliest days of European settlement, Kawsmouth was infamous for illegal whiskey sales to displaced Native Americans, with some merchants losing their trading licenses in the process. By the time Van Horn suggested that the city produce its own whiskey supply, Westport alone had numerous "grocery stores," which were synonymous with saloons. The English travel writer Francis Parkman Jr. remarked that whiskey "circulates more freely in Westport than is altogether safe in a place where every man carries a loaded pistol in his pocket."[19] Saloons likewise filled Independence streets and crowded the levy between Westport Landing and Chouteau's Landing. After the Civil War, several whiskey distilleries were operating in Kansas City, among them the Old Pioneer Distilling Company and Edward Lowe Martin's Kansas City Distilling Company (Edward Lowe Martin, a Kentuckian, also served as Kansas City's mayor in 1873). In nearby Weston, Missouri, Ben Holladay's distillery, established in 1856 and later bought by the Shawhan family, became the largest and most famous regionally. Located near underground limestone springs, the distillery produced bourbon that supplied Kansas City saloons. It was eventually sold to Isadore Singer, who renamed the distillery McCormick, and it remains in robust operation today.[20]

Along with the Border War and Civil War, attitudes regarding alcohol highlight an important historical difference between Kansas and Missouri. Depending on whether a person enjoyed her shot of whiskey or was a teetotaler, the state line bisecting the two Kansas Cities was a boon or menace—nothing in between. Kansas's early endorsement of temperance cast Kansas City, Missouri's wide-open attitudes toward alcohol in sharp contrast, particularly in 1881 when Kansas officially became a dry state. A stretch of West Ninth Street between State Line Road and Genessee Street on the Missouri side became home to two dozen liquor stores and saloons, crowded in together among the stockyards. It was popularly known as "the wettest block in the world." In spite of the ratification of the Eighteenth Amendment in 1919, Kansas City remained "wide open," in large part because of city boss Tom Pendergast's involvement in a massive multicounty bootlegging network that operated under the umbrella of the Pendergast Distribution Company. During Prohibition, distributors, sellers, and drinkers were largely left alone, but only if they were willing to play by Boss Tom's rules.

Whiskey fueled the city's reputation for wildness, but beer production was important indirectly to the city's reputation for a more wholesome hospitality. The Muehlebach fortune that came from brewing beer enhanced Kansas City's tourism industry, its downtown commerce, and also the city's early reputation for capturing professional baseball and football franchises. George Muehlebach and his brothers were Swiss-German immigrants who arrived to Westport in 1859 and opened a harness and saddle store. In 1879, George Muehlebach bought George Hierbe's Main Street Brewery; by 1879 the Muehlebach Brewery was producing roughly four thousand barrels a day.[21] The brewery's success resulted in money for real estate investments, including the lux Hotel Muehlebach that opened in 1915 and hosted presidents, dignitaries, well-heeled visitors, and convention-goers. Its status spawned numerous competitors in the hospitality businesses, from hotels to restaurants to theaters that clustered in the vicinity around Twelfth and Baltimore. The Muehlebach fortune also built the city's first major athletic stadium, which opened in 1923 as Muehlebach Field, home to the Negro League Monarchs, minor league Blues, and later the Kansas City Athletics. As the renamed and enlarged Municipal Stadium, it became the first home of the Kansas City Royals and Kansas City Chiefs. Hotels, restaurants catering to all tastes, plenty of beer, and a major sports venue can be attributed indirectly to the Muehlebach fortune and from there, to Kansas City's love of German pils.

THE 1951 FLOOD

Kansas City's location facilitated its economic good fortunes, but only at a price: routine, devastating floods. The Chouteaus were not the only entrepreneurs to see their entire property wiped out in a deluge of water—twice. Indeed, Kansas Citians recount the past by referring to the floods: 1844, 1903, 1951, and 1993 were the Big Ones. In terms of Kansas City's food biography, the flood that seared itself into the collective consciousness was the Flood of 1951. It was the death knell of Kansas City's provisions industry, and it forced a self-reckoning, given that the identity of Kansas City was so intricately tied to that industry. The aftershocks of the flood persist, and how Kansas Citians eat, how they understand their food heritage, and how they commemorate their foodways, can often be traced back in some fashion to the Flood of 1951.

Early spring that year had been particularly rainy and had caused some minor flooding, but between July 9 and 13, record-breaking levels of rain fell almost constantly over eastern and central Kansas, swelling the Kaw River and its tributaries. As a result, the Missouri River, right below the Kawsmouth, experienced a flood that wiped out entire communities, including Kansas City, Kansas's Argentine and Armourdale districts. Neighborhoods, businesses, the stockyards, and the meatpacking plants were largely under water. The industry suffered damages of roughly $140,000,000. By July 12, the waters had swelled so high that hundreds of bloated animal carcasses were bumping up against the Lewis and Clark Intercity Viaduct, the freeway bridge that rises up over the West Bottoms and connects Kansas City, Missouri, to Kansas City, Kansas. Walter R. Scott, secretary to the Kansas City Board of Trade (the body that oversees the futures market for hard-red winter wheat) estimated the grain loss between $5,000,000 and $10,000,000. The crippled railroad industry sustained upwards of $100,000,000 worth of damage.[22] After the flood waters retreated, it made little sense to rebuild what was already going away.

The Great Depression and World War II rationing had made butcher's meat too expensive for many Americans to afford and at times unavailable regardless of the cost. With postwar prosperity, beef was in demand, a situation that mirrored pent-up consumer desire for meat following the Civil War. This time, however, Kansas City's meatpacking industry was not positioned to satisfy a quickly changing consumer market, in part because of grocery store innovations happening on the West Coast. Entrepreneurs such as Dwight Cochran, Safeway Stores Inc.'s marketing vice president, wanted to make a profit by offering consumers superior, marbled beef but at a more affordable price. Cochran left Safeway to organize the publicly held Kern County Land Co. in Bakersfield, California, a farm-to-feeder complex that could process fifty thousand head of cattle a year. Instead of feeding them only grass, Cochran finished them on a fattening diet of an "advanced nutritional formula" that probably included corn. As a result, his operation produced a higher volume of USDA Choice and Prime beef at an acceptable cost for many consumers.[23] When rationing ended, new grocery store chains did a tremendous volume of business. Traditional stockyard operations such as those in Kansas City inevitably suffered.

Iowa, a pioneer of farm-to-feeder operations, helped persuade ranching states such as Kansas and Oklahoma to abandon using the railroad to haul livestock to meatpackers. The tapping of the Ogallala Aquifer in the 1960s made this decision possible, as it allowed High Plains ranchers and farmers to incorporate center-pivot irrigation. Abundant water made it possible for large farm-to-feeder operations to water thousands of cattle and also irrigate the forage crops (mainly corn) necessary to produce marbled beef.[24] With the advent of long-haul highway trucking, neither the Kansas City stockyards nor meatpackers could survive with its nineteenth-century model of operations; the Flood of 1951 helped expose this truth.

The rise of agribusiness also adversely affected Kansas City's milling and baking operations. Mergers had defined the milling industry as early as the 1920s, but they accelerated in the early 1950s for interconnected reasons, ranging from people's changing consumption habits, global competition, technological innovations, and transportation. Independent flour mills throughout the United States suffered declines, and even very large corporations such as General Mills and Pillsbury were bypassed by ADM, ConAgra, and Cargill, none of whose headquarters or primarily milling operations were (or are) based in Kansas City. Falling grain prices left farmers in a vulnerable position. The 1960s saw the acceleration of corporate factory farming across Kansas, as agribusiness and nonfarm interests both began buying up land from bankrupt farmers and as Kansas itself experienced the challenges of rural flight. All of these factors resulted in shrinking Kansas City milling and baking industries. The 1951 flood furthered that decline, and a series of mill and grain elevator explosions in the mid-to-late twentieth century both symbolically and literally signaled the end of what had once been a robust Kansas City industry.

KANSAS CITY SPIRIT

The Flood of 1951 also exposed Kansas City's painful split personality when it came to image. While residents took pride in showcasing their city's native foods and their city's role in feeding the nation, they also suffered from an inferiority complex from doing just that. Barbecued ribs, corn dodgers, chili, fried catfish, smothered pork chops, and biscuits are foods that Kansas Citians have long enjoyed, but many were self-conscious of how that cuisine marked them as hayseeds and country bumpkins, and their city as a backwater or worse, a cowtown. The inevitable stench of cattle was lamely justified as "the smell of money," but those who could do so lived far away from the smell, in graciously appointed mansions and along boulevards designed to detract their and their visitors' attention from where exactly a lot of that money came from.

As early as the 1870s, those who took charge of Kansas City's image deliberately measured their own and their city's growing sophistication by its cuisine. The 1900s-era Baltimore Hotel à la carte menu set a culinary standard that was simultaneously sophisticated and sterile, one virtually identical to upscale hotel restaurant menus nationwide, with its Blue Point Oysters, Green Turtle *a l'Anglaise*, *Consommé*, Chateaubriand with Truffles, and caviar on toast points. In other words, Kansas City fought hard to convince visitors and itself that it was not a burg where buffalo, cowboys, and Indians went roaming through Union Station, or by the 1950s, the Municipal Downtown Airport. The fountains, Nelson-Atkins Museum of Art, the Kansas City Symphony (then Philharmonic), the Country Club Plaza: these were what postwar residents wished to show off to their visitors, and when food had to be involved because visitors grew hungry, it made many Kansas Citians feel better about themselves and their city if they dined at a fancy Continental restaurant rather than a barbecue joint or a fried chicken roadhouse.

In some ways, then, the Flood of 1951 was devastating, but it also allowed Kansas City to modernize and to seek new forms of commerce, to leave behind some of its cowtown identity. It attracted cleaner industries, including telecommunications, fiber optics, and STEM research. Grain elevators were largely replaced by skyscrapers and suburban corporate campuses. Meatpacking plants and stockyards were replaced by office parks. Ice manufacturing warehouses and old breweries became luxury condominiums and loft apartments. The old freight house district, now the Freight House District, became prominent for its art galleries and a host of new restaurants. While the vestiges of the city's agricultural past are still very much here, present in the Kansas City Board of Trade, the Polled Hereford Association, the Dairy Farmers of America, and the

American Royal Livestock Show, the stench of cattle and the haze of grain dust are long gone.

In the twenty-first century, more than half a century since the Flood of 1951, it might be argued that Kansas City has come far enough along to have gained the necessary distance to come to terms with, appreciate, and *celebrate* its provisions-based past; equally important, its residents have gained a profound appreciation for the natural resources that created the city in the first place. Many have studied its food history and heritage and have considered how to reinvigorate its provisions and hospitality economies, but in ways that reflect the importance of sustainability, heritage, and region. As a result, Kansas City has become a culinary destination, more than merely a crossroads.

Our paying homage to Kansas City's past meat industry has led to the resurgence of the butcher and the raising of grass-fed beef cattle that again graze the tall-grass prairies, along with bison. The city's meat markets have a loyal patron base who respect the art of fabrication and who have tired of feedlot beef. New butchers oftentimes run both meat markets and connected restaurants. As in the past, Kansas City's food identity is again intricately tied to producers who live outside of city limits. Burger's Smokehouse, based in the Missouri Ozarks, depends on Kansas City grocery stores to sell its bacon and country ham, just as the Good Shepherd Poultry Ranch in Lindsborg, Kansas, relies on area stores to sell its heritage-breed turkeys. Shatto Milk Company in Osborn, Missouri, supplies the community with milk in glass bottles, cheese curds, butter, and ice cream. The Good Natured Family Farms' collective of local farmers and artisans produce everything from raw clover honey to heritage chickens to free-range, pastured eggs for sale at area grocery stores and farmers' markets.

Bread is also back, after Kansas City's Farm to Market Bread Company began selling loaves first out of a small rented space in Westport, and then, as the operation took off, out of a much larger bakery in the Crossroads District. Farm to Market, perhaps the city's largest and most prominent bakery, has itself regenerated enthusiasm for the corner baker, with most people in the city and surrounding suburbs now able to buy artisan loaves from a number of independent bakeries. In 2009, one hundred acres of Turkey red was planted by Bryce Stephens from Decatur County, Kansas,

milled by Heartland Mill in Marienthal, Kansas, and used by WheatFields
Bakery in Lawrence and by Fervere Bakery in Kansas City.[25] Both are accustomed to long lines forming around opening time, and they know that
within hours, they will sell out.

Brewing has also seen a renaissance with microbreweries, such as Boulevard Brewery, which is so popular that it is now distributed nationwide.
Boulevard's success has prompted many others to begin brewing, and the
city is literally awash in microbreweries, nanobreweries, and gastropubs.
Area liquor stores stock many local and regional beers. Regional spirit
distilleries include the historic McCormick in Weston, Missouri, and also
(gleefully or ironically, depending on how one views Kansas's dry past)
the High Plains Distillery in Atchison, Dark Horse Distillery in Lenexa,
and the Good Spirits Distillery in Olathe. Even wine, which prior to
Prohibition made Missouri the second-largest wine-producing region in
the United States, has made an explosive comeback, again with urban,
suburban, and exurban wineries offering their bottles and casks at local
restaurants and liquor stores.

And of course, there's barbecue, Kansas City's favorite way of paying
homage to its cowtown heritage, but also the importance of its Southern settlers, especially African Americans, who perfected the art of taking the flesh
of an animal and treating it to slow cooking over native hickory and oak.
The remaining chapters in this book will look at all these foods, trends, and
people more carefully, exploring a culinary past and legacy that encourages
its residents to revel in good food, good spirits, and good fortune.

Chapter Two

Prehistoric and Native American Foodways of the Kawsmouth Region

Roughly twelve thousand years ago, northeastern Kansas and northwestern Missouri were becoming progressively drier and warmer, and Pleistocene animals such as the mammoth and mastodon began slowly dying out due to climate change and also to the skill of the Paleoindians who hunted them. These earliest known people associated with the Clovis, Folsom, and Plainview cultures roamed North America, crossing and crisscrossing the region that would someday include Kansas City. They followed big game and water sources, camping where food was plentiful, and moving when it was not. The purpose of this chapter is to introduce the foodways of the Kawsmouth region's prehistoric cultures and those of the historic Native American tribes with whom Europeans first interacted. Inevitably, many of the artifacts that archaeologists have uncovered are related in some fashion to food.

ARCHAIC HUNTER-GATHERERS ON THE CENTRAL PLAINS, 2500 BCE TO 500 BCE

As the previous chapter details, Kansas City is situated in a transitional zone on the eastern edge of the Central Plains. Hence, Kawsmouth flora and fauna comprise two distinct ecosystems: tall-grass prairie that characterizes land to its immediate west, and deciduous forests that characterize the land to its immediate east. A patchwork quilt or more technically, a mosaic, are ways to describe the region. Archaic peoples who inhabited the Central Plains region during the Holocene epoch (four to three thousand years ago) were strictly hunter-gatherers, and as

continues to be the case with all civilizations past and present, survival
depended on people's exploitation of natural resources and also their
ingenuity when it came to utilizing everything they could find to ensure
that they had sufficient food to eat.

From around 5000 to 4000 BCE, a complex known as the Nebo Hill
people lived on the Missouri River bluffs in the vicinity of Riverside,
Missouri, roughly four miles from downtown Kansas City. Dense timber
provided cooking and heating fires as well as wood for their shelters. The
prairie woodlands and rivers offered a diversity of foods, such as water-
loving great bulrushes (*Scirpus validus*) and cattails that grew like forests
along the Missouri River bottoms. All parts of the cattail were useful to
prehistoric peoples as well as historic Native Americans. Pollen thickened
soups and was sometimes mixed with flours to create cakes or bread;
the peeled roots were eaten raw or boiled. Young shoots were likewise
boiled.[1] Away from the wet marshy areas, the upland prairies offered big
game, including the *Bison antiquus* that roamed the tall grass prairies
roughly ten thousand years ago, and in more recent times, the modern
bison (*Bison bison*), herds of which astonished Coronado's Conquistadors
when they came upon them in 1541.

Along with using spears and atlatl-propelled darts to hunt game, hunter-
gatherers fashioned traps of tough plant fibers. Hunting clubs, scraping
and cutting tools, bone fishhooks, bifacial knives, hand stones (manos),
and grinding basins (metates) also offer archaeologists clues about hunter-
gatherer foodways in this region, as do the traces of acorn, tubers, roots,
and seeds left behind on manos and metates. Dry cave sites in eastern
Kansas and much of Missouri have turned up evidence of fire pits, hearths,
earth ovens, and burned limestone with traces of ash and charcoal. To eat
many foods or to make them more palatable, they first had to be cooked.
Carbohydrate-rich acorns were boiled in rock- or hide-lined fire pits that
were waterproofed with wax. Hot stones were added until the water boiled,
at which point the food was placed in the pit as well; alternatively, food
was cooked above the fire in a suspended skin bag.[2] Chenopodium seeds,
from lamb's-quarters (*Chenopodium berlandieri*), were roasted directly
over the fire and ground into a buckwheat-like meal that could be eaten as
mush or used for breads and griddle cakes. The seeds were energy-packed
and lightweight, so they could also be eaten out of hand when people were

in transit. Protein-rich insects such as grasshoppers and moths were also essential food sources for people in transit, as were nuts.

Lamb's-quarters' leaves were as valuable as the seeds they produced. They were probably eaten thousands of years ago just as people consume them today: raw when the leaves are young, or as a potherb when the leaves are mature. Traces of other food found at Paleolithic sites in the region include charred wild onion, hackberry, wild grape, and Solomon's seal (*Polygonatum biflorum; P. pubescens*), whose boiled rhizomes offered long-burning nutritional fuel rather than short bursts of energy provided by berries.[3] Other foods were best roasted on rocks placed alongside the hearth, such as sunflower seeds and edible gourds. Meat was prized for flavor and sustenance. It was roasted on a stick held over the fire, while the roots and tubers that accompanied the meat were placed on rocks close to the heat and turned frequently to roast them. The hearth, in other words, was sacred for the food it provided and the community it fostered.

Around 1000 BCE, hunter-gatherers in the Central Plains region also began using earthen ovens, and with this technology, a greater variety of foods could be consumed. Packets made of animal skins, intestines, or stomachs were filled with food, placed on a heated rock bed, covered with grass or hides, and covered again with earth. The food inside the packets cooked slowly, conserving energy and regulating heat. Plant bulbs and tubers benefited from being cooked in such a manner, not only becoming edible, but sweet, tender, and caramelized. Large marrow bones likewise benefited from this slow cooking technique, along with cuts of bison, elk, or antelope.

Prior to the introduction of the modern horse by Spanish explorers in the 1500s, many prehistoric Plains cultures relied on dogs as beasts of burden, camp guards, and as a food source; most importantly, dogs assisted with big-game hunting.[4] One of the oldest hunter-gatherer sites in Kansas was located at 12 Mile Creek in Logon County and was affiliated with Clovis and Folsom cultures; it included numerous *Bison antiquus* skeletons. It is clear that these animals were killed by highly skilled hunters. Because stalking had to take place on foot, a well-coordinated hunt was essential. The easiest way to attack such large animals was to lie in wait around a watering hole. When the animals began to approach, men prepared their weapons, set traps, and waited for the animals to begin drinking. When the lead hunter gave the signal, the rest would immediately attack, hurling and jabbing their spears. A swampy area was particularly ideal for hunting large prey, as the weeds and reeds slowed down trapped animals. When it was possible, hunters and dogs might also crowd bison into a narrow chute and run them over cliffs, where other hunters finished off the stunned and maimed creatures.

When food shortages occurred, hunter-gatherers turned to other, less coveted foods such as mussels. Although plentiful along rivers and streams, these bivalves offered low nutrient value for the extensive labor it took to collect and prepare them. Turtles, frogs, and other amphibians were also consumed when larger animals were scarce. Pools of water could be poisoned by placing broken walnut husks in them, thus allowing hunters to fish for smaller, less desirable food without the need of hook or bait. People were also thought to consume the large, but not very tasty, root of the bush morning glory (*Ipomeoea leptophylla*) if there was no other choice.[5]

Depending on their needs, hunter-gatherers moved en masse, or some members of a clan went on extended hunting expeditions and left others in a semipermanent location. When away, hunters lived in skin-covered tents and brush-covered wikiups (huts) supported by poles that were easy to set up, dismantle, and transport via dog travois. Those at more stationary sites lived in cave enclosures or semisubterranean structures covered with logs, branches, and sod; these were common throughout the Central Plains by the middle Holocene epoch.

WOODLAND PERIOD, 500 BCE TO 1000 CE

Kansas City Hopewell

During the Woodland period, gardening was added to hunting and gathering activities, in part because societies recognized the value of cultivating some plants whose harvests could sustain them during late winter and early spring when supplies ran low, or if game was unusually scarce, or nuts difficult to come by. People during this period also produced ceramic pottery to hold, cook, and eat the food they prepared. Little is known about the earliest Woodland people who resided at Kawsmouth because their artifacts are scarce. However, recent excavations around present-day Riverside, Missouri, in the same vicinity where the Nebo Hill people lived earlier, have uncovered pottery associated with the Early Woodland Black Sand culture, a people who likely migrated to the Missouri River Valley from the Lower Illinois River Valley around 600 BCE and who resided in small camps on terraces of tributary streams until around 1 CE. The brevity of their occupation in the area has led archaeologists to speculate that like the Archaic peoples before them, these Early Woodlanders built seasonal habitations, moving around frequently to follow their food sources rather than settling for long in any one place.[6]

Better understood because of the duration of their culture, the size of their villages, and the number of artifacts and food traces left behind are Kansas City Hopewell, a Middle Woodland people who lived in the lower Missouri River valley and flourished from 100 BCE to 500–700 CE.[7] Foraging and hunting continued to play a dominant role in this culture's sustenance and economy, with white-tailed deer the most common game they evidently consumed, along with wolf, coyote, beaver, fish, and turtle.[8] Kansas City Hopewell and neighboring Middle Woodland cultures began using bows and arrows in addition to the atlatl and dart when hunting, and reasons for this added technology might have been ingenuity born of necessity: increases in the human population put pressure on game, and hence competition increased.[9]

Forays into agriculture are oftentimes the reason for an expanding population, but it is also possible that an expanding population necessitated agriculture. Unlike Early Woodland people who might have done some limited experimenting with cultivating plants, Middle to Late Woodland peoples, including Kansas City Hopewell to a degree, were culling wild species and moving them from their native habitat to isolated fields in order to avoid cross-pollination; from there they developed better varieties of edible native plants. Marsh elder or sumpweed (*Iva annua* var. *macrocarpa*) was the most prominent cultigen (a plant altered by humans) in the analyzed remains at a Kansas City Hopewell food processing site near Smithville, Missouri. Kansas City Hopewell people convened at this site and others like it where they processed harvests for winter sustenance.

It is helpful to think about how families today might store certain shelf-stable foods that can be used in an emergency or if they need food to fall back on if money runs out before the end of the month. Scores of college students know that ramen noodles can be purchased for mere pennies, and although they don't taste great, if money is tight, those noodles can help keep their stomachs full until a financial aid check comes in. Kansas City Hopewell forays into agriculture might well have been for similar reasons.[10] Hickory nuts were a favored food, for example, but wildlife competed for them along with people, and so sometimes the harvest was slim. Thus, it made sense for people to cultivate marsh elder, working toward a variety that produced seeds up to one thousand times larger than those found in the wild. These larger, oily seeds were roasted and ground into meal-like flour. It was extremely nutritious, offering people a concentrated source of protein and calcium along with essential B vitamins.[11] Although marsh elder was an important food source, its cultivation fell out perhaps because it was not very tasty; it was replaced in people's diet by sunflowers (*Helianthus annuus*), squashes and gourds, and most importantly maize, by around 1000 CE.[12]

MISSISSIPPIAN PERIOD, 1000–1450 CE

Steed-Kisker Culture

Why the Kansas City Hopewell died out is not fully understood. When it disappeared from Kawsmouth, other variants of the Hopewell Culture, including to its east and north, were disappearing as well. The people who lived in the Lower Missouri Valley from roughly 900 CE to 1500 CE, part of a wider Central Plains Village culture, are referred to as Steed-Kisker, and their diet and cookery were not only more reliant on crop cultivation, but they also share many similarities with the cultures who followed them, including the Native Americans living at Kawsmouth at the time of European contact. Steed-Kisker pottery also altered to accommodate new foods and cooking technologies. Fashioned from clay and tempered primarily with shell, Steed-Kisker pottery is often plain-surfaced, and its globular-shaped thin walls could better withstand repeated expansion and contraction that happened when the vessels were filled with food to be heated and then cooled.[13] As with European Neolithic people, Central Plains Village people maintained and expanded their connections via trade, marriage, and kinship links. Individuals and small groups probably migrated into other areas carrying different foods, cooking techniques, and technologies for planting, growing, and preserving food. Their range might have taken them along well-known trade routes eastward along the Missouri River as well as westward onto the plains.[14]

Plains Village people grew large quantities of maygrass (*Phalaris caroliniana*), chenopod, and marsh elder, but they also cultivated plants that were becoming more integral and that would eventually replace these seeds altogether. Along with tobacco, their gardens included beans, little barley, gourds and squash, and sunflowers.[15] Sunflower seeds were tasty, nutrition-packed, and used in many ways. They were knocked out of the flower head with a stick and then parched over a fire. Once toasted, they were hulled and pounded into meal, shaped into cakes along with some fat (bison tallow, for example), and then baked. The meal could also be made into a thick mush, or the seeds themselves could be ground into nut butter. Sunflower oil was extracted by taking the seed head, crushing it, and boiling it in water. When the oil rose to the top, it could be skimmed off and mixed into nut butter, or the oil could be used for other food preparations.[16] Most important was maize, the staple cereal grain of all of American indigenous populations, hence called "the Mother" by numerous tribes. Steed-Kisker people were farming an evolving form of Eastern Eight Row maize and varieties of Midwestern Twelve Row maize.[17]

As with other Mississippian cultures during this era, Plains Village people were increasingly sedentary, living in established villages situated on river and stream bluffs away from flooding. Their earth lodges ranged from four to fifteen meters in dimension and were typically rectangular or square; each included a central basin hearth for cooking and heating, and up to five cylindrical or bell-shaped cache pits both inside and outside for food storage.[18] When not planting and harvesting crops, Plains Village people went on long-range hunting expeditions in search of big game, including but not limited to bison. Woodland fauna, including white-tailed deer and cottontail rabbit, and the occasional bear remained integral to these people's diet.[19]

LATE PREHISTORIC TO HISTORIC PERIOD, 1450–1700

Oneota

Central Plains Village cultures such as Steed-Kisker flourished and then slowly waned during the early fourteenth century as they interacted with and possibly intermarried with other cultures, including Oneota, a Mississippian culture whose artifacts have been found in the Kawsmouth region.[20] These people continued to exploit the same Woodland flora and fauna that had sustained people for many centuries, but they extended their culture westward, taking fuller advantage of highland prairie flora and fauna, particularly bison, on which their health and prosperity depended. Hunters probably pursued the herds by building a three-sided ring of fire that forced animals toward them. While hunting required young men to be gone for long periods, many women, children, and elders resided in permanent villages. Increasing population made moving en masse unnecessary and impractical. Women worked the soil with bison scapula hoes, planting crops on the silt-rich floodplains to ensure plentiful irrigation. They experimented with and became accustomed to cultivating new varieties of maize, squashes, and beans due to influences coming from Southwest cultures, who in turn were influenced by cultures in Central and South America. Among the maize varieties in this region at the time of European contact were dent, flint, flour, sweet, and popcorn.

Oneota and other Mississippian cultures abandoned their large villages (or in the case of Cahokia its fortified city) sometime in the late 1300s to early 1400s. However, this culture did not just simply disappear, nor did its foodways. Because some earlier Oneota sites in Kansas City's vicinity were eventually occupied by historical Native American tribes, it is possible that these cultures cohabitated, or that Native Americans took over the abandoned sites and tools for their own use, or that they drove out the earlier inhabitants.[21] The foodways of these two cultures bear important similarities, demonstrating how over centuries people utilized native flora and fauna and based daily lives around the seasonal cycles of hunting and planting, storing and eating, their food.

HISTORIC TRIBES AT KAWSMOUTH, 1700–1750

The *Canceres* that the French allied themselves with in the early 1700s were most likely the Kansa or Kaw, a historic Native American tribe aligned linguistically and culturally with the Osage. While the next chapter details the effect Europeans had on fundamentally changing Kansa and Osage foodways, this chapter concludes with some description of how Osage and Kansa were cultivating their crops, hunting, and cooking before significant disruption. Along with the Omaha, Ponca, and Quapaw, the Osage and Kansa peoples speak of an ancient homeland in the Ohio River Valley and their westward movement in the early to mid-1600s. While the Osage settled along the Osage River in Central Missouri and spread out to cover much of Missouri, Kansas, Arkansas, and Oklahoma, the Kansa moved up the Missouri River and stopped at the Kaw River for a little over a decade. In the 1880s, the Kansa informed ethnographer James Owen Dorsey that it was during this time that they first encountered Europeans who offered them brass kettles, knives, and cups. From there, the tribe moved almost to the Iowa state line; however, battles with the Cheyenne led them to retreat south to Kawsmouth, and from there again, up the Kaw River. During these various migrations, the Kansa had more encounters with Europeans who offered them presents.[22]

Some early descriptions of Kansa village life come from August 1819, when Stephen H. Long's expedition explored along the Missouri River. Long journeyed from Fort Osage in Missouri Territory to a Kansa village consisting of about 120 circular lodges fashioned of oak pillars and covered with woven twig and grass mats that were partly earth-covered. Most lodges housed two to three extended families, and each family possessed its own fireplace over which kettles of food were cooked by means of a pole extended over the fire. A hole at the roof's apex allowed for smoke to escape.[23] Lodges included wood platforms roughly two feet from the ground where food, weapons, skins, and personal property were stored. When engaged in their seasonal bison hunts, the entire village participated, living in skin-covered tipis for its duration. Prior to their use of the horse, all goods were transported via dog travois.[24]

The Kansa and Osage relied on subsistence agriculture in addition to annual bison hunts. Maize was the primary crop, but they also planted squashes (pumpkins), grayish white and brown mottled beans (also called peas), and melons. Early twentieth-century ethnobotanist Melvin Gilmore noted that these crops were probably of Mexican origin.[25] In a typical year, Kansa and Osage harvested two maize crops. Women, who owned the fields and the crops, planted in mid-March or after frost danger had passed, and in mid-May before the village removed to the plains. When the village returned from the hunt in late July, the maize was in the "milk" or "green" stage and was ready to be eaten as roasting ears. It was left in the husk, placed in large earthen pits, and buried with earth. Several inches of burning coals were then lowered on top of the earth, and the ears beneath slowly roasted. When they were ready, the ears were rubbed with bison grease or bone marrow: a much-anticipated treat.[26]

Excess roasting ears were boiled briefly to halt enzyme action and help preserve the kernels. They were removed from the cobs, thoroughly dried, placed in loosely woven sacks, and stored high in the lodge rafters. When combined with a meat stew, the maize added bulk and flavor. It could also be crushed for pemmican or reconstituted in stock and eaten as a side dish.

After the green maize had been eaten and/or stored, women planted the pumpkins and the beans in among the remaining maize before the village left for the summer hunt. When they returned in September, the second maize harvest took place, along with pumpkins and beans. This mature maize was essential for numerous recipe staples. One way to prepare it was to shell, parch, and soak the dried kernels in lye-ash water. When the outer skins slipped from the kernels after a long soak and repeated washing, it was often boiled with bear side meat or bear bacon. The Osage referred to this recipe specifically as "hominy." Mature maize also was ground into cornmeal. When the French Creoles settled along the Missouri River, they most likely learned to thicken their gumbos or bouillons by copying the Osage method of doing the same thing. Cornmeal was also mixed with acorn flour to make "squaw bread," or what today is known as Osage "fry bread." Fried in melted bison fat, it was then topped with box-elder syrup.

The remaining maize was left to dry on the cob with the husks pulled back and tied in strings; it too was stored high in the lodge rafters. However, limited space meant that a lot of dried food was transferred to secret cache pits that were double lined, first with tiers of split wooden posts and then dried grass. As much as eight feet deep and round at the bottom and sides, these pits had a narrow neck just large enough to admit a person to enter, descend a ladder, and retrieve the maize. The pits could be covered with earth and trampled down. Sometimes a fire was built over the cache so that thieves could not detect that the soil was a different color or texture.[27]

Pumpkins were preserved by drying strips of flesh partially in the sun, mashing the strips into flat mats, and then drying them completely before storing. They could be reconstituted along with meats and maize to create a savory stew.[28] Indeed, a lot of Central Plains Native cookery might be described as one-pot stews, where dried or fresh vegetables and fruits were used to accent the meat (ideally the bulk of the meal). In 1858, Balduin Möllhausen, a German explorer and artist, wrote of being taken in by a group of Otos who were in their winter hunting encampment some distance from the Missouri River. Möllhausen, an honored guest, was seated in the large tipi of the medicine man between tribal elders. While they smoked the "medicine pipe, with a bowl cut out of some red stone," they waited for their meal to be served. It was a meat stew prepared by a woman and her daughters whose attention "was exclusively devoted to the vast kettle and its bubbling contents; a row of roughly-cut wooden platters" stood before them, and "by means of a pointed stick [the woman] fished up from the cauldron large joints of bear and half turkeys, and loaded each of the platters with a huge portion of the savory smelling food" that was then passed around to the seated men.[29]

While cultivated plants such as maize and pumpkin supplied vital nutrients, wild flora continued to sustain Kansa and Osage as well. The Osage relied on the roots and nuts from the yellow lotus (*Nelumbo lutea*), which they called *Tse walla* or water-chinquapin. It flourished in oxbow lakes close to Osage villages and campsites. To retrieve both it and cattails, women waded into the water and probed the mud with long poles. When they hit the plant's long, arm-like roots, they used the pole to extract them. The roots were peeled, cut into one- and two-inch pieces, and then left to dry or to eat fresh.[30] The Kansa lived in drier upland prairie areas, so more essential to their diet was the prairie potato or turnip (*Psoralea esculenta*), which they foraged and cultivated.[31] Once peeled, the egg-shaped root was eaten raw, boiled, or roasted; it was also dried and used in winter stews or pounded into flour for breads and griddle cakes. Early European settlers called the prairie potato *pomme blanche* due to its white color.

The ground nut (*Apios tuberosa*) produced tubers that resembled beans and that were prized by the Kansa for their high starch content. Because the beans resembled beads, the French called them *les racines des chapelets*. Arrowhead (*Sagittaria*), which grew abundantly in wet areas, also produced an edible, starchy tuber. The hog peanut (*Falcata comosa*) was another Central Plains staple. A terrific protein source that resembled lentils in flavor when cooked, the hog peanut was likewise a favorite of voles, who stored them in underground burrows.[32] Enterprising boys would root out the voles' hideaways and steal the peanuts.

Fruit was prized for flavor and for the general sense of well-being it provided. To brighten the heavy, fatty taste of pemmican, crushed choke-cherries and/or juneberries were included. When dried, juneberries resembled raisins and were eaten out of hand as such. The very tart gooseberry cut the richness of game stews. Wild black cherries, a pea-size fruit from the native black cherry tree, were also used in pemmican, and they were crushed and dried as patties to be added to winter meat stews.

Pawpaws, persimmons, and wild plums were highly valued. The pawpaw was eaten fresh in season, and it was also dried and pounded to make flour for cakes and bread. The Osage considered the pawpaw a sacred tree and used both its fruit and its bark. One Osage camp in central Missouri, *To shon He* (Pawpaw Bark), supplied the Osage with enough bark to make the twine that they used to string together buffalo ribs after a hunt. These sewn-together "rib blankets" were thrown over racks for drying.[33] Persimmons were eaten fresh, but many people preferred to dry them or cook the pulp into a thick pudding or bread studded with hickory nuts. Writing in April 1811, the Kawsmouth explorer John Bradbury was invited to Osage Chief Waubuschon's lodge. "A wooden bowl was . . . handed round, containing square pieces of cake, in taste resembling ginger-bread. On enquiry I found it was made of the pulp of the persimmon, mixed with pounded corn. This bread they called staninca."[34] Technically, Osage called the persimmon fruit itself *Sta en ka*. To prepare this gingerbread-like sweet, the Osages gathered the fruit after the first frost and laid it on a screen composed of numerous rod-like saplings. By forcing the soft, ripe pulp through the screen, they could extract it from the sticky, hard-to-remove seeds. The pulp could then be flattened on a board and baked over coals. The finished product was called *Sta en ka Ka he*.[35] A modern-day version of staninca, often mixed with cornmeal, hazelnuts, pecans, or hickory nuts, appears in Missouri cookbooks as well as area restaurants that feature native foods.

While persimmons were almost tooth-achingly sweet and pulpy once they had ripened, smooth sumac was prized for its astringency, and strawberries for their sweet-tartness. Boiled with box-elder syrup (box elder is a maple species native to this region), sumac berries and strawberries could be made into jam. Sumac berries, when bruised, were mixed with box-elder syrup and water to make a lemonade-style drink; dried sumac leaves were good for tea or smoking like tobacco. Understandably, "all the tribes were fond of wild strawberries and luxuriated in them in their season," wrote Melvin Gilmore.[36]

When food was scarce because of a particularly dry or wet season, Kansa and neighboring tribes turned to less palatable foods. Prairie rose-hips, for example, were considered famine food. Although nutritious, picking and preparing them took more labor than they were worth if other food was plentiful. When times were even more desperate, Native people relied on the native red haw tree. The fruit was easy to collect, but it was bitter and unpalatable. The fruit of the red-osier dogwood was even more so, but such food could save people from malnourishment.[37]

While most game and fish were protein sources for Osage and Kansa people, bison was the most favored meat, followed by deer (the Osage called it the "small animal"), followed by bear (the Osage called it "no sinews"). While some people enjoyed eating fish, small game, and fowl, others commented that these animals did "not feel good in the mouth" and hence avoided them if possible.[38]

As a cornerstone of the diet, bison was integral to Osage and Kansa rituals and traditions. Among the fifteen or sixteen Kansa gentes, or kinship groups, were the Earth People, Thunder People, Deer People, Buffalo People, and the Ghost People. The Earth People consulted with the Deer and Buffalo People to determine when it was time to move a hunting camp; this privilege allowed the Earth People to put up their camp first, but it also meant that they were not allowed to eat roasted maize, a ceremonial food, until all others had eaten. Similarly, the Buffalo People were not allowed to partake of buffalo meat until all others had finished.[39] The Osage, like the Kansa, also relied on the wisdom of specific tribal members to ensure a successful hunt. The spring and fall grand hunts (which were exclusively for bison hunting) were overseen by the Director of the Hunt, who was selected in a ceremony, along with his eight assistants. En route, two Grand Division chiefs were in charge, responsible for choosing the routes to and from the hunting ground.[40]

Kansa and Osage relied on various methods to ensure a successful kill that resembled those of the prehistoric peoples before them. Stampeding required everyone in the hunting party to participate. The animals were approached downwind and frightened so that they stampeded toward a gully or cutbank. A decoy dressed in a bison robe complete with bison head stood near the gully's edge. Seeing what appeared to be a content cow or bull grazing, the herd would move toward the decoy, who then had to gamely jump below the bank and run to avoid the falling bison. Similarly, a decoy dressed in bison robe and head would move into the herd upwind, "grazing" closer and closer, and secreting under his robe a bow and arrows. When within easy range, the decoy would (with luck) aim his first arrow at the targeted bison's lungs, distressing the creature and causing other bison to gather around it. From this point, the hunters, again (with luck) could kill the entire cluster. If the shots were inaccurate or not powerful enough, however, winded buffalo could easily kill the hunters before they escaped.[41]

The gun and the horse made some of these strategies obsolete, and they fundamentally altered other strategies. Because early gun technology made it difficult to fire repeatedly from the back of a moving horse, some decoys hid the gun under their buffalo robes instead of bows and arrows. When hunting on horseback, the Osages and Kansa continued to prefer bows and arrows, given the time it took to reload a gun and how easy it could be to accidentally kill a fellow hunter if the rifle discharged or the aim was off.

The conclusion of a successful bison hunt resulted in feasting. In 1819, a party of explorers participated in one at the Blue Earth village, near present-day Manhattan, Kansas. The men sat in the tribal leaders' lodge and were presented with "two wooden bowls, filled with Buffaloe [sic] meat, soup and corn" and handed "spoons made of the Buffaloe horn." The men found the food "very palatable." After they had eaten, they were encouraged to eat again, and so they enjoyed a second feast. They finished and left the lodge but were immediately invited to yet "another feast, and [were] conducted to another lodge." They ate heartily, took their leave "in the same unceremonious manner as before," but attended yet another feast, this one including some watermelons. "During the course of the day," the men wrote, they were "invited to partake of nine or ten feasts."[42]

A successful hunt resulted in two weeks' worth of such merrymaking and feasting, significantly more than was customary for the tribes at any other time of the year. Nonetheless, these rituals and traditions, not to mention the food itself, were threatened and in some cases destroyed as French, British, and Spanish settlers began making inroads into the North American middle section. It is to actual European settlement in the Missouri Territory and at Kawsmouth specifically that this food biography will now turn.

Chapter Three

The Old World Meets the New

When traveling by steamboat to his new Parish of Kansas post in May 1845, Father Bernard Donnelly received a visit from Mr. Northrup, a clerk for the P. Chouteau Fur Trading Company. Northrup and Madame Berenice Chouteau were on the same boat making their way home, and Northrop stopped by Donnelly's berth to extend Madame Chouteau's regards. As the men talked, Northrup filled Donnelly in on the habits and customs of his soon-to-be parishioners. While Donnelly's primary residence would be Independence, Jackson County's seat, he would also have the Kawsmouth mission church, St. Regis, and its two hundred or so French Creole and Metis parishioners. They are a "very honest, simple, virtuous, and yet very social" people, Northrop explained. He cautioned that "some of them loved their glass rather to [sic] well, but seldom quarreled." They had their social reunions where they "danced to the music of the fiddle."[1]

Although the Town of Kansas was increasingly Anglo-American in terms of its public life, it remained French in regard to its social life and traditions. Donnelly's quick perception and acceptance of this somewhat complicated status quo, and his ability to work as intermediary and spiritual advisor to many people, make his memoirs some of the most authoritative information available concerning life at Kawsmouth in the antebellum era.

Of course Donnelly was arriving relatively late in the game. Although it would be five more years before the "Town of Kansas" became an official municipality, the boomtown feel of the levy and nearby Westport had largely erased all vestiges of Kansa and Osage culture. The area where many of the French and Metis lived was also rapidly disappearing in part due to flooding. The region by this decade was a polyglot of languages and ethnicities with roughly sixty steamboats a day unloading people, livestock, and supplies. The Town of Kansas Company had transformed a rock shelf into a steamboat loading area. Everything was in the process of being "improved." What had happened to make it so? And in the course of this transformation of "Kawsmouth" into the "Town of Kansas," what had happened to its food? More importantly, what role did the food play in that transformation? This chapter explores some answers to these questions.

THE FRENCH AMONG THE OSAGE, MISSOURIA, AND KANSA

As is always the case, before one can discuss the food or the food-ways, one must have some understanding of the history, economics, and politics of the area in question. From the mid-to-late 1600s when Osage, Kansa, and other Siouan-speaking peoples came to the Missouri and Kansas River Valleys, they had lived largely unencumbered by European ways and influence. While French and British settlements in the St. Lawrence River Valley and along the eastern Atlantic seaboard might have indirectly prompted Native inhabitants to leave the Ohio River Valley and move west, it is also likely that their decision had to do more directly with food. Possibly, these Siouan-speaking peoples were following buffalo herds on which their diet and way of life depended. It could also have been that they found the river bottoms and terrace-lined valleys between the Mississippi River and the western prairies more conducive to cultivating maize.[2] In all cases, as they traveled west, these tribes were moving through and into lands that were the hunting grounds of other tribes. Part of their settlement patterns, with Osage spreading out along the Osage River, and Kansa moving on to Kawsmouth and up the Kaw, were based on the shifting boundaries of other people's domains. The information that Europeans initially received about the Kansa and the Osage came from other Native informants who had relationships with, or secondhand knowledge about, these peoples.

At the time that French exploration began at the confluence of the Missouri and Kaw Rivers, the main motivation was to determine the direction of the waterways; a secondary motivation was to trap mammals to supply Europe's insatiable desire for fur. Related to both motivations was the need to administer and control the boundaries that harbored such rich natural resources. In all cases, France was engaged in what might be described as colonial one-upmanship as it competed with Spain and Great Britain for its share of the North American continent.

When King Louis XIV ascended the throne in 1643, New France was restricted to the St. Lawrence River Valley, but the nation wanted a colony that matched, if not superseded, that of New Spain in size and importance. Columbus's 1492 voyage had ignited Spanish exploration of the Americas. Juan Ponce de León reached "La Florida" in 1513; Cabeza de Vaca reached the Gulf Coast in the early 1500s. Reaching closer to the Kawsmouth region but not yet to it was Francisco Vázquez de Coronado, whose 1541 *Entrada Conquista* brought soldiers and missionaries up from Mexico and as far north as present-day Rice County in Central Kansas. Importantly, Coronado also brought horses, sheep, and cattle, all of which would affect indigenous foodways. At roughly the same time, Hernando de Soto was exploring present-day northeast Arkansas, also with livestock in tow. Based on such expeditions, Spain claimed an extensive region northeast of Santa Fe and Taos, but knowledge of precisely what the region consisted of and its actual borders remained virtually unknown during the 1500s and 1600s.

Taking significant risks and racking up large debts to pursue its colonial ambitions, France sponsored explorers who traversed North America's middle section, with attention focused on what the Algonquin called the *Missi sepe*, or Great River, and also the river's westward-moving tributary, the *Pekittanoui*, or Muddy Water.[3] When Jacques Marquette and Louis Joliet were commissioned in 1673 to explore these river systems, they were attempting to locate a passage from the *Missi sepe* (or Mississippi) to, as Marquette put it in his journal, a river "that discharges into the Vermillion, or California Sea." Kawsmouth lay at a critical juncture of that supposed passage.[4]

Due to unforeseen problems, Marquette and Joliet did not reach Kawsmouth, but they made it to (and past) the confluence of the Mississippi and that westward-moving tributary, the *Pekittanoui*, as Marquette labeled it on his 1673–1674 map. Soon thereafter, *Pekittanoui* became known as the *Emissourita*, the name French explorers took from the Native people who lived at its confluence with the Mississippi, and the name that the French in turn called those Native peoples.[5] Eventually, *Emissourita* gave way to *Missouri* for river, territory, and the people. Marquette also recorded the names of other tribes along the Missouri and at its bend to the north, including the Kansa and the Osage.

When French explorer Robert Cavelier, Sieur de La Salle, descended the Mississippi River all the way to the Gulf in 1682, he claimed the river, the land drained by it, and its tributaries for France, including the Missouri River. While it had become clear that the Missouri did not lead directly to the Pacific, its thickly timbered banks were home to a seemingly endless supply of mammals whose pelts would bring significant money on the European market, and the Osage clearly knew the terrain and contours of that area.

The Osage had covered their nation with a system of interconnecting roads and trails that spread throughout present-day Oklahoma, Arkansas, Kansas, and Missouri and that served multiple purposes. Some were for hunting, others for gathering plants or harvesting timber, others for avoiding enemy ambushes, and still others for communicating and visiting.[6] Intimate understanding of this topography was essential if the French were to profit in the fur trade, and thus, their explorers were interested in fostering good relationships with the Osage, and when they met with them, the Osage's linguistic cousins and allies, the Kansa.

A people "of an extraordinary height and bigness" was how the Huron and Ottawa described the Osage to explorer Pierre Esprit Radisson. "They live only upon corn and citruls [pumpkins] which are mighty big. They have fish in plenty throughout the year. . . . Their dishes are made of wood. . . . They made a store of tobacco."[7] The Osage were considered formidable by allies and enemies alike. Their success as hunters was renowned; their later antagonism toward the Spanish and ability to best them, combined with their disregard for the British, meant that the French had a lot to gain if they coexisted peacefully with these people.

Through negotiations, gifts, and intermarriages, the French did make alliances with the Osage and Missouria, and as they pushed west to Kawsmouth, with the Kansa. In the 1720s when Etienne de Véniard, Sieur de Bourgmont, established Fort Orleans along the Missouri River, these tribes and the French had relatively peaceful relationships, and there was little adverse effect on the Osage food supply. What did change early on because of European influence were their gardening, hunting, and cooking technologies.

The first Osage and French contact in the Missouri region probably occurred in 1693 when traders left Kaskaskia in present-day Illinois to form a trading relationship with Native tribes. From that encounter, but perhaps from even earlier interactions with the Spanish or neighboring tribes, the Osage acquired European goods. The earliest known Osage camp in Missouri, the Utz site, included glass bottles, digging tools, iron scrapings, iron arrowheads, and guns that predate 1700.[8] Europeans offered the Osage an array of products as gifts or in exchange for fur, including goods such as those uncovered at Utz, as well as hoes, traps, fishhooks, knives, hatchets, thread, rope, and cookware.

In some respects, these tools were more durable than what the Osage had used previously, or they came in multiple sizes, or they were lighter weight and easier to use. When the Osage deemed European products flimsy, or in the case of brass and copper pots dangerous because of food poisoning, they rejected them. The Osage did like the heavier but safe iron cookware, however, and adopted it readily.[9] They also valued European traps and muskets. For French traders, Osage adoption of these technologies could mean more pelts acquired; for Osage, they could increase their meat supply.

Thus, in the earliest decades of French-Native contact, the relationship was often mutually beneficial. While Native people adopted some European cooking and gardening techniques to facilitate their traditional foodways, the French relied on Native foodstuffs and know-how to keep themselves fed. Native people's interaction was often with *coureurs de bois*, unlicensed trappers who did not often work according to official government or bureaucratic rules and who were themselves navigating successfully within and among Native communities. Pierre-Jean DeSmet, the Jesuit missionary who visited Kawsmouth and published information on the French trappers' culture and foodways, wrote about how they survived and what they learned from the Native Americans. Trappers enjoyed beaver flesh, for example, because it was "fat and savory." "The feet are deemed the most dainty parts. The tail affords a substitute for butter," DeSmet wrote.[10]

Bison was as coveted among the French trappers as it was among the Osage and Kansa. "It may be called the daily bread of the traveler, for he never loses his relish for it," DeSmet wrote. Some men preferred tongue, others the hump. They also made a hash of pounded meat mixed with bone marrow "called bull or cheese"; it "is generally served up and eaten raw, but when boiled or baked it is of more easy digestion, and has a more savory taste to a civilized palate." Men also preserved much of the meat by cutting it "in slices, thin enough to be dried in the sun," DeSmet added.[11] When in unfamiliar territory or experiencing food shortages, trappers did as Plains Natives did: they used their own stores of pemmican, jerky, dried fruit, prairie potatoes, and nuts. When convenient, they traded goods or purchased maize from the Kansa, Osage, Omaha, and Pawnee.

It took time for the French at Fort Orleans and later at the various Chouteau fur-trading posts to establish their orchards, vineyards, and pastures, as well as to harvest sizable crops of European cereal grains. Furthermore, prior to the steamboat era and Santa Fe commerce, goods such as olive oil, cane sugar, coffee, tea, wine, and spices were rare and thus expensive. With transportation slow and river travel nearly impossible during winter and early spring, French settlers depended on native cultivated crops, foraged foods, and game. Hazelnut bushes grew so densely that the only way through them was to hack paths with axes. These nuts, along with walnuts and hickory, figured heavily in people's diets. The French added their own culinary expertise when it came to preparing native foods. Wild grapes and gooseberries were turned into wine, for example, and wild plums, cherries, and blackberries into cordial. The French began raising dairy cows, pigs, and fowl. The honeybee likewise flourished in apiaries, and indeed became, as Louis F. Burns put it, "the vanguard of the American Frontier"; Native Americans knew that if they located a honeybee, American settlement would follow within two or three years.[12]

Food was more consistently available at the French forts themselves, including one at Cahokia established in 1699, one established on the Mississippi River at Natchez in 1716, as well as one at Fort Orleans, which was, as Kansas City historian Charles E. Hoffhaus described it, a "microcosm of the Regency period."[13] Established in the 1720s as the base from which expeditions could be sent out to make peace between the French, Plains tribes, and the Spaniards, Fort Orleans was relatively close to present-day Kansas City. Although a small stockade, it was nonetheless a largely self-contained and self-sustaining village. Within it, soldiers maintained barracks, a warehouse, kitchen gardens, stores, poultry houses, an ice house, maize and tobacco crops, and perhaps some wheat. The gardens presumably produced European vegetables (radishes, cabbages, beets, carrots) alongside native ones (melons, squash, beans).[14] De Bourgmont, who oversaw the fort, lived at least part of the time in a neighboring Osage village, and men came and went between fort and village. It is likely that some Native Americans worked within fort walls, interacting regularly with the soldiers and personnel. In such exchanges, ideas about food and cooking would have taken place, but without especial comment or notations made in the various logs and correspondence.

Larger forts in the region were established primarily to process furs; they maintained a strict hierarchy among employees that directly affected their diets. *Engagees*, the lowliest of trappers and personnel, were allowed only meat for their board; they had to supply all other wants or go without. *Voyageurs*, the licensed trappers, were allowed meat, biscuit, and black coffee with sugar. Clerks and managers ate the best, supplied with meat, bread, soup, and fruit pies.[15] Fort kitchens were overseen by French cooks who delegated the majority of basic cooking and cleaning tasks to conscripted soldiers or *engagees*, although the lower echelons of fort personnel would have seen to their own cooking needs.

Outside the fort, some trappers lived largely solitary lives, depending primarily on themselves for survival; others turned to Native women because they were skilled at procuring and cooking food. Frenchmen's and Native women's liaisons often were initially based on satisfying physical hunger, but sometimes the liaisons became sexual as well. It might be said that the need to eat gave rise to a distinctive society, one largely opaque, even unfathomable, to the higher echelon of New France colonials, as well as some Jesuit missionaries, who looked on *marriage à la façon du pays* as evidence of a "Scandalous and Criminal life."[16] If forced to defend themselves, trappers argued that "their wives ground the corn to make the staple food known as *sagamité*." They also prepared hides for trade while preparing meat for the pot.[17]

Among the French traders and merchant class, those whom historian Jay Gitlin identified as the bourgeois, relationships with Native American women were likewise common, but they were not for matters of survival; rather, such marriages or partnerships *à la façon du pays* ensured that trade went smoothly and that trust among the French, Osage, and Kansa grew, irrespective of what colonial power actually controlled the region.[18]

Some years before Francois and Berenice settled at Randolph Bluff along with fifteen other St. Charles and St. Louis French Creole families, the Chouteau clan (including Francois) had actively made inroads into Kansa territory farther up the Kaw River. The intermarriages and alliances that resulted thus facilitated the establishment and ensured the success of the Randolph Bluff post.

This French-Native alliance was not without problems, but prior to the French-Indian War in 1754, it allowed the Osage and Kansa to maintain much of their traditional culture, including the alternation of planting and harvesting crops with annual hunting expeditions. The Osage were powerful middlemen who controlled French access to fur and to the other goods traded between farther-away western and southern Native nations. Osage people were overall healthy, lived to old age, suffered few debilitating diseases, and rarely had significant tooth decay or other dental maladies. Osage women bore on average three to four children and nursed them two to three years. Access to a varied and plentiful diet also helped protect the Osage from European diseases.[19]

INDIAN REMOVAL AND ITS EFFECT ON NATIVE FOODWAYS AT KAWSMOUTH

From the start of the French-Indian War to the Louisiana Purchase in 1803, alliances between the French, Osage, and Kansa frayed as they and other European powers and ultimately the United States fought for dominancy over North America. Indian removal policies that began to take shape after the American Revolutionary War and particularly after the War of 1812 intensified problems. In all cases, Native foodways were jeopardized, and the overall health of Native peoples declined dramatically.

Missouri and eleven other states joined the Union between 1816 and 1848, and Washington officials thought that large portions of central and southwestern Missouri, part of the Osage Nation, were the best areas to forcibly relocate Native tribes. In this respect, the French were often in an optimum position to help broker such deals and to benefit from them. Hence, from the early 1800s on, the Osage contended with displaced tribes encroaching on their hunting grounds, resulting in hostilities and violence. Potawatomi, Iowa, Sac, Mesquakie, and Kickapoo came into

Osage land from the north in their own search for game, while Cherokee, Choctaw, Chickasaw, Shawnee, and Delaware entered Osage land primarily from the South.[20]

When these incursions happened, the Osage Nation's first priority was to protect the native flora and fauna on which their immediate alimentary needs depended. The delicate food balance was further compromised, however, as European settlers and their African slaves also competed for decreasing supplies of game and edible plants.[21] The Osage and Kansa became dangerously used to purchasing European foodstuffs and goods on credit, repaying Chouteau and other merchants the debt when an annual fur harvest took place. This financial relationship undermined whatever autonomy and power the Osage Nation still exercised.

Long-established alliances between the Osage and French did in some instances mitigate tensions; however, as Jay Gitlin put it when discussing A. P. Chouteau's and Frederick Chouteau's willingness to supply Native communities with resources, "in the end, there was always a bill to pay."[22] Many of Francois's letters detail this credit-debt merry-go-round that defined his life at Kawsmouth, particularly as the displaced Shawnee competed with the Kansa and Osage for dwindling fur supplies. "And what upsets me with [the Shawnee] is that they do not pay their credits," complained Francois in his January 12, 1829, letter to his father-in-law, Pierre Menard Sr., who had been instrumental in relocating the Shawnee to Indian Territory close to Francois and Berenice's enterprise.[23] Traders competing with Chouteau also felt pressure from banks and supervisors, and as the U.S. government began doling out annuity money as payment for Native land, traders were eager to balance their books by taking the annuity moneys as well as furs to repay outstanding debts.

Inevitably, the annuities system was abused. Paid out once a year, typically in silver coins to a tribal leader who in turn paid traders and merchants to cover his tribe's debts, such ready cash was irresistible to settlers who came to the area purposely to open stores. They often made the case to Native Americans that it was risky for them to extend credit; hence, they charged tribes so much interest that price inflation was commonplace, as much as 500 percent (even 900 percent in some rare cases).[24] Hence, Kansa, Osage, and displaced tribes found themselves indefinitely in debt.

To protect villages and remaining food caches from raiding enemy tribes, some Osage and Kansa men were compelled to stay behind during hunting seasons, thus hindering their ability to bring in enough bison meat to sustain the tribes through winter months.[25] When tribes could not depend on bison, they had to resort to smaller mammals and wild plants, and hence, another nightmarish merry-go-round ensued as even more pressure was put on native flora and fauna. In many areas near Kawsmouth, some animals and plants alike were driven nearly to extinction.[26]

Given these circumstances, many native peoples' diets changed for the worse, although this topic is complicated. For one, the Ohio Shawnee, Delaware, and Creek had already adapted their diets to accommodate European foods and cooking techniques before their forced removal; they were excellent farmers, both with milpa and Western farming techniques. The Wyandotte, whose reservation land would become a key portion of present-day Kansas City, Kansas, were likewise excellent farmers and were accustomed to European foodstuffs. Ironically, these tribes had been advised to farm on their reservation land in spite of the fact that it had been deemed by Zebulon Pike little more than a desert.

Exacerbating an already terrible situation was erratic Kansas weather. Long periods of drought (what might have led to Pike's initial observations) compromised bison fertility and the health of the herds, but then, extended seasons of spring flooding also hampered planting crops. The flood that destroyed the Chouteaus' Randolph Bluff post also destroyed the Kansa's maize at nearby Mission Creek, and flooding happened the following spring. By 1836, after failed promises of the U.S. government to deliver livestock to his starving and disease-ridden people, Kansa Fool Chief told the damning truth with few words: "Of the hogs due us, one hundred and seven were wanting, and seven of the cattle, but I do not know how many chickens."[27]

When Kansas and Nebraska Territory was opened to Anglo-American settlement in 1854, the Osage, Kansa, and displaced tribes were repeatedly left with diminished lands. During an earlier 1825 removal, the federal government ordered "full-bloods" (the government term for full-blooded Kansa), to move to reservations far west of present-day Kansas City. French fathers were allowed to remain in the region, and their offspring, the people that historian Charles E. Hoffhaus called the French-Kansa, were allotted twenty-three sections of farmland extending north of Topeka to Lecompton, Kansas.[28]

The complexity and scope of intertribal warfare, wars between European powers, U.S. treaty negotiations, diminishing fur supplies, and Indian removal policies are beyond the scope of this study and have been dealt with masterfully elsewhere. What is important to understanding early Kansas City food heritage is that much of the metropolitan area sat in the western portion of what had been the Osage Nation, a place where inhabitants had successfully utilized and managed two ecosystems for their food supplies. By 1845 when Father Donnelly disembarked and took up his parish duties, Westport, Independence, and the soon-to-be Town of Kansas were on the western border of Missouri, with Indian Territory and Mexican-controlled land on the other side of that border; few full-blooded Kansa or Osage remained in the vicinity.

The people who would determine Kansas City's food culture from this point in time were a diverse mix, including French Creoles, or people of French descent who had been born in New France; Americans, or people of English, Scotch-Irish descent who had been born in the British colonies or the United States; increasing numbers of first-generation immigrants from Western Europe; African Americans who were brought here as slaves; and Metis, those of mixed blood heritage that the U.S. government designated "half-breeds" and who were the offspring of (predominantly) French fathers and Native American mothers. The food that people ate in this preindustrial time was still largely based on native flora and fauna, but the ways these foods were prepared, and the increasing availability of imported ingredients with which they were combined, reflected culinary traditions that were as diverse as the people themselves.

The remainder of this chapter takes into account some of the most prominent features of Kansas City's antebellum culinary makeup with focus on the French settlement at Kawsmouth, and then after Mexico won its war of independence from Spain and the Santa Fe Trail began in earnest, the American settlements at Westport and Town of Kansas.

FRENCH FOOD CULTURE AT KAWSMOUTH

In language, social habits, customs, and religion, Kawsmouth was a Francophone community. Although small, it resembled any other such community in regard to its hierarchies and alliances. The Chouteaus were the "First Family," both literally and figuratively speaking. They had their established stake in the fur trade, significant real estate holdings, and investments in what would become Kansas City. Also prosperous were Louis Roy and his sister, the Widow Revard, with their families who were descendants of Andre Roy, an independent trader.[29] Critical to this story are Gabriel and Susan Prudhomme, whose 257 acres of farmland would eventually be purchased after Gabriel's death by the Town of Kansas Company to become Kansas City. Susan was a Cree Indian artisan who, with Gabriel and her older children, ran the community's store and tavern.

The majority of these settlers were subsistence farmers, second- and third-generation Metis who lived in the "French Bottoms," the land along the Kaw and Missouri Rivers. Many men left for extended hunting and trapping expeditions while wives and children cultivated crops in a pattern that resembled what Kansa and Osage had done previously. As the fur trade declined, many French turned exclusively to farming, marking their plots into *arpents*, or long, narrow strips of land roughly seven-eighths of an acre. Some were successful enough to sell excess produce, milk, and honey to Chouteau fort personnel, soldiers bound for Fort Leavenworth, and travelers. Others opened hostelries and made their living by boarding hunters and trappers. Accounts of French life at Kawsmouth left by its earliest Catholic missionaries and priests inevitably involved information on farming and food, both in times of hunger and plenty.

When Father Benedict Roux's "petition to be sent among the Indians" was granted by his bishop, he joined the Chouteaus at Kawsmouth in 1833.[30] He arrived shortly after the missionary priest, Father Lutz, resigned—disgusted by the "slothful bellies . . . addicted to drink"—as he characterized his French parishioners.[31] As first resident priest, Father Roux likewise wrote detailed letters to his superior, Bishop Rosati in St. Louis, of the hardships he endured "from the mouth of the Kansas," and how his enthusiasm for the venture faded.

Roux wrote from the perspective of a man whose satisfaction and dissatisfaction in life hinged on his stomach: "Board, fire, lodging, everything is prepared for me with the greatest care," Father Roux wrote enthusiastically of his arrival to the Chouteau estate. Living as they did in a large house, complete with slaves to see to their needs, it is understandable why Father Roux was pleased. Of course—he hastened to assure his bishop—"I do not expect to remain long with them." Father Roux's challenge was the distance he needed to travel to minister to the Kickapoo and Potawatomi who had received him (as he saw it) "as an angel sent from heaven," and his need to minister to the French who lived roughly three miles from his temporary home with the Chouteaus. "I intend to go and settle in the midst of the French congregation; provided I have corn-bread and milk I am content," Father Roux explained to Bishop Rosati.

Father Roux yearned for more than corn bread and milk, however. While living with the Chouteaus, he indulged in whatever heady imported luxuries were on hand—salads dressed with olive oil, coffee with cane sugar, bread made from wheat flour—foodstuffs that Berenice and Francois relied on family in St. Louis to supply them with.[32] Five months later, Father Roux again wrote Bishop Rosati, reiterating that the Chouteau family continued to "lavish a thousand cares on" him, and that to help him minister to the French, they had "arranged very decently a house for this purpose, to which house two others are attached to serve as presbytery for the priest." Alas, this presbytery still required Father Roux to journey "ten long miles" from the Chouteaus' home in the course of his duties. He left on Saturday, but on reaching his presbytery, he found there "neither breakfast, dinner, supper, nor fire. . . . If I want to eat," Father Roux continued, "I must go in search of food, often several miles away. Hunger gives a seasoning to everything however coarse the dish," he observed morosely. "It is impossible, then, to say Mass. Not being taken care of by anybody, the most robust health would fail there in a few weeks." Roux did place some hope, however, in persuading "a respectable widow" to prepare his meals, "giving her to understand that the Catholic congregation would defray" whatever expense he should put her to. The battle to fill his stomach and "the rough, undisciplined life of a frontier settlement" defeated Father Roux's morale. Before St. Regis could be finished, Father Roux left in April 1835 to return to the more civilized comforts of Kaskaskia and St. Louis.

Father Roux was not only tired of frontier life; he was frustrated and at times outraged by what he perceived as the immorality among the French. Plenty of food was fine, but only in a pious context. In a letter to Bishop Rosati written shortly before his departure, Father Roux criticized Madame Chouteau's unholy love of "bals," the winter parties where the community gathered to eat bullion and *croquignoles* (deep-fried crullers similar to *beignets*), drink homemade cherry bounce and cordials, and dance to the fiddling of Messrs. Joe and Peter Rivard—and when it arrived, to the tinkling strains of Madame Chouteau's piano, reportedly the first to be brought into western Missouri, strapped to the deck of a keelboat.[33] Roux wanted to ban these parties, but Madame Chouteau set the community standards, and it was largely her own strong Catholicism that had brought the priests—including Roux—in the first place. As Tanis C. Thorne pointed out, "In attempting to ban these weekly dances and feasts enjoyed by the Creoles, mixed-bloods, and Indians, Roux faced a formidable opposition."[34] Given the size of their home, the Chouteaus frequently hosted the balls, thus bringing Father Roux and Madame Chouteau to an impasse. Desperate to win the battle, Father Roux appealed to St. Paul, informing her that women were "not to teach, nor hold authority over man, but to be in silence." Madame Chouteau remained unmoved, reminding *him* that the nearby Anglo-Americans, largely Episcopalian, Presbyterians, and Methodists, did not have any issue with such frolics. The balls would go on.[35]

More equipped for the challenges of frontier life and also appreciative of the people was Father Donnelly. He also alluded in his records to food, particularly when it pertained to celebrations; indeed, he apparently enjoyed the balls when he was in residence. Recalling those customs in surprisingly vivid detail in 1876, Donnelly wrote:

> A select committee waited on some settler and informed him that a dancing party would visit his place on a certain evening. The party waited on was reminded that his friends expected he would have indispensable pot de Boullion for his guests, but what was in this pot de Boullion? It was a rich palatable soup, cooked in a large pot, composed of chicken, wild fowl, venison, and sometimes slices of fresh buffalo meat, to all which was added a few handfuls of corn meal with seasoning of salt and pepper. The soup was quaffed from gourds, cups and dishes.[36]

No one seemed to fret or mourn the lack of "civilization," Donnelly maintained. Indeed, gourds among the cups and dishes, and the *bouillon* itself, symbolized the mixing of Native, African, and French people at this settlement.

The French are traditionally credited with creating stock, or *bouillon*. By boiling animal bones and vegetables in water, hundreds of broths, gravies, and sauces are born. In the mid-1700s, the French also called some *bouillon* a *restaurant* or restorative broth, championed for its simplicity and healthful qualities. However, in fundamental ways, the *bouillon* that the Kawsmouth French were eating resembled the one-pot soups and stews that Native women had been feeding their families for centuries. The difference was in the thickening agent and of course the available plants and protein. Native women used pounded rehydrated pumpkin along with cornmeal and beans to give a certain luxury to their meat stews, while the French, if they wanted to thicken the *bouillon*, used a roux of fat and flour. Given the initial scarcity at Kawsmouth of wheat flour and butter, French women adjusted their palates.

Donnelly's *bouillon* was also characterized as a gumbo, the most popular dish in Missouri during the 1820s, according to historian Charles Van Ravenswaay.[37] It came into Missouri by way of Louisiana French Creoles, the Virginians, and their African slaves. The word *gumbo*, which means okra, is of probable West African origin, and the seeds for this vegetable traveled with slaves through the Middle Passage. Slaves passed their culinary traditions on to their children as well as their masters, thus infusing Southern cuisine with the flavor of this unique vegetable, one that grew prolifically in hot climates and that could thicken stews. On the nights when the ball was at the Chouteaus', it was likely a slave who made the *bouillon* Donnelly recalled.

AMERICAN ENTREPRENEURS AT WESTPORT

Americans who moved into Missouri from the South, primarily Virginia and Kentucky, were also fond of gumbo. Their numbers began to dwarf the French population by the 1840s. Some came to Kawsmouth to missionize, some came to farm, and a significant number came to capitalize on the Santa Fe trade, pioneers, and also Indian annuities. It was for this last reason that John Calvin McCoy decided to establish his trading post at Westport.

European foodstuffs were of course highly profitable because they were in demand by Native Americans forced to make do with them, and also because Americans needed to stock them before continuing west. Even basic supplies were expensive, costing much more than the prices charged in St. Louis. Motivated to find the best prices, Shawnee and Delaware men would travel from their villages in Indian Territory over to Independence to see what was on offer, comparing prices and quality with what they could get for their money at the Chouteaus' various posts along the Kaw. John Calvin McCoy intended to compete with these merchants, and his success at Westport led to others joining him there; the settlement began to grow.

Westport's proximity to the Missouri state line became even more important in 1848 when the United States acquired and annexed New Mexico after the Treaty of Guadalupe Hidalgo ended the Mexican War. Santa Fe Trail commerce picked up increasing momentum. Based on the route established by Captain William Becknell in 1821, the seven-hundred-mile trail crossed through what was to become Westport. During the first two decades, traders transferred lead, cotton cloth, glass bottles, cookware, fine china, and other wares from steamboats docked near Independence onto Conestoga wagons. The traders returned from Chihuahua, Santa Fe, and Bent's Fort, Colorado, with silver coins, processed gold, wool, and mules. Missouri farmers also sold home-cured hams and bacons, cornmeal, tobacco, flour, and beef to the Santa Fe Traders to feed the men, but also because such foodstuffs were desperately needed and highly profitable in the expanding West.

Pioneers added to the Santa Fe traffic by the 1830s and 1840s. Given that a wagon journey took three or more months and that people had to store enough staples to survive the journey, anyone going into the provisions business at a critical juncture along the trails stood a chance at profit, and indeed McCoy profited handsomely. His double-pen log store stocked virtually any foodstuff or cookware a pioneer needed.

McCoy's was not the first business in this area, however. Prior to his arrival, both Daniel Yoacham and James Jennings recognized that food and/or lodging were potentially profitable occupations. Jennings operated a water mill, presumably to grind corn, and Daniel Yoacham, a Tennessean, ran a tavern and hostelry.[38] Kansas City lore has it that Yoacham offered terrible food, but travelers either partook of Yoacham's "overdone beef and raw whisky; biscuits, corn bread, sow belly, coffee, [and] beans," or they did without. Edward R. Schauffler, whose 1945 vignette offered this description, wryly imagined that "Daniel must have been a two-fisted man to have survived his customers, and they needed to be copper-lined to endure his whiskey."[39]

Yoacham's Tavern: Westport, 1812–1912 (Franklin Hudson Publishing Company, Kansas City 1912). Author's personal collection

Travelers meant that the Westport hospitality business grew, giving Yoacham competition. Those who could not afford any room or board relied on open prairies to feed their livestock and to camp. Those with wealth found their dinner and lodging at the Harris House Hotel, what became the area's finest restaurant, and one where frontier cuisine was given a distinctive Southern flavor and served with Southern hospitality. Harris House standards arguably influenced fine dining in Kansas City for decades to come, and its popular dishes, particularly pan-fried catfish and chicken, remain integral to Kansas City's culinary identity.

Kentucky natives John and Henrietta (Simpson) Harris came to the Kawsmouth region in 1832. After buying land and establishing a farm, the Harrises decided to start a Westport hotel, or what was initially a hostelry. Located on the corner of Main Street and Main Cross Street (now Westport Avenue and Pennsylvania Street), it "was famed far and wide," according to early Kansas City historian Carrie Westlake Whitney.[40] After two fires, Colonel Harris built a three-story brick hotel, complete with a large, comfortable dining room.

Known colloquially as the Catfish House, the Harris House saw to the gustatory needs of Missouri politicians such as Senator Thomas Hart Benton, celebrity authors such as Washington Irving, military personnel, and numerous well-to-do travelers and locals. Its culinary fame, however, rested squarely on the backs of the Harrises' slaves. Harris designated a slave boy or elderly man to spend much of his day fishing so that the kitchen always had a plentiful supply of catfish.[41] Nellie McCoy Harris,

Harris House at the time of the Civil War, Battle of Westport.
Westport, 1812–1912 (Franklin Hudson Publishing Company, Kansas City 1912). Author's personal collection

daughter of John Calvin and Virginia Chick McCoy, recalled that the Harris House was renowned for "hot waffles, buck-wheat cakes, chicken pie, fried chicken, turkeys, broiled vension [sic], prairie-chicken, buffalo steak, and such other toothsome viands! These were supplied at all times at the Harris Inn, good and plenty."[42]

Southern specialties were well suited to the Kawsmouth climate. Pigs throve on acorns and groundcover in the dense forests, making it easy for settlers to fatten them for slaughtering and smoking. Hams, bacon, and salt pork were used to flavor wild greens as well as all manner of garden vegetables. Unlike pigs, chickens were more difficult to raise because the area was thick with predators who raided even the most secure chicken coops. The Harris House's ability to feature pan-fried chicken on a regular basis testified to its reputation for offering luxurious cuisine during a time of limited industrialization, and at a hotel restaurant that was literally on the frontier. Nonetheless, the Kawsmouth climate, which resembled that of large portions of the southern United States, ensured in good years huge gardens full of potatoes, collard greens, cowpeas, butter beans, and squashes, all of which appeared on dinner tables.

While the French community had its balls and saint's day feasts, the Westport community had its dining days and quilting bees. While bees allowed women to complete a quilt in one day, they also involved food and parties. The women arrived at the hostess's house around nine o'clock. At noon they broke for dinner and returned to quilting. The entertainment began around four o'clock when the husbands and eligible bachelors arrived. First, a "court" was convened and the quilt was "condemned" to "guilty and hung." Once the quilt was drawn up to the ceiling, the floor was left clear for "the dancing or a 'kissing' game according to the religious tenets of the host," wrote Westlake. When the guests ate supper, they enjoyed "pumpkin pie, peach pie, spice pie and buttermilk, after which there were more games." The evening concluded with young men escorting girls home.[43]

Dining days were more exclusive, involving Westport's wealthiest traders and travelers keen on experiencing the frontier life in comfort; the event was hosted by settlers who depended on these visitors for their own entertainment. They took turns hosting dining days, where guests gathered for dinner, conversation, and music. For these affairs, as well as for regular evening parties, everyone dressed up, with men in their best suits and women in the latest East Coast fashions. Some of the most famous hosts included Allen McGee, Joab Bernard, Finis Ewing, and Colonel Albert G. Boone, remembered specifically by Carrie Westlake Whitney as "a great entertainer, and after the custom of the times kept open house where many distinguished visitors stayed weeks at a time."[44]

Hence, by the mid-1840s when Father Donnelly arrived to Kawsmouth, Westport was a prosperous, albeit noisy, rowdy, and dirty town, complete with thirteen stores, the majority of which sold provisions and livery for the journey west. It was a place where "ponies, pelts, furs, trinkets, and annuity monies, were received by our early traders in exchange for powder, lead, tobacco, sugar, coffee, candies, and beads, and as there was at that time no temperance orders among these buyers and sellers, a little bad whiskey was also sold," wrote C. C. Spalding in his description of Westport in the 1858 *Annals of the City of Kansas*. It was, Spalding continued, "what our yankee neighbors would consider, in their vernacular, as a 'truck and dicker trade,' mainly done with the neighboring Indians, the employees of the mountain traders and freighters, the Mackinaw boatmen, &c., &c."[45]

Activity along the Missouri River levy was equally robust by the time Donnelly's steamboat arrived, but critical to sustaining the levy's growth was investment in its infrastructure. Joining his father-in-law, William Chick, John Calvin McCoy and a group of other investors now known as the "Historic 14" formed the Town of Kansas Company to begin building docks and platting the Town of Kansas. They bid on and won for $4,220 what had been part of Gabriel Prudhomme's property: acres that encompass present-day Broadway east to Holmes, and south to Fifth Street. While the final sale of the plats was held up for some years in litigation, improvements on the levy and increased services allowed pioneers to outfit directly in the Town of Kansas. By 1853, a formal charter gave the town a new name, the City of Kansas.

The cultural makeup and the economic character of Kawsmouth changed significantly from 1822 to 1853, but in some fundamental respects, its foodways and customs were codified during this antebellum era, not transformed. This had to do largely with the preindustrial nature of life as it was lived here prior to the Civil War. The disruption of the Border War and the following Civil War made technological innovation difficult and slow. Furthermore, for all their religious and cultural differences—and there were many—the French and the American elites privileged many of the same things: hospitality toward guests, the love of a groaning table replete with jellies, pickles, beaten biscuits, pies, gumbos, fried chicken, and catfish. They did their best to make meals a leisurely affair. French women enjoyed breaks with neighbors where they ate bread and cheese and drank wine; American women enjoyed teas and calling-card parties. Balls in French homes had their Westport equivalent in the quilting bee dances. And fundamental to both of these cultures were their Southern roots: Louisiana and Southern Illinois in the case of many of the French; Virginia and Kentucky in the case of many of the Americans. As large and diverse a region as the South was and is, its agrarian traditions gave many early settlers a common ground on which to build Kansas City's food traditions and its enduring legacy of hospitality.

Chapter Four

Contributing to Kansas City's Greater Good

Immigrants and Their Food Traditions

Given Kansas City's reputation as provisions center and crossroads, many immigrants who put down roots here found work in one or both of these industries. A father and older son worked in the rail yards while a younger son worked nearby in a meatpacking plant. A mother cooked for a wealthy family while her daughter stayed home and cooked for their family plus a boarder. For many immigrants, employment in these occupations was plentiful, although it tended to be brutal, with long hours and low wages. Inevitably, numerous immigrants recognized that what they did on an industrial level, meatpacking for Swift & Co., for example, could be done on a smaller level: a Jew leaving Swift & Co. and becoming the *shochet* who supplied his community with kosher meats. Kansas City's culinary richness emanated from many immigrants going into the catering and provisions business for themselves, creating restaurants, bakeries, grocery stores, butcher shops, and small food manufacturing businesses, many of which survive today.

Irrespective of their ethnicity, Kansas City immigrants' foodways followed a similar course. Initially, Old World recipes were adapted to use more readily available ingredients, but as they gained financial stability, immigrants often enhanced the Old World recipes that had once been beyond their means to eat: Italian families who had subsisted on hard dark bread could now afford not only soft white bread, but also pasta, and for that matter, they could top the pasta with meat on Sundays. From there, foods that at one time indicated impoverishment often became "heritage" foods, connecting immigrants to their roots and identity. Swedish *potatis korv,* a humble sausage comprised primarily of potatoes, appeared on lavish smorgasbords amidst *köttbullar* (meatballs) and *bakad skinka* (baked ham); it reminded a Swede of where she came from, lest she forget. In many cases, Kansas Citians' enthusiasm for trying new foods made it possible for immigrants to open restaurants. This chapter explores Kansas City's growth from edge of wilderness to metropolis by focusing on the waves of immigrants who came here to build it: what they ate and what they shared.

THE SANTA FE TRAIL AND THE RAIL YARDS: HISPANIC FOODWAYS

Kawsmouth has always been a "jumping-off" point given its location on the border of two ecosystems and two river ways. During the prehistoric Mississippian era, it is likely that Central Plains people made annual trips to the midsummer fair in Taos, where they traded commodities, including foodstuffs, with Western Plains people and those who came north from Mesoamerica. When John Calvin McCoy founded his emporium at Westport in 1832, the Santa Fe Trail on which Westport's prosperity partially depended was a continuation of that ancient journey and exchange. Beyond Westport was Indian Territory and beyond that, the Spanish Borderlands, a stretch that in the 1830s included present-day Colorado, Southern California, Arizona, New Mexico, and South Texas. From 1762 to 1800, the Kawsmouth Region and the Louisiana Territory had likewise been part of *Nueva España*, after France and Spain signed the Treaty of Fontainebleau and gave the land over to Spanish control. Given this history, it makes sense that many of the foods Kansas Citians enjoy eating are associated with the lands and cultures to their southwest.

Santa Fe Trail commerce connected Kawsmouth settlers primarily to the inhabitants of Northern Mexico and New Mexico. By the 1820s and 1830s, personnel engaged in the day-to-day logistics—the grunt work—of moving freight along the seven-hundred-mile trail were often of the same socioeconomic class, irrespective of national boundaries and ethnicity. Santa Fe, New Mexico, was home to ten thousand to fifteen thousand Spanish-speaking citizens and roughly ten thousand Pueblo Indians. Established in 1610 as a provincial seat of Spanish colonial government, Santa Fe was removed from the cultural sophistication and tastes of Mexico City, the colonial capital. It was more like a backwater, similar to

Westport, which U.S. government officials often referred to as the Edge of Wilderness. Aside from a minority of *hacendados*, government officials, and mission priests who lived on estates, most New Mexicans were lower-middle-class *mestizos*, descendants of Indian and Spanish parents. Their diet was relatively conservative and uncomplicated, based on the maize, squash, and beans of their ancestors, and due to the influence of missionaries, the chili pepper. Game, berries, and piñon nuts rounded out the average person's diet.[1]

Along the Santa Fe Trail, American traders often adopted the cuisine of the *mestizos*. Chilies, what culinary historian Keith J. Guenther Jr. rightly described as a "culinary revelation that added the missing fourth dimension to the major staples of corn, beans and squash," joined wild onions, garlic, and oregano in the prototype of a modern-day chili seasoning mix. Traders favored meals that included boiled and/or refried beans, vegetables, and meat. Because meat was often "green," or unaged, it tasted better if it was slow boiled, if time permitted. Jackrabbits, antelope, bison, and occasionally mutton, beef, or fowls, ended up in the campfire stew pot along with beans and chilies to create savory meals. They were often accompanied by quick-to-cook tortillas fashioned of *masa*. As Guenther explained, traders were "unencumbered with gastronomic amenities or inbred culinary sophistication"; they were "as rough and ready as the Mexican cuisine was hot and spicy."[2]

Santa Fe commerce also influenced the diets of Missouri and New Mexico settlers. Missouri farmers sold cereal crops and cured meat to traders headed to Mexico, and traders coming north brought food imports along with mules, silver, and woolens. In the 1600s, Spanish mission friars planted vineyards in the Rio Grande River Valley that produced a sought-after mellow wine, El Paso or "Pass" wine. It became one of Mexico's most valuable trade items.[3] *Aguardiente*, a powerful brandy distilled from the same grapes, was also a valued Santa Fe Trail commodity, along with oranges, lemons, olive oil, black pepper, chocolate, ginger, and nutmeg. But most important were chilies, the food integral not only to Mexican and New Mexican cuisine, but foundational to Southwest cuisine as a whole and to varying degrees, Kansas City cuisine.[4]

The Civil War and railroads ended Santa Fe Trail commerce around the time that Kansas City's culinary tastes became increasingly influenced by European immigrants and pioneers moving in from the Southern United

States. While thousands of Mexicans also immigrated to Kansas City later in the century, their arrival did not result in the dominant society suddenly embracing tortillas and pinto beans; in fact, the arrival of Mexicans often-times resulted in a conscious rejection of their cuisine, or as I will detail below, the Anglicization of it.

The Kansas City railroad industry recruited many Mexican men from Michoacán, Jalisco, and Guanajuato in the late nineteenth century. With little desire to settle in Kansas City permanently, these men often lived in box cars set up in camps adjacent to the freight yards. The Foreign Exclusion Act passed by Congress after World War I increased the num-ber of Mexican immigrants to Kansas City, particularly in the meatpack-ing industry, where newly arriving Mexicans and Central Americans began replacing Slavic immigrants who had traditionally been recruited. Out of convenience and also due to racism, these men lived close to their work. As families joined their menfolk, large Mexican communi-ties were established in Argentine in the midst of the Atchison, Topeka, and Santa Fe yards, and on the Westside in Kansas City, Missouri, near the Frisco rail yards.[5]

All along Southwest Boulevard, which roughly follows Turkey Creek and crosses the state line in the West Bottoms, *carnicerías* and *tienditas* sprang up, offering meats and other foodstuffs that allowed these immi-grants to re-create the flavors of home. Some houses had small gardens with maguey plants as well as a fire pit to prepare *barbacoa* for celebra-tions. Offal and other less desirable parts of cows and pigs were in plenti-ful supply, given the Mexican communities' proximity to stockyards and meatpacking. When a cow's head was wrapped in maguey leaves and buried in the ground with live coals, a delicious Mexican-style barbecue resulted. Women created tortillas, *birria* (a spicy Jalisco stew originally made from sheep or goat), *chorizo,* and for special occasions, particularly at Christmas, *buñuelos* and tamales. Women stuffed them with pork or beef, often incorporating the fatty, succulent meat from pig snouts before steaming the tamales in corn husks.[6]

For many Kansas Citians such foods, like the Mexicans themselves, were largely invisible. The exceptions were tamales and chili. Their success with a wider Kansas City population was likely the result of Anglo-Americans who adapted these Mexican specialties to mainstream tastes. Jim Shepard, the "Tamale Man," came to Kansas City in the

1920s from Springfield, Missouri. To earn a living, he sold hot tamales from a cart in downtown Kansas City.[7] His long, cylindrical tamales were not steamed in corn husks, but in waxed paper, and then simmered in meat-chili broth. They were not spicy hot, but rather, steaming hot. By the 1940s, Shepard employed fifteen to twenty "tamale men" who hawked tamales in front of bars, downtown department stores, and on weekends, in urban neighborhoods. Their cries of "Hot tamales! Meat in the middle and mush on top! Makes your tongue go flippity flop!" were eagerly awaited by hungry children.[8] When tamale vendors disappeared in the early 1980s along with home-delivered milk, eggs, and bread, Jim's Tamales opened as a small drive-in in East Kansas City, Missouri, where it did business up until 2013.[9]

Jim's Tamales paired particularly well with Dixon's chili, another Kansas City mainstay that owes its roots to Mexican culinary traditions. The advent of commercially available chili powder, first manufactured in Texas in the 1890s, resulted in chili parlors opening up throughout the Midwest.[10] As with Jim Shepard, Vergne Dixon started his career by selling chili from a cart in downtown Kansas City in 1919; from there, Dixon opened his first Dixon's Chili Parlor at Fifteenth and Olive Street. After Dixon's death in 1964, the family franchised the restaurant. The last remaining Dixon's Chili Parlor does a brisk business in Independence.

Dixon's chili was and remains distinctly bland. Customers order a plate of steamed ground chuck, barely seasoned. It is up to them to top their chili with condiments, including the house-mixed blend of chili powder and a fiery chili-infused vinegar (a condiment that was also found at most 1930s- and 1940s-era Kansas City diners). Also available is "two-way" chili, where California pink beans (Santa Maria *pinquitos*) are ladled on top of ground chuck. While Dixon allowed customers to season the chili, ketchup was anathema, and if he caught a customer sneaking it in, he fined them ten cents. Dixon's now charges customers ten cents for ketchup in memory of the founder's aversion to the condiment. Incidentally, Dixon's Chili received national recognition because President Harry S. Truman, an Independence, Missouri, native, routinely patronized it. In December 1950, he was photographed by *Life Magazine* enjoying a plate of chili at Vergne Dixon's original Olive Street location.

Chili remains a Kansas City mainstay, although it is almost always a spicy, tomato-based concoction complete with beef (ground chuck is popular) and kidney beans. Another variation, a very spicy chili made with barbecued burnt ends (the charred bits of beef brisket), is also popular. Remaining diners that date back to the mid-twentieth century, including Town Topic Hamburgers and Hayes Hamburgers, keep chili simmering in a pot over to the side of the grill, there to top hot dogs, hamburgers, and Tater Tots, or to serve in a bowl along with vinegar and saltine crackers.

On a more sophisticated level, chef Jess Barbosa helped introduce Mexican and Spanish tastes into the Continental repertoire. Barbosa grew up in Kansas City's West Side neighborhood, and after returning from the Navy in the mid-1950s, he was hired by hotelier Phil Pistilli to work in the Muehlebach Hotel kitchens. There he was under the tutelage (or command) of German and French chefs. As Barbosa climbed the culinary ladder, moving from dishwasher and eventually to chef, he infused classic dishes with the Spanish and Mexican flavors of his childhood. He poached game hens in a cilantro-jalapeño broth, and he added chicken mole with pinto beans and *sopa de arroz* to the lunch menu, much to his patrons' delight.[11] Later, as executive chef at the Alameda Rooftop Restaurant (which architecturally paid homage to Kansas City's Spanish roots), Barbosa prepared entrées that were often Latin in flavor and execution. Poached salmon accompanied by saffron-infused rice and chicken amandine finished in an almond-orange liqueur sauce were representative.

New waves of immigrants from Mexico, Central, and South America came to Kansas City after World War II, and they continued to work in restaurant kitchens and also open their own establishments. The Muehlebach Hotel started Jess Barbosa on a distinguished career path, as it did Manny Lopez, one of Kansas City's most popular Mexican-American restaurateurs. Lopez began as a Muehlebach bartender, but eventually he and his wife Vivian started their own Mexican restaurant at 207 Southwest Boulevard, which the family has owned and operated since 1980.[12] Southwest Boulevard continues to support a vibrant Mexican restaurant and food service economy. Nearby neighborhoods are likewise crowded with Mexican food manufactories that produce salsas, tortillas, chorizo, taco and tortilla chips, chili seasonings, and *paletas* (ice cream pops). *Taquerias*, *paleterías* (ice cream parlors), *panaderías* (bakeries), along with generations-old *carnicerías* and *tienditas* join sit-down Mexican restaurants and Spanish tapas bars. Such establishments are now found throughout the Kansas City Metro. Restaurants and groceries that once catered exclusively to Hispanics are patronized by Kansas City residents in general and are often destinations for out-of-town visitors.

THE GIFTS OF THE IRISH

Kansas City's preindustrial growth rested literally on the backs of the people who carved paths and leveled bluffs separating upland prairies from the Town of Kansas and the levy. Without such labor, Kansas City's transformation from trading post to major metropolis could not have happened. Arguably, then, the city owes its modern existence to the Irish. Downtown Kansas City, from Wyandotte, Delaware, Main, Grand, and Holmes, began to take shape as Irish immigrants were recruited to Kansas City in the 1840s.

How the Irish ended up on the frontier is an interesting story, although as is true for Irish immigrants elsewhere, their mass migration was triggered by *an Gorta Mór*, the Great Hunger, when potatoes in Irish fields rotted on the vine during the mid-to-late 1840s. Although Father Bernard Donnelly came to Kansas City to serve as a priest, he was also by training a civil engineer who understood that if Kansas City were to grow, it would need roads cut through the bluffs. After seeking permission from city officials, Donnelly posted ads in New York and Boston Irish newspapers to recruit men to Kansas City, enticing them with a one-way train ticket and promise of higher wages than what they were making in the East. He recruited men specifically from the Connaught Province (an area that bordered Donnelly's own native County Caven) in order to assure harmony, to create as fraternal an atmosphere among the men as possible. What began as a call for three hundred soon led to a steady stream of immigrants, men and women, from all over the Emerald Isle.

Vestiges of an Irish presence in Kansas City do not often show up in its restaurant offerings. The Irish did not come to Kansas City with a strong culinary identity, given that their ruthless subjugation to English landlords and subsequent malnourishment did not allow for a distinctly Irish cuisine to manifest itself in the nineteenth century. Instead, their culinary offering to Kansas City rested in their deeply rooted understanding that food and drink are a host's manifestation of his or her generosity. The Southern hospitality discussed in this book's previous chapter was in part because many Southerners were themselves Scotch-Irish descendants. The Irish who arrived in Kansas City in the 1840s enhanced that reputation further by opening many taverns or saloons, the frontier equivalent of Irish pubs, as well as boardinghouses and hotels complete with grills, bars, and oftentimes, as the century progressed, the basement cabarets that would ultimately lay the foundation for Kansas City jazz.

Father Donnelly's initial recruits lived in boardinghouses close to Sixth Street and Delaware, in "Connaught Town." The parish saw to it that these laborers were fed and looked after by two families.[13] As they settled into a routine of back-breaking labor cutting the roads and laying the sewers, the Irishmen punctuated their evenings with "kitchen rackets," dance parties complete with whiskey (or poteen from the Old Country) and whatever food was on hand. Rackets, along with the wake, exemplified "hospitality and openhandedness," both of which became "enshrined as virtues" among the Irish, wrote the historian William V. Shannon. Hard games and hard drinking, Shannon continued, "gave vent to cramped passions."[14] The warmth and enthusiasm that Irish poet John Livingston Wright evoked in his poem "Kitchen Racket" was transferred directly to Kansas City's Irish enclaves, where visitors came to the host's quarters to dance under "the rafters hung wi' pots an' things, / From cod to herrin', tong an' rings, / The old brown cupboard, hinting shtore [within] / O' things ter dhraw ye miles or more."[15]

By 1870, the census put Kansas City's Irish-born population at 9 percent, and nearly one-third of Kansas City's population was recorded as second- and third-generation Irish.[16] With two Catholic parishes, both with Irish priests (one of whom was Father Donnelly), and "jobs for the asking," land- and cashed-strapped Irish immigrants made Kansas City a destination. Although the majority of Irishmen initially worked in excavation and bricklaying, and Irishwomen as servants, plenty found opportunities in the hospitality industry.

Irish enclaves began to spread throughout the West Bottoms, particularly around Twelfth Street and State Line, an area referred to as "the Irish Patch." It filled with Irish-owned hotels and modest boardinghouses, as well as saloons. It was cheap to rent a narrow room, buy a crank phonograph or old piano, put up a countertop with a leaning rail, and sell whiskey and five-cent Tom Keene cigars. The venture required little capital and even less education, as Pat O'Neill humorously noted in *From the*

Bottom Up: The History of the Irish in Kansas City.[17] With more men than women population-wise, and with thousands coming through Kansas City on their way elsewhere, whiskey sales were robust.

Saloons did more than facilitate fistfights and roustabouts, the stereotypical and demeaning image of the drunken, violent Irishman that was propagated in the press. Men also talked politics and banded together to protect common interests, and some became civic leaders due to support they garnered by campaigning in saloons; indeed some of the most prominent started their careers as saloon owners, including James (Jim) Pendergast and his brother, Tom, who controlled city politics up through the 1930s.

The Pendergasts were sons of Irish immigrants from County Tipperary. Jim moved to Kansas City in 1876, taking with him several of his siblings from their home in St. Joseph. He did what thousands of other immigrants did when arriving in Kansas City: he worked as a meatpacker. While Tom stayed in St. Joseph to complete his schooling, Jim, with his winnings from a horse race, bought the American House, a hotel on St. Louis Avenue, close to the Union Depot. While living upstairs, the Pendergast siblings tended bar below and took care of the hotel. Through networking and his gregarious personality, Jim became the most powerful Democratic Ward boss in Kansas City. Along with his brothers Michael and John, Jim extended his saloon business, and when Tom joined his brothers, he tended bar on Main Street near Market Square and went on to own the Jefferson Hotel (along with the Ready-Mixed Concrete Company and a liquor distribution business). When Jim was elected alderman to the First Ward in 1892, the era of Pendergast machine politics began.

Corruption, including kickbacks, collusion with the Mob, bouts of violence, prostitution, and gambling defined the Pendergast era, but a lot of votes that kept Jim and his more powerful brother Tom in control were due to their commitment to the poor and ensuring that they did not go hungry, irrespective of their race or ethnicity. Many poor people were happy to pledge loyalty to "Boss Tom" because of the largesse they received. During the Depression, residents of the First Ward were assured that if they suffered from hunger, they could turn to the Machine for relief. Kelly's restaurant at Sixth and Main was only one example of the charity extended to people who suffered. Subsidized in large part because of Tom Pendergast's kickbacks, it offered poor families a free Thanksgiving and Christmas Day dinner. The line often stretched three

blocks long. Holiday baskets of essentials like coal, bread, and potatoes, alongside extravagances like fruit, were delivered to hundreds of
hungry families, the elderly, and the infirm, while Tom himself donated
thousands of dollars during his reign to the Little Sisters of the Poor at
Fifty-Third and Highland.[18]

Perhaps even more ironically, considering the violence and corruption
that the Pendergast Machine perpetuated, it also ensured Kansas City's
cultural relevance, not merely its importance as a meat and wheat processing town. During the 1920s and 1930s Kansas City's "wide open" reputation gave jazz musicians from all over the nation steady work, given that
music and booze flowed together. Musicians in turn attracted writers and
other artists, bohemians, flappers, and throngs of visitors who participated
in a cultural awakening on par with the Harlem Renaissance. "Paris of
the Plains," Kansas City's moniker, was the result of Pendergast and an
underlying Irish sensibility that equated generosity with drink and a full
belly. The Irish did more for Kansas City's legacy than blasting through
cliffs and laying sewers.

GERMAN, AUSTRIAN, AND SWISS
BREWERS, BAKERS, AND RESTAURATEURS

In Westport in December of 1882, cabinetmaker Oswald Karl Lux was
eager to re-create the sights of his native Germany at Christmas. This
marked the first time in the town's history that a full-size Christmas
tree was decorated and lighted. The procedure was not easy, however.
Lux tried to purchase a fir tree, and when that failed, he made do with a
broomstick for a trunk and curved barrel staves for branches. However,
with candles and garlands, the tree managed to put him and his neighbors in a festive frame of mind. Soon thereafter, other families joined
Lux in the tradition, and by 1884, Kansas Citians could purchase Christmas trees that had been shipped in from Michigan.[19] What had been a
German tradition was now a Kansas City tradition, or more accurately,
an American tradition.

In some cases, it is just as easy for Kansas Citians and Americans
in general to take German culinary traditions for granted. The fir tree
is embraced as a traditional symbol of Christmas irrespective of one's

ethnicity, and so too are ballpark pretzels, brats, lager and pils beer, and for that matter, hamburgers and hot dogs. They are beloved, yes, but they seem American, not German. And yet, without a steady flow of German immigrants into Kansas City throughout much of the nineteenth century, Kansas City's culinary heritage would be markedly diminished.

By 1860, roughly 12 percent of Kansas City's population was German, made up largely of professionals and artisans. Their assimilation was eased significantly by the fact that many German families were already established in Missouri well before the Civil War. Germans who moved to Kansas City often had families in St. Louis or elsewhere in the state, and those connections and support networks remained strong. A second wave of German immigration began in the 1870s when economic strife spread throughout Continental Europe, bringing not only Germans, but also Austrians and Swiss. As James Shortridge pointed out, Germans as a whole did not face enough discrimination to "cleave only to themselves," and so distinctly German enclaves in Kansas City were smaller than Italian, Irish, Jewish, Hispanic, and Eastern European enclaves.[20] German food itself did not stand out to many as "exotic," given that its flavors and preparations were somewhat similar to those of Anglo-Americans.

Among these immigrants were highly skilled butchers, brewers, grocers, bakers, and chefs; their arrival from the 1870s past World War II had enduring effects on Kansas City's economy, including in hospitality and in brewing. Although no information exists on "Dutch Joe," Theodore S. Case's memory of arriving in Kansas City in 1859 and gazing down Market Street (now Grand) is revealing: "There was one decent-sized two-story brick [building] owned and used as a bakery and Lager beer Saloon by 'Joe the Baker,' or 'Dutch Joe.'"[21] Clearly the lager-bakery combination was prospering, given its solidity in a town of largely flimsy wooden-framed buildings.

Importantly, German immigrants slowly transformed a town of whiskey drinkers into a town of beer drinkers. While the popularity of whiskey has never gone away, beer was often marketed, and accepted, as a more wholesome beverage, the perfect way during Kansas City's notoriously long, hot summers to slake one's thirst after a hard day at the mill or plant. Some German brewers started their companies in Kansas City, while others who had started in St. Louis (a brewing capital) located branches and depots in Kansas City. This was in part because the Hannibal Bridge facilitated shipping beer to remote sites via rail. Whether it was brewed in St. Louis or Kansas City, a lot of lager ended up in Kansas City saloons, restaurants, and grocery stores as well.

Up to Prohibition, Kansas City's levee and downtown were crowded with breweries and brewery depots, including the Kansas City Brewery, the Green Tree Depot, and the George Wiedemann Brewing Co. Along with George Muehlebach's brewery, whose legacy will be covered in full later in this study, the Heim Brewing Company was one of the most famous. It was started by an Austrian immigrant, Ferdinand Heim, who at one point operated a brewery in St. Louis with his brother. In 1899, shortly after his brother died, Heim, his wife, and their three sons moved to Kansas City and purchased the Star Ale Brewery from F. H. Kump & Company. Heim became Kansas City's largest brewery during that era. To accommodate demand, the Heim family expanded their operation, purchasing an old sugar refinery in the East Bottoms.[22]

The Heims brought more to Kansas City than great-tasting lager; they also brought Kansas City its own version of Coney Island. Looking to promote and sell even more of their beer, the Heim brothers opened Electric Park, close to the East Bottoms brewery. On opening day, people waited in breathless anticipation, and when a hundred thousand electric lights blazed to light up the night sky, the park's legacy was secured. The brothers piped lager directly from the brewery into Electric Park's Beer Garden. For a modest price, customers could buy refreshments as well as ample mugs of frosty lager while listening to German band music. The park quickly outgrew its location and was moved in 1907 to Forty-Sixth and the Paseo, where its magic awed young Walt Disney, who lived north of the park. Possibly, some of Disney's earliest inspiration for Disneyland came from evenings spent under the blanket of electric stars at Electric Park.[23]

Anti-German sentiment, passage of the Food Control Act in 1917 that conserved grain for the war effort, and from there, the passage of the Eighteenth Amendment in 1919, decimated beer and wine production throughout Missouri. World War II likewise compromised the abilities of German brewers to do successful business. Many breweries went bankrupt, and some were converted to making soft drinks, malt syrup, yeast, and breakfast cereals. Mergers and acquisitions of national breweries did not help the situation either. Kansas City brewing was particularly slow

Heim Electric Park Beer Garden.
Missouri Valley Special Collections, Kansas City Public Library, Kansas City, Missouri

to rejuvenate. However, time and perspective persuaded a new generation of entrepreneurs to begin resurrecting that past. Today Kansas City has gone from virtually no brewing to supporting numerous microbreweries.

The largest and most successful of these operations is the Boulevard Brewing Company on Southwest Boulevard, the creation of John Mc-Donald. A Kansas native and University of Kansas graduate, McDonald was a passionate home brewer interested in making the distinctive pre-Prohibition beers that defined Kansas City. After attending a course in microbiology at the Siebel Institute in Chicago, McDonald worked with a German-trained brewer, Charlie McElevey, to refurbish a fifteen-thousand-square-foot warehouse and outfit it with repurposed brewing equipment from a brewery in Vierkirchen, Germany. The first business to take a risk with serving Boulevard Brewery's offerings was nearby Ponak's Mexican Restaurant. The success of Boulevard Beer eventually took McDonald and McElevey back to Germany in the early 1990s to purchase a bottling line to move to Kansas City.

Boulevard remains committed to brewing beers first for the Kansas City market, and second, for the region, and at this point beyond it. The brewery creates distinctive flavors and labels, some of which recall Kansas City's German heritage. One of its most successful seasonal brews, for example, is Bob's 47. This Munich-style lager pays homage to Bob Werkowitch, retired brewmaster and mentor to McDonald who was head brewer for Muehlebach Brewery in the late 1930s. Bob's 47 is so popular that many Kansas Citians buy up crates to sustain themselves until next October's release.[24] Boss Tom's Golden Bock (a maibock) is another example of Boulevard's interest in Kansas City's past, both Pendergast's legacy and the enduring popularity of German brews. KC Pils is yet another example. This American-style beer recalls the "full-flavored but easy drinking classic American lager" that small breweries produced in an era where baseball and beer were intricately linked.[25] Boulevard currently produces thirty-four beers, many of them seasonal, artisanal brews, with seven available year-round.

Beer and sausage inevitably go together. Enhancing Kansas City's long identification with quality meats are German butchers, including Fritz's Meats and Superior Sausage, which opened in 1927 when Fritz and Rose Plapp moved to Kansas City from Germany. Fritz's, an old-fashioned smokehouse, is in its fourth generation and produces handcrafted wood-smoked bratwurst, knackwurst, hams, and pork loins, as well as turkeys, chickens, and other specialty meats. Another long-standing German enterprise is Bichelmeyer Meats, whose story begins in 1880 when Mathias Bichelmeyer, a professional butcher, left Füssen, Germany, and came to Kansas City, Kansas. He found work at Swift & Co. and taught his son, George, how to butcher as well. George started his own meat market in 1906, but the 1908 flood ruined the shop, and for a time, George and his wife lived in Eudora, Kansas, where they butchered for local farmers. The family eventually returned to Kansas City, Kansas, in 1946, where George's son, John, also worked in the meatpacking industry before wishing to resurrect the family business. To ensure quality, John and his sons began their own livestock operation in Williamsburg, Kansas, which supplies the bulk of the meat that Bichelmeyer Meats fabricates and in the case of beef, dry-ages. Bichelmeyer Meats remains in operation today, now catering to a large Hispanic market as well as producing classic German specialty cuts and sausages.[26]

From the 1870s on, Kansas City has always had German, Austrian, and/ or Swiss restaurants and cafés, even during decades where German food fell out of fashion nationally. André's Confiserie Suisse is one of Kansas City's most popular cafés and pastry shops. It opened in 1955 when André Bollier, a Master Konditor-Confiseur, and his wife Elsbeth emigrated from Basel, Switzerland, to start a confectionery business currently in its third generation.[27] German chefs have always commanded respect and authority in Kansas City, so much so that in 1973, they established the Greater Kansas City Chefs Association, chartered by the American Culinary Federation. Among its founding members was Klaus H. Sack, who grew up in Germany during World War II and arrived in the United States with no more than his chef's tools and a suitcase. He became an executive chef at the Muehlebach.[28] The Rhineland in Independence, Missouri, was started by Heinz and Rosie Heinzelmann and remains popular, along with two newer restaurants: Martin and Katrin Heuser's Affäre, on Main, and the Austrian restaurant Grünauer, run by Peter Grünauer, his son, Nicholas, and Viennese restaurateur Klaus Piber.

KANSAS CITY'S JEWISH CONTRIBUTIONS

Jewish people did not emigrate from just one country but from several, primarily Russia, Germany, and Poland. Prior to 1881, Kansas City was home to roughly 175 Jewish families, many of whom were involved in Kansas City's civic and business affairs, including positions on the Kansas City Board of Trade and City Council.[29] When Czar Alexander II was assassinated in 1881, the political upheaval led to Jewish people fleeing violence and persecution, and a significant number came to Kansas City through the aid of the Jewish Educational Institute in conjunction with the Immigration Bureau at Galveston, Texas. *The Social Prospectus of Greater Kansas City* (1913) recorded that 3,403 foreign-born Russians (primarily Jewish) joined a corresponding number of native-born Russians who already resided in Kansas City.[30]

Most of these immigrants were not fluent in English, and they arrived with few financial resources. As such, they joined scores of other immigrants who took menial positions in the packinghouses and related industries. Many Jews and Italians lived in tenements between the

Missouri River and the City Market, with the poorest crowded into the notorious McClure Flats. Some two thousand other Jews lived along Independence and Lydia in the Belvidere slum, neighbors with many African Americans.[31]

Kansas City's Jewish immigrants during this era (1880s up through the 1950s) were determined to assimilate into, rather than separate from, mainstream American culture. Their success thus makes it more challenging to trace Jewish foodways in the metropolitan area. Kansas City native Calvin Trillin remembered that no one in his immediate family would "have struck anybody as foreigners." That his father had "been born in the Ukraine seemed almost a technicality," Trillin wrote in *Messages from My Father*. The "Old Country" was a constant in their lives, but more as a reminder of hard work and sacrifice essential to ensuring that the next generation—he and his sister, in other words—would "have the opportunity" to be real Americans. Anglicizing one's surname was common among immigrants, but many Jews also melded their foodways into the mainstream as well.

Again, Trillin's background is illustrative. His father was a grocer and later a restaurateur; both businesses were Midwestern in flavor and character, not Jewish. Blue-plate specials, including turkey and stuffing, open-faced roast beef sandwiches and mashed potatoes, and apple pies were more typical at Trillin's Restaurant than kugel, bagels, and lox. "Making Chopped Liver with Miracle Whip" was how Trillin titled a lecture he gave on Midwestern Jews' upbringing in postwar America. When a person came up after his speech to remark that his title was "an interesting metaphor," Trillin replied with his usual Midwestern bluntness, "It's a recipe. That was how my mother made chopped liver. I believe she considered schmaltz déclassé."[32]

Of course, some restaurants did have a more distinct Jewish character, although Kansas City's most famous, Bretton's, is remembered as much for its raucous Bali Hai Room as it is for its "Nasch Table." From 1945 to 1976, Max Bretton, a former Jewish rabbi, offered patrons some of the best Continental food available in Kansas City. It was a classy place, with music, elegant trappings, a charming maître d'hôtel (often Max Bretton), and table-side service. The menu featured Kansas City steaks, roast duck and capon, Maine lobster, Wiener schnitzel, and baked Alaska. The "Gourmet's Nasch Table" was more Jewish in offerings, but it was also suave, reaffirming for diners who had traveled to great European cities that they, too, were urbane. It was popular for lunch, as it allowed patrons to choose from a variety of smaller plates, including chopped liver, pickled herring, knishes, and blintzes.[33]

Bretton's basement Bali Hai Room opened in 1954 after *South Pacific* made the song "Bali Hai" a hit; it was Kansas City's first tiki restaurant and hugely popular with trendsetters. While more staid diners upstairs ate classically prepared roast duck, the patrons downstairs were eating Mandarin deep-fried duck drenched in plum sauce. Most of the offerings were Cantonese style, which in 1950s and 1960s Kansas City meant unadventurous entrées such as shrimp with mushrooms, sweet and sour chicken, and pork with pea pods. People did not go to the Bali Hai Room for authenticity, though; they went for drinks and atmosphere. Men routinely bet one another whether they could walk upstairs and out of the restaurant without assistance after imbibing two Atomic Bombs (the menu limited customers to a *maximum* of two). In other words, few knew—or cared—that such heady concoctions were overseen by a former Jewish rabbi.

Delicatessens catered to Jewish patrons as well as a broad array of customers, including downtown shoppers and businessmen who enjoyed eating at Wachter's for lunch and locals who depended on the corner deli for bagels, pastrami, and prepared salads. Esther and Isadore Becker's New York Bakery and Delicatessen at Seventy-Fifth and Troost stood out in this regard. It opened in 1905 and catered to a large Jewish neighborhood up into the 1970s. When the delicatessen was purchased in 1981 by Jim Holzmark, its patron base reflected shifting demographics, with increasing numbers of African Americans standing at the order counter alongside Jewish patrons. Indeed, what made the New York Bakery and Delicatessen important was the blending of two cultures to create a new Kansas City classic: the hickory-smoked kosher brisket, "the best combinations of Jewish and black cuisines," author David Sax claimed. It was created by New York Deli's head cook Sonny Taborn, who rubbed raw briskets with a blend of seasonings before smoking them for five to six hours in a specially designed metal box with a puck of hickory wood.[34]

When the New York Deli closed in 2009 after more than a century, it followed the demise of the other Jewish delis, and nothing came along to replace them, in part because franchises served up cheaper sandwiches. However, an increase in Kansas City's Orthodox Jewish population resulted

in the creation of Vaad Hakashruth in 1994, which oversees kosher certifi-
cation and supervision for many of Kansas City's retail vendors and food
production companies. Area grocery stores carry many Vaad Hakashruth
certified products. One Hen House Market in Overland Park also offers
Kansas City's only extensive kosher deli, as well as a branch of Kansas
City's Farm to Market Bread Company, where loaves are baked in ovens
that are also overseen by the Vaad (as it is colloquially known).

ITALIANS IN KANSAS CITY: FAMILY AND FOOD

Italians also crowded into North End tenements in the 1880s and 1980s.
However, unlike many Jews, Italians were largely disinclined to assimilate their cultural values or culinary traditions into the American mainstream. They understood food as the essential tie to the home that many
of them had unwillingly left behind, and for those who settled in Kansas
City, they put an indelible mark on the city's culinary heritage as a result.

Among the first to arrive were a dozen or so families from Genoa, and
they settled in the eastern part of Kansas City's original townsite in the
1880s.[35] By the 1890s, these Northern Italian immigrants were joined by
Sicilians and Southern Italians fleeing both oppressive poverty and also
La Mano Nera, or the Black Hand, an underground ring of extortionists
who forced families to pay "tribute" or risk murder (and who came to
Kansas City right along with those so desperate to escape it).[36] "Little
Italy," as the Italian enclave in the North End came to be called, was home
to many landless sharecropper immigrants, the *contadini*, who now found
themselves in Kansas City's rough urban core. What value would their
knowledge of farming and food production serve them in such conditions?

Fundamental to answering that question was the location of the Kansas City Market. Since the 1830s when the Town of Kansas Company
purchased Gabriel Prudhomme's land to lay out the first plats, a thriving
market had been in operation. However, the brick building along Walnut,
near Fifth Street, was not constructed until 1888, and when it was doubled
in size in 1910, the expansion was due partly to Italians.[37] While men
worked in the rail yards, packinghouses, and mills, women who needed to
be closer to home to care for children sought employment at the market.
By 1910, Italian men and women were both working at the market, hawk-

ing fish and produce from wheelbarrows, working for area bakers and grocers, and ultimately, as they gained a financial foothold, buying their own produce companies, grocery stores, and bakeries. The market grew to accommodate these businesses and increased patronage.[38]

Italian immigrants' tendency to enter food-related industries in Kansas City surpassed that of other groups. The numbers of Italian-owned produce wholesalers, bakeries, groceries, and restaurants—many still in operation—had to do with the importance Italians place on food. Although most Italian immigrants suffered deprivation in their homeland, wide-scale famines in Italy were rare, and Italian Catholicism celebrated, rather than suppressed, the sensual pleasures of feasting. Traditionally, Italian peasants had subsisted on hard bread, polenta, or rice (depending on the region). Nonetheless, they produced the wine, sausages, cured hams, olive oil, cheeses, breads, and pasta that their wealthy landlords consumed. Italian peasants thus understood and appreciated the quality of food, given their intimate connection with producing it, even if, as Hasia Diner has noted, they "could only eat what those with power allotted." Catholicism also mandated that on certain religious holidays, such as the Feast of the Assumption, the rich make lavish gifts of food to the poor. When communities celebrated holidays in general, including Christmas, Easter, and Carnival (the day before Lent), the rich again offered food to the poor, including pastries such as *cuccidati* (fig-stuffed cookies), *nucatoli*, and *mustazzoli* (both are almond-based cookies). Families themselves worked to save money to enjoy macaroni, minestrone, and meat at least a couple of times a year, primarily for weddings and christenings.[39]

A degree of prosperity for first- and second-generation Italian Americans in Kansas City allowed women to focus on cooking, rather than merely procuring, food, and they incorporated into recipes ingredients that had been beyond their means in Italy.[40] Kansas City Italian restaurants were thus built on the recipes and experience of grandmothers, mothers, and wives. Jennies Italian Restaurant opened in 1938 in the North End because a widow, Jennie Barelli DeSimone, needed to help her son complete college; she began cooking meatballs, and her operation became a popular Italian restaurant (it closed in 1998). This was true for the Italian Gardens, discussed later in this study, and it was true for Cascone's Italian Restaurant in Kansas City's Northland, started in 1954 by two brothers, John and Leroy Cascone. They relied on family recipes that dated back

to Ragusa, Sicily. Sixty-one years later, Cascone's sugo (red sauce) sur-
rounds ravioli, lasagna, and cannelloni that remain guarded recipes. While
Cascone's does offer Northern Italian specialties, its co-owner, Frank
Cascone, champions the family's commitment to doing what they have
always done best and resisting culinary fads.[41]

Jasper's, one of Kansas City's oldest restaurants, is similar. It started
as a small restaurant in 1954 when Jasper Mirabile Sr. and his wife, Josephine, purchased Rose's Bar at Seventy-Fifth and Wornall and renamed
it Jasper's. Jasper Sr. relied heavily on his mother's Sicilian recipes while
Josephine prepared bar snacks and helped in the restaurant. Jasper Mirabile Jr., who is the current executive chef, continues to use his family's
Sicilian recipes as inspiration, as well as those his father and mother col-
lected and developed when they began traveling to Italy and Sicily in the
1970s. Jasper Jr. champions their legacy in his own cooking, adding to the
repertoire creations that are likewise inspired by his work for Slow Food
Kansas City. Jasper's and its attached market, Marco Polo, moved from
their Waldo location to the current Watt's Mill Shopping Center on State
Line Road in 1998.[42]

Italians also began many food manufacturing and wholesaling businesses that remain in operation today. Initially, entrepreneurs marketed
their goods to other Italians, but as they became established, their reputation for high-quality foods grew, and Kansas Citians from all over sought
out their imports and house-made specialties. Roma Bakery began in the
North End in 1923 when Sicilian-born Joseph Filardo joined his cousin
Joseph Cusamano and brother-in-law Jack Binaggia to purchase a small
grocery store. While they provided neighbors with staples, their specialty
was pastries and breads. Eventually, the company outgrew its space and
moved to a larger facility on Independence Avenue. Although Roma was
purchased by Rotella's Italian Bakery in Omaha, Nebraska, after a 1992
fire destroyed its operation, both a distribution branch and the Roma
brand of Italian bread and rolls are mainstays in Kansas City Italian restaurants and on family dinner tables.[43]

Scimeca's has also reached iconic status. In its fifth generation, this
family of grocers and sausage makers began in 1935 when Sicilian-born
Fillipo Scimeca and his son Frank started a grocery store. For over sixty
years, Scimeca's Market on Independence Avenue offered Kansas Citians
a large selection of Italian imports, but more importantly, its house-made

sausage. In 1996, Phil Scimeca, Frank's son, started a wholesale operation, Scimeca's Famous Italian Sausage Co., and in 2001 sold the grocery store to focus on wholesale.[44] Widely available at area supermarkets, Scimeca's sausages are simultaneously ubiquitous and celebrated. If grocery store cases were emptied of Scimeca's sausage, or for that matter, V's Italian ravioli and tortellini, or Jasper's pasta sauce, or Roma's breads, the loss of such products would impact Kansas City families who depend on these kitchen staples.

EASTERN EUROPEANS: MEAT AND POTATOES

Croats, Poles, Slovenes, Slovaks, Serbs, and Russians were heavily recruited to Kansas City in the early 1890s because of disruptive strikes at the meatpacking houses. After a brutal crackdown in 1893, management accelerated recruitment among less picky immigrants who chose low wages and terrible conditions on the killing floors in Kansas City, Kansas, over the tyranny of the Austro-Hungarian monarchy. By 1920, some four thousand émigrés had arrived from Eastern Europe, with the majority of them settling first in the "Strawberry Patch," houses close to the packinghouses in the West Bottoms, and then after the 1903 flood, on "Strawberry Hill," a neighborhood higher up from the floodplains in Kansas City, Kansas.[45] With its rows of neat homes and Catholic and Orthodox churches to serve parishioners' needs, Strawberry Hill became, and remains, synonymous with excellent food, much of it largely based on the specialty meats and butchering skills that these immigrants brought with them.

Although part of Kansas City's love affair with meat comes from its location and its stockyard industry, many immigrants also came from cultures where meat was the cornerstone of the ideal diet. In spite of low wages, many immigrants earned enough money in Kansas City to afford at least some meat on a weekly basis, and this fact was fundamental to Kansas City's evolving culinary identity. In this regard, the Eastern European contribution to Kansas City's passion for meat is worth noting. The late Joe Krizman Sr., founder of Krizman's House of Sausage, used to refer to his fellow Croats as "meat-and-potatoes" people and non-Croats as *zec*—rabbits, or salad eaters. Joe Krizman III, who carries on the family's business, likewise agreed that Croatian cooking is not about vegetables, with the exceptions of potatoes and sauerkraut (or when the entire cabbage is pickled intact, sauerheads).[46]

Seventeen-year-old Joe Krizman Sr. came to Kansas City to escape World War I, and he started as a meatpacker in Kansas City, Kansas. As he became skilled, he opened a small grocery store with his wife, and by 1939, he made sausage in the back room. Afraid that he would lose his job at the plant, Joe Sr. sold the product as Grisnik's (his brother-in-law's name) to hide his identity. When he left the packing plant at three o'clock in the afternoon, Joe Sr. would continue making his own sausage. His success was secured because World War II made it difficult for people to buy butcher's meat; they turned to sausage instead. When his son, Joe Jr., took over, he changed the name officially to Krizman's House of Sausage in 1969. In Kansas City, Missouri's, Northeast, Peter May's House of Kielbasa shares a similar story. It started as a neighborhood grocery where Peter May specialized in crafting kielbasa based on recipes he carried with him from Poland. May's House of Kielbasa is now in its sixth generation, and the sausage, made in-house, is smoked slowly over walnut wood to give it a distinctive, delicious flavor.[47]

Eastern Europeans also brought new types of bread and pastry to Kansas City, including *povitica*, a holiday favorite. Several area bakers specialize in creating this intricate bread made by rolling paper-thin yeast dough around a filling of finely chopped walnuts, honey, butter, and eggs. Strawberry Hill Povitica Company is one of the most successful of these bakeries. In business since 1984, it was founded by Harley O'Leary, who married into a Croatian family.[48] Now owned by O'Leary's two sons, Marc and Dennis O'Leary, Strawberry Hill Povitica sells thousands of loaves in area grocery stores and by mail order out of its bakery in Merriam, Kansas, particularly during the holiday season. Along with Strawberry Hill Povitica Company is Mema's Old Fashioned Bakery in Kansas City, Kansas, owned by Loraine Waldeck and named in honor of her mother. It too specializes in strudel and povitica.

ASIAN CONTRIBUTIONS TO KANSAS CITY FOODWAYS

Kansas City's Asian population stands at approximately forty-five thousand, with around thirty thousand from China, South Korea, Vietnam, the

Philippines, and Laos; roughly seven thousand arrived here from India, Pakistan, Sri Lanka, Nepal, and Bangladesh.[49] These numbers are conservative, and Asians continue to settle in Kansas City. Most Asians arrive here to take jobs in STEM industries (science, technology, engineering, and medicine), but significant numbers have also become caterers, an avenue to financial and social stability that remains lucrative. Few suburban strip malls are without an Indian, Korean, or Chinese grocery, and large Asian supermarkets also add to the city's food offerings. Asian restaurants of all types are numerous as well.

Kansas City's first Chinese community was made up of men from Guangdong Province who worked in laundries and Chinese apothecaries before World War II. Three Chinese-owned grocery stores and as many as twenty Chinese restaurants catered to this small community. Most of these businesses were obscure and did not advertise in the *City Directory*; they were simply known in the Chinese community.[50] To attract a wider patron base, some Chinese restaurant owners began to capitalize on stereotypes of Chinese restaurants as exotic spaces of opulent interiors while also "Americanizing" their offerings. Chop suey and egg foo yong figured heavily on Chinese menus.[51] The city's most famous twentieth-century Chinese-owned restaurants, King Joy Lo and the House of Toy, were destinations for Kansas Citians who wished to enjoy not only a meal, but also the atmosphere.

King Joy Lo was located at 1217 Grand Avenue in downtown Kansas City in the early twentieth century. Advertised as a Mandarin restaurant, it featured tomatoes with beef, egg foo yong, and other relatively bland combinations, although it probably followed the custom of offering those who asked for it a separate menu that featured more authentic fare. King Joy Lo advertisements also touted the health-giving properties of Chinese food, noting that "dishes are based on the best Vegetarian laws—meat is never served in true Chinese fashion without its proper proportion of vegetables added—and this proportion has been determined by 6,000 years of experience."[52] When King Joy Lo moved to its second location, near the corner at Twelfth and Main, it was presided over by Don Toy and his cousin, Lem Toy.[53] This second-floor restaurant looked down on the bustling streets below, and its proximity to Kansas City's downtown cinemas made it a popular place for dates, as well as memorable events such as anniversaries.

The House of Toy offered many of the same menu selections that had made King Joy Lo successful. Chef Billy Chill Youn Choi oversaw the back of the house while Harry Toy oversaw the front.[54] Writing about House of Toy in the early 1980s, the *Clarendon Guide to Kansas City* reaffirmed loyal patrons' own opinion when it noted that the restaurant "is heaven for aficionados of egg rolls."[55] Pea pods with beef was also a popular selection. With its upscale Country Club Plaza address, parqueted floors, and a light tan and wood interior, the House of Toy offered reserved elegance in contrast with the more riotous goings-on at the Bretton's Bali Hai Room downtown. Severe flooding on the Country Club Plaza in the late 1970s damaged the House of Toy, and although it rebounded temporarily, it closed for good in the 1980s. Chinese food remains popular in Kansas City, but the mild Cantonese and Mandarin cuisines of the past have fallen out of fashion (with the exception of Chinese chain and franchise buffets) and have been replaced with more Szechuan and Pan-Asian, or fusion, cuisine. Bo Lings, Princess Garden (which offers a kosher menu), and more recently, the Blue Koi, have particularly loyal patrons.

While Chinese citizens have contributed to Kansas City's culinary landscape since the early 1900s, Vietnamese citizens have done so since the aftermath of the Vietnam War. As had been true with many immigrants, first-generation Vietnamese began their lives in Kansas City by living in the North End. "Little Italy," as it was still called, had been suffering from urban blight. Instead of allowing it to fall into total disrepair, Italian caterers joined with Kansas City leaders to write grants to help settle Vietnamese refugees in the area. Chief among them were Carl J. DiCapo, owner of the Italian Gardens, and Tom Barelli, owner of Jennies Italian Restaurant. These restaurateurs and others worked with the Don Bosco Center and Holy Rosary Parish to ensure that the Vietnamese had homes and could also find employment, including in the restaurant and City Market industries.[56] Jennies Italian Restaurant is now the Kim Long Asian Market and Restaurant, and although radically different in cuisine and concept, it anchors the North End community while also offering the city a large selection of Vietnamese specialty items, as well as a restaurant. Other Italian restaurants remain in the area, such as LaSala's. Its owner hired Vietnamese workers and again, cross-pollination of cooking ideas and techniques occurred.

Figuratively speaking, Kansas Citians resemble children in a candy shop: enthusiastic, overawed, and momentarily paralyzed by the array of treats on offer. This chapter has only covered the larger immigrant groups, but adding to the culinary landscape are also Japanese, Indian, Thai, Scandinavian, Greek, and most recently, Ethiopian cuisines that tempt and delight as well. From Mexican *carniceritas* and *taquerias*, to Vietnamese restaurants and pho houses, to locally produced meatballs and matzo balls at area stores, Kansas Citians are fortunate when it comes to the foods that they take for granted to make their lives better, their stomachs fuller.

Chapter Five

African American Contributions and Kansas City's Southern Traditions

Kansas City owes a tremendous debt of gratitude to African Americans for the city's rich food heritage. The flavors and offerings at restaurants, on family dinner tables, at church suppers, reunion picnics, and barbecues can often be traced in some fashion to African American techniques, flavors, and customs. While they did not single-handedly build Kansas City's reputation for fine food, without their efforts and contributions to the catering and provisions industries, Kansas City cuisine would be blander, and the city's reputation for equating food with hospitality would likewise go by less noticed. African American slaves in this region often worked as butchers, millers, bakers, railroad porters, barkeeps, waiters, and cooks; after the Civil War, many continued to work in kitchens and dining rooms; the toughest positions in the provisions industry were reserved for them. That African Americans made the best of their options, that some discovered fulfillment in cooking, and most importantly, that such talents brought them status, has been in Kansas City's best interest.

SLAVERY IN ANTEBELLUM KANSAS CITY

The decision that Missouri Territory would remain open to slavery after the Louisiana Purchase had immediate and lasting repercussions on Kansas City's foodways. The first documented African American to see Kawsmouth was York, property of Captain William Clark. Roughly eighty leagues from Kawsmouth on June 5, 1804, Clark tasked York with swimming to a sandbar in the Osage River "to geather Greens for our Dinner." It goes without saying that York would have also hunted game (for food, not sport), jerked meat, built fires, made salt, and cooked the food.[1] While he would have been assisted in these tasks by other Corps members, York's race alone determined his role as provider and preparer of food, a foreshadowing of what was to come for slaves when "in the winter, spring, summer, and autumn of 1816, [Southerners] came like an avalanche," as Baptist minister John Mason Peck described those moving into Missouri. "It seemed as though Kentucky and Tennessee were break-ing up and moving to the 'Far West,'" Peck marveled.[2] Many wealthy settlers brought their slaves.

Slaves and their owners also brought with them Southern food and food customs that were relatively easy to adapt to Kawsmouth climate, flora, and fauna. Oak and hickory wood continued to be used for cook-ing, a fact that had repercussions for Kansas City barbecue. Much of the game was recognizable as well. Often relegated to nighttime hunting to satisfy their own families' hunger, slaves trapped the same opossums, raccoons, woodchucks, rabbits, and squirrels that they had trapped in the South, while they prepared better, equally familiar game—venison, quail, pheasants—for their masters. Unusual game, including bison, antelope, jackrabbit, and the prairie chicken, were readily adapted to fit family recipes. Pigs and chickens were as easy (or as challenging) to raise at Kawsmouth as they had been in the South, so while masters ate "high" on the hog, enjoying cured hams, the best bacon, and fresh pork roasts, slaves ate bacon rinds, spare ribs, chitlins, brains, feet, ears, and snouts. Some families kept cows for milk, cheese, and meat, although lard remained the preferred cooking and flavoring fat among many Southerners, more so than butter.

Maize figured heavily in slaves' rations as well as on the master's dinner table. Hominy grits and cornmeal-based quick breads were cor-nerstones of Southern diets, although slaves often had little equipment to prepare their corn other than by boiling it in a pot with field peas (the other slave staple) and with "this or that." While in the fields, slaves often used a greased chopping hoe on which to shape cakes of cornmeal, water, and salt. With dexterity, they could slant the hoe into a bed of burning coals, bake the cake on one side, and then turn it to bake on the other.[3] It was also easy in the long Kawsmouth summers to grow green peas, toma-toes, peppers, onions, cucumbers, okra, yams, and all manner of greens that Southerners enjoyed. The heat also meant that the Southern arts of pickling and curing remained essential well into the 1900s; hence, whites and blacks maintained a liking for spicy, vinegary, salty fare.

Southern food customs came to Kawsmouth along with recipes. For Christmas, many families tasked their slaves with finding and preparing the Yule log. Victor Clarence recalled that the ceremony on his father's farm was to grant slaves a holiday for the duration of the Yule log's burning, and so slaves searched for the biggest and hardest log they could find well before Christmas morning. After the log was shaped to fit the master's hearth, it was "dragged by oxen to the big pond in the woodland pasture, rolled in, and there permitted to rest in the mud and water" until Christmas Eve "when it was rescued and brought to the kitchen door." After Christmas breakfast, the family and slaves "assembled in the dining room. All the wood, embers and ashes in the great fireplace were drawn and the backlog was rolled into place." Festivities for slave and free alike commenced. Another custom was to indulge in a cup of eggnog after the Yule log was burning. Victor Vaughan remembered that "his mother stood at the table with an immense bowl of eggnog" and that each family member, whites and then the blacks, received from her a glass of the beverage and drank to her health.[4]

Weddings were also based largely on food customs, and wealthy settlers could serve up copious amounts because of slave labor. When John Calvin McCoy married Virginia Chick in December 1837, it was a momentous occasion for the frontier community. Nellie McCoy Harris, their daughter, remembered being told that "Aunt" Rachel, the slave cook, had no shortage of ingredients with which to prepare the wedding feast: "more than one hundred pounds of ingredients—sugar, eggs, butter, flour, . . . were used in the cakes for the wedding supper." The menu featured "venison, turkey, chicken, home-cured hams, jellies, preserves, salads, pickles, custards, beaten biscuits, syllabub, and the hundred pounds of cakes."[5]

In 1850, Jackson County had approximately 14,000 residents, with 2,969 enslaved African Americans and 41 free. By the 1860s, the number of enslaved persons had increased to 3,944.[6] Prosperous settlers pocketed the profits from their businesses, but oftentimes slaves ensured their masters' revenue streams. James H. McGee made a substantial income from his gristmill, but he had slaves to grind meal, sack it, and haul it. John Calvin McCoy built Westport's first provisions store, but his slaves cut roads through the brush so that McCoy could transport supplies; they also helped create Westport's roads. Recalling the odd layout of the town, Nellie McCoy Harris humorously explained that although her father was a surveyor, he "laid out his town with but slight regard for the points of the compass." What mattered was the shortest route to his parents' dinner table: "I have heard my father say that he told old Tom, the colored factotum on our place, to take a yoke of oxen, and a plow, and open up through the timber and hazel-bush, a road from the store, the nearest way home to dinner" at his parents' house across the stream on what is now Wornall Road.[7]

Travelers coming through Westport were often catered to by African Americans. The kitchen and dining room at the Harris House were overseen by a slave couple, Minerva and Mark. "Mark would 'roach' up his hair, put on a white apron and soft slippers and fly into the dining room where he turned into head waiter," early historian Carrie Westlake Whitney recalled. "He presided over the meat table and carved venison, wild turkey, three year old home cured ham, or a whole roast pig with a flourish and distinction that made him famous.[8]

Meanwhile, in Independence, Emily Fisher (circa 1808–1898) created a culinary legacy that was continued by her granddaughter, Vietta Garr (1896–1973). Not only did Emily Fisher operate the first hotel in Independence, but she did so as a freed slave. Adam Fisher, Emily's owner (and likely father), ran a gristmill and large farm, and while she was a young woman, Emily served as Adam's housekeeper and cook, honing her craft. When Adam allowed Emily to buy her freedom, he wanted to ensure that she would be able to earn her own way, so sometime in the 1850s, Adam put Emily in charge of an Independence hotel. It was a success, renowned for cleanliness and excellent food. Travelers looked forward to staying there, eager to enjoy home comforts and cooking one final time before setting out West.[9]

While we have no record of what Emily served her guests, Emily's granddaughter, Vietta Garr, probably learned some of her craft from her grandmother. Born and raised in Independence, Garr was at one point hired to cook by Madge Gates Wallace, Bess Truman's mother, and ultimately Garr cooked for Harry and Bess Truman after they married. The Trumans asked Garr to accompany them to the White House so that she could advise the White House kitchen staff as to "the Missouri way" when it came to cooking. Poppy Cannon and Patricia Brooks rightly observe that "like the Roosevelts, the Trumans did not care for elaborate food," but unlike them, they "demanded it better-cooked."[10] The Trumans' food preferences can be traced to Garr's cooking, and from there back to a slave whose cooking guaranteed her livelihood after freedom. Corn pudding, corn dodgers, biscuits, Southern-style greens (made by adding salt pork or ham hocks), Old Missouri ham, fried chicken, watermelon pickles, and transparent pie were beloved foods that Southern settlers and their slaves had brought with them to Kansas City. These foods continue to characterize Kansas City's wider culinary heritage, particularly during the holidays and at large celebrations.

Southerners equated excellent food with hospitality, and this was the case no matter who cooked, served, and ate the food, and it was the case no matter where the food was served. This fundamental fact of Southern culture meant that African Americans who excelled at cooking were often immortalized while countless others who labored just as hard and often in more brutal occupations died forgotten. "Aunt" Rachel, Minerva and Mark, Emily Fisher, and Vietta Garr are only a handful of examples from the annals of Kansas City history.

In 1925, Frayser T. Lane, executive secretary of the Kansas City Urban League, explained that although Kansas City "can neither be termed [a] Southern nor Northern city," there is no doubt "about the prevailing atmosphere being definitely Southern."[11] After the Civil War, African Americans continued to work in the catering industry and were in demand aboard trains after the invention of the Pullman car allowed passengers to dine en route. As a major rail hub, numerous young African American men responded to Kansas City newspaper ads calling for cooks and waiters with promise of "good wages and working conditions."[12] Significantly, many gained their start working on steamboats or trains and would later return to Kansas City to start their own restaurants.

African American women were by nature of their sex even more limited in their career paths than African American men. In 1920, the fourth most common occupation for this demographic was boardinghouse keeper, followed by housekeeper; most of them cooked meals for borders and families alike.[13] As such, they often had direct influence over menus that came from their mothers' and grandmothers' recipes. Evan S. Connell, a Kansas City native, accurately depicted that cuisine in his novels *Mrs. Bridge* and *Mr. Bridge*, set in the 1920s through the 1940s in a fashionable Kansas

City neighborhood. *Mr. Bridge* offered a glimpse of the gustatory satisfaction that better-off Kansas Citians took for granted when they employed African American cooks:

> Around dinnertime it usually occurred to Mr. Bridge that there were, in fact, three women on whom he depended and Harriet was not the least of them. She was such a marvelous cook that he resented the occasions when he and Mrs. Bridge were invited out. There were traces of the South in her cooking. Such dishes as jambalaya appeared on the table, and frequently she served barbecued ribs which he loved with a love he held for very few things on earth. She could prepare sugar-cured ham with red-eye gravy far better than any restaurant, and hot biscuits and honey, and turnips which tasted like no other turnips, and candied yams with the flavor of marshmallow. She never used a cookbook. She knew.[14]

Pork in particular remains as fundamental to Southern cuisine as it does to Kansas City cuisine, and after the Civil War, thousands of African American laborers turned pigs into pork in Kansas City meatpacking plants.

THE KILLING FLOORS OF THE "BIG FOUR"

In the late 1870s, African Americans came north from the Deep South, lured by printed handbills promising free farmland to "all colored people that want to go to Kansas." Between six and ten thousand people began the journey, but many ran out of finances and settled in Kansas City instead. Many of these Exodusters, as they were called, competed for employment in the packinghouses and stockyards alongside newly arriving immigrants.

By the end of the 1930s, Kansas City was home to eleven packinghouses, with the "Big Four," Wilson, Armour, Cudahy, and Swift, employing the majority of laborers. As the previous chapter detailed, Eastern Europeans were heavily recruited, and so too were African Americans as a means to break strikes and keep wages low. Melvin B. Tolson, a graduate of Kansas City's all-black Lincoln High School who went on to a distinguished literary career, remembered that when it came to the brutality of the packinghouse, workers sometimes overcame their racial prejudices because all their bellies were empty, and their children and women were "without proper food and clothing."[15] Tolson gained such insights while working in a Kansas City, Kansas, packinghouse the summer before he left for Fisk University; later, he described the realities of the killing floors where a grisly racial cooperation manifested itself.

Five men worked "The Tub" and thus set the pace for ten thousand workers. A "huge German . . . stuck the hogs as they passed on a long chain. In five minutes, he was covered with blood. He drank blood—and said nothing to anybody. Everybody feared him. Some said he'd cut a man's throat as soon as a hog's." After the hogs were attached to the chain, a "Negro dropper . . . stood above The Tub and dropped hogs from a turntable into tons of boiling water. He sang blues as he set the killing pace." Tolson recalled that one day, he tried to do the dropper's job, and "a mammoth hog, in its death agony, almost hurled [Tolson] into The Tub." Next was "Old Man Jeff. Old-timers said he was slipping; yet he could souse hogs faster than a cat can lick its paw." Next on the line "was the little Mexican who hooked the hogs to the dehairing machine. His hands were faster than Joe Louis's punches. Fifth, there was the big black man who split the hogs. With one mighty blow, he could half [sic] a 600-pounder."[16]

Those who could survive the pace and demonstrate talent and courage advanced skill- and pay-wise. Some seventy-nine African Americans held skilled jobs as managers, butchers, and foremen; more than eight hundred did semiskilled work.[17] For those who rose to the top, their pay allowed them to leave notorious Kansas City slums such as Hell's Half Acre and instead live on the bluffs overlooking the Kaw River, away from the pollution and stench of the meatpacking plants below.

THE AFRICAN AMERICAN CONTRIBUTION TO KANSAS CITY–STYLE BARBECUE

Just as immigrants often saved enough money to leave the packinghouses altogether and start their own businesses, so too did many African Americans. The most successful often specialized in barbecue. African American contributions to the art of slow-roasting meat have been covered in numerous accounts. Suffice it to say that by George Washington's birth in 1732, Virginia slaves were already experts at preparing barbecue for the large parties that their masters hosted. While Virginians danced to banjo and fiddle music and enjoyed mounds of succulent pork and its accompaniments, the slaves performed the labor: "digging trenches, butchering animals, chopping wood, making grates, tending fires for hours on end, and serving food—bowing and scraping all the while," as Kansas City barbecue historian Doug Worgul characterized it.[18] Missouri also became a barbecue state, and if a Missourian owned male slaves, barbecuing was their responsibility.

Kansas City festivals, political rallies, and the Fourth of July inevitably featured barbecue. A particularly memorable Fourth occurred in 1858 when Colonel McGee hosted a citywide party and offered up a bison for the barbecue pit. The celebration was under way by ten in the morning, and the men in charge of butchering and barbecuing would have been McGee's slaves.[19] More memorable was the citywide barbecue on July 3, 1869, when upwards of forty thousand spectators gathered on the banks of the Missouri River for the opening of the Hannibal Bridge. Father Bernard Donnelly wrote that after the celebration, many revelers "reformed and marched to the barbecue grounds, located in Col. Steen's pasture at the eastern terminus of Ottawa Street—near what is now Twelfth Street and Troost Avenue." Patrick O'Neill rightly credits the Irish, including Colonel Steen and Sara Malloy, wife of the police captain Dennis Malloy, with overseeing the preparation of "a ton of barbecue and other refreshments." Likely Malloy was overseeing the logistics while African American men, the experts in this art, prepared the barbecue.[20]

What had been forced on African Americans could also be a pleasure if it was done voluntarily, for compensation, or privately for friends and families. In Jim Crow–era Kansas City, African American neighborhoods were hazy with hickory smoke on the weekends. "During those days," recalled "Amazin'" Grace Harris, Kansas City's beloved barbecue queen, "there was a limitation of where black people went. . . . So [neighbors] would have a little hole in the ground, put a rod in it and barbecue. They would go from house to house, play the blues and dance until the day."[21] Tough meat and offal were relatively cheap if neighbors pooled resources, and wood was free or virtually free.

Henry Perry (1875–1940) is credited with being the first man in Kansas City to take barbecue, what had traditionally been offered up for free, and make a substantial living selling it. He was born in Shelby County, near Memphis, Tennessee, and started learning the art at age seven; by age fifteen, he was barbecuing for others. As with many African American restaurateurs, Perry had gained additional experience as a steamboat cook.[22] That work took him to Kansas City, Chicago, and Minneapolis, but he settled in Kansas City in 1907, perhaps because he saw the money to be made. After all, generations of Kansas Citians knew about and loved barbecue, and to be able to purchase excellent sandwiches and ribs for a modest price would appeal to them. Perry, the consummate marketer and self-promoter, explained that he had a "special way" of preparing meat that was irresistible. "Cooking only over a fire made from hickory and oak woods, the meat gets that delicious flavor which is the cause of the tremendous popularity of barbecued meats," he explained to his admirers and acolytes. He also insisted that there was "only one way to cook barbecue," and it was his way: "over a wood fire, with a properly constructed oven and pit."[23]

While working as a saloon porter on Kansas City's West Side, Perry started a stand on Banks Alley in the Garment District.[24] Lack of refrigeration necessitated that Perry sell out, and apparently, he had no difficulty doing so. By 1916, Perry was listed in the *City Directory*, and his advertisement bills were pitched to customers of varying incomes and tastes. During the holidays, one bill encouraged people to "stop in at Perry's for your Barbecued Turkey, Duck, Pig or Goose," and on another, he encouraged people to "call on Perry for your O'Possum, Ground Hog, Coon, Beef, Pork, and Mutton." This bill resonated with older African Americans who hunted nocturnal animals on their own time, given that daylight hours belonged to the master.[25] Although the term "soul food" would not be used in any publicized fashion until another Kansas Citian, Inez Kaiser, published the *Soul Food Cookbook* in 1968, this particular Perry advertisement also got to the heart of what "soul food" meant: taking humble meats and making them delectable.

Perry operated numerous establishments over his long career, including one at 1514 East Nineteenth Street from 1915 to 1925, one at 1403½ East Seventeenth Street, and later, one at 1900 Highland. For one year, 1934, Perry's barbecue was also available at 502 Westport Road.[26] His success attracted loyal patrons but also competitors looking for a way out of poverty and seeing the potential that barbecue might offer them, too. A September 9, 1916, *Kansas City Sun* newspaper advertised not only "Henry Perry, Barbecue King," but also Mrs. A. D. Turner's Barbecue at 1747 Forest Avenue and R. W. Alexander's at 1172 East Eighteenth Street among others.[27] By the 1930s, close to one hundred establishments were operating, including Red Devil Bar-B-Q at 2109 Campbell Street, operated by Mrs. Pearl Monroe, and Black Hawk Barbecue at 1410 East Fourteenth Street, run by Mr. and Mrs. William H. Spivey. The city had so many barbecue restaurants that even a couple of New York City restaurants started serving "Kansas City Barbecue."[28]

Barbecue had traditionally been learned by apprenticeship. Children learned from their elders and did the heavy work of lifting and hauling in return for the lessons. To make money, Perry needed help, and the young men who worked under Perry's tutelage thus learned a valuable skill that allowed them eventually to operate their own businesses. Perry's most famous apprentices were two East Texan brothers, Charlie Bryant (1892–1952) and his younger brother, Arthur (1900–1982). These men's legacy permeates Kansas City barbecue culture today.

Charlie had come to Kansas City as a boy and at some point began working for Perry. After he mastered the technique of slow-roasting meat over coals, Charlie started his own barbecue business at Fourteenth and Woodland. He created his own sauce, a "formula . . . that spread his fame as a barbecue man far and wide," his obituary in the *Kansas City Call* noted.[29] Arthur had not planned to become a Pitmaster, but on an August 1931 visit to see Charlie after graduating from Texas Prairie View A&M, Arthur changed his mind. As had Charlie, Arthur credited Henry Perry for his skill, explaining in a 1980 interview that both he and Charlie "learned the game under him."[30]

In 1929, Charlie Bryant started his own restaurant at 1921 East Eighteenth Street, where he and Arthur worked to make their establishment stand out from the competition for the flavor of the meat and the fiery sauce that accompanied it. In 1946, Charlie retired because of failing health and sold his enterprise to Arthur. Not wanting to destroy a good thing and adamant that Charlie and Henry Perry were "the greatest barbecue men [he] ever knew," Arthur nonetheless altered the establishment to reflect his own style, starting with the sauce. His was less fiery than his brother's, although it retained its distinctive vinegar-paprika base and noticeable absence of sugar.[31] He also replaced the sawdust planks with linoleum and replaced wooden tabletops with easier-to-clean Formica. In the late 1940s, Arthur also installed electricity and refrigeration. Along with homemade pickles, he introduced hand-cut French fries boiled in lard to create what remains in many Kansas Citians' opinions the best plate of fries to be had at any Kansas City restaurant, barbecue or otherwise.

Eventually, Arthur Bryant moved his establishment to its current location at 1727 Brooklyn. It continues to attract dignitaries, out-of-towners, and even though the Municipal Stadium around the corner at Twenty-Second and Brooklyn was closed in 1972, Chiefs and Royals fans still descend on Bryant's on game day, patiently waiting in a cafeteria-style line for their barbecue fix. Its space fills also on weekdays when the noon whistle (now more figuratively than literally) blows.[32]

In Kansas City barbecue lore, Arthur Pinkard (1880–1963) was Henry Perry's other most important apprentice, although information on Pinkard and his connection to Perry is hard to come by. Most of what barbecue aficionados and historians understand of the Perry-Pinkard connection comes from an interview with Ollie Gates, son of George and Arzelia Gates. In 1946, George and Arzelia purchased from Johnny Thomas the run-down Ol' Kentuck Bar-B-Q on the northwest corner of Nineteenth and Vine Streets. The Gateses were eager to start their own barbecue legacy and Pinkard, as Doug Worgul described it, "came with the place." Pinkard's barbecue was certainly similar to Perry's in that he, too, believed that meat must be slowly roasted over a pit of hickory and oak coals, and that the meat juices must drip directly onto the coals, as Ollie Gates recounted. As George and Arzelia transformed Ol' Kentuck into their own restaurant, Pinkard mentored George and Ollie, who was fourteen when his parents bought Ol' Kentuck. "Arthur Pinkard *did* learn from Henry Perry. He was a student of Henry Perry's. And that is how we came to learn how to barbecue the Henry Perry Way," Ollie stated. "That's why we have his picture hanging in all our restaurants."[33] When Ollie decided to enter the barbecuing business in earnest, George changed the name to Gates & Sons, and six currently exist in the Kansas City Metro.

When Arthur Pinkard retired in the early 1950s, dying shortly thereafter, he left little information as to his past, but the *Kansas City Directory* indicated that in 1917 he was a cook at Selah Fassett's Owl Lunch Room, at 21 East Twenty-Fourth Street, and that up until 1941 he worked as a janitor and at one point on a WPA road crew. Pinkard started to cook at Ol' Kentuck Bar-B-Q in 1942. While Perry, the Bryant brothers, and Ollie and George Gates became established businessmen and expert promoters of their product, Arthur Pinkard remained someone else's employee, back there with the meat and the pit. He did his job expertly but without fanfare, and as a result his own contributions have been easier to overlook.[34] What also makes Pinkard important to the story of African American culinary contribution, however, was his connection to Johnny Thomas. While the establishment might have been rundown and largely forgotten when the Gateses were looking to start their business, Ol' Kentuck had previously been one of Kansas City's most important barbecue and jazz venues.

FOOD AND JAZZ DURING KANSAS CITY'S PENDERGAST ERA, 1920–1939

Most Kansas City barbecue establishments in the early twentieth century were clustered in one of the few areas where African Americans could buy or rent property, both commercial and residential. Following the Civil War, African Americans lived close to their employers or in whatever areas they could afford to live in, often in shantytowns near West Bottom packinghouses. By the early 1900s, Kansas City's African American population doubled, going from 17,567 to 30,719. The City Beautiful Movement created parks, boulevards, and exclusive residential and commercial developments where it was illegal for African Americans to reside unless they were "legitimate" live-in servants. The largest area of African American housing and businesses was bounded on the north by Independence Avenue, Troost on the west, Twenty-Seventh on the south, and Benton Boulevard on the east. Starting at Twelfth and Troost and continuing south to Eighteenth, one soon arrived at the pulsing heart of "Paris of the Plains," the Eighteenth and Vine district.[35]

While Ol' Kentuck's decline took place in the early 1940s after Tom Pendergast was sent to prison and Kansas City's reform era began, at its zenith, Ol' Kentuck epitomized what a blend of machine politics, Mob violence, and a "wide-open" culture could do to make Kansas City a magnet to out-of-work jazz musicians, bohemians, curious travelers, and crooks. Ol' Kentuck was one of Kansas City's "pig iron" houses, as young saxophonist Henry "Buster" Smith called them, a place where "pork was served, liquor was drunk, and the bands played the blues all night in the keys of B, D, and E."[36] Ol' Kentuck was a favorite among poor musicians because the barbecue was so cheap. Particularly in demand was "barbecue soup," a large bowl of which sold for a dime. Johnny Thomas drew in customers with the aroma of smoking meat and the sound of what was becoming known as Kansas City jazz, a hard-swinging dance music indebted to the blues and fashioned initially by musicians such as Count Basie and the Bennie Moten Kansas City Orchestra. Thomas wanted musicians to see Ol' Kentuck as their "second home." If he could fill them up with barbecue and offer a stage with a piano and drum set, Thomas could count on them to perform and bring in more patrons. Ol' Kentuck's sawdust-covered floor lent itself to swing, and the music pulsed all night long. Ol' Kentuck was particularly popular with a band of Lincoln High School students, the Deans of Swing, which featured among their ranks young Charlie Parker.[37]

Numerous club owners kept the music going by tying it directly to food. They put out kitties to collect musicians' tips, and they offered them cheap chili, coffee cans brimming with hot and spicy crawdads, and newspapers holding mounds of barbecue. Thus it is that when someone says "Kansas City," it often calls to mind jazz and barbecue, both tied to African American artistic and culinary culture, both rooted deeply in the South. Furthermore, jazz and barbecue are often associated with celebration and optimism, a real good time. However, such an association should not come at the expense of what was at the foundation: hunger—unrelenting, physical hunger. Jazz great Orville "Piggy" Minor summed it up: "Things come in threes: Eat food first, then it was a toss-up between the habit and the horn."[38]

Minor was referring to Charlie Parker, but such was also the case for many African American musicians. Hunger powered musical innovation while a wide-open culture of booze lubricated it, and periodic Mob violence punctuated it. "In Kansas City, all them big clubs were [run by] them big gangsters, and they were the musicians' best friend. They give you a job, and something to eat, and work regular. We didn't know nothing about their business, they didn't know nothing about ours," recalled Buster Smith, a sentiment echoed by many musicians attracted to Kansas City during the 1920s and 1930s. In fact, so many unemployed jazz musicians came to Kansas City and found work that it became a mecca, a place to satiate one's hunger by blowing on one's horn.[39] Bandleader Jay McShann explained the appeal of Kansas City's opportunity this way: "So the hours are passing, you're up there sweating and swinging, and your stomach is still crying the blues, louder by the minute. With all this activity, you knew you had to get something down in your stomach, and by the end of the gig, you wanted it to be hot, it had to be a solid, and it better be *right*."[40] Kansas City offered up barbecue joints, lunch wagons, chili parlors, cafeterias—these were all popular with the musicians.

Charlie Parker's early career illustrates the interrelation of food and jazz to the African American psyche and by extension, how it came to be intricately tied to Kansas City's identity. As a teenager, Parker snuck into the Reno Club on Twelfth, between Cherry and Locust, to listen to saxophonist Lester Young and the Count Basie Orchestra. Because his age barred him from legal entry, Charlie had to edge past Rusty, the large ex-boxer doorman. To do so, Charlie walked down Cherry to the alley behind the club where during breaks, musicians, hookers, and patrons congregated. A John Agnos lunch wagon parked there, so laden with wares that it leaned against the Reno Club's northeast corner, wrote jazz historian Ross Russell.

Everyone lined up to buy the sandwiches favored by Kansas Citians of modest incomes, including "liver, pig snoots and ears, hog maws, fish, chicken, and pork tenderloins." Also available were chicken "short thighs" that Charlie favored.[41] He would purchase two or three, as much as his allowance money afforded, and while he ate he watched for musicians coming out on break. They too ordered from the lunch wagon, dousing their fried brain sandwiches or tenderloins with plenty of hot sauce, talking and joshing. Noticing Charlie hanging around, gnawing on his chicken, what people called yardbirds, they would call out to him, "Hey Yardy! Hey Yardbird!" and the nickname stuck: Charlie "Yardbird" Parker, or "Bird," was born. Meanwhile drummer Jesse Price would squeeze Charlie in among the band members when they headed back into the Reno. Because Rusty's size hindered him from climbing the narrow balcony stairs, Charlie sprinted up, found a corner overlooking the stage, and spent his nights absorbing that music.[42]

Indeed, Midwestern jazz, wrote historian Nathan W. Pearson Jr., was nurtured in the South and in food served up by poor rural blacks at their Saturday night suppers. Families gathered at a host's house, where they paid a small entrance fee to listen to a musician. While banjos, pianos, guitars, or saxophones supplied tunes, people supped on fried fish, chicken, chitlins, or barbecue; dancing would follow. Whiskey, moonshine, beer—whatever was available—flowed freely. These Saturday night suppers remained important as African Americans migrated north to Kansas City and farther on, although they were often called rent suppers. The host needed money for rent or perhaps a medical expense. People gathered, paid what they could, and then settled in for food, drink, music, and dance. Roger Searcy, a Kansas City jazz musician in the early 1940s, remembered that he got his start as a twelve-year-old when hired to play for a rent supper. The hosts, Searcy recalled, "really didn't have to give me the fifty cents, because I was so anxious to play. And then they'd give me a fish sandwich."[43] Local jazz historian and KCUR radio host Chuck Haddix does not call his Friday and Saturday night music show the "Fish Fry" just because of his name; it pays homage to those rent suppers.

Supper clubs offered a similar vibe in a public setting. Patrons came for a meal, and then the music started. Countless nightclubs were in fact supper clubs, often operated by the Mob in collusion with Pendergast and the police who received kickbacks. Wiggle Inn at 2607 Troost billed itself as Kansas City's oldest nightspot, offering dinner, dancing, and drink. Club Mardi Gras advertised "always delicious food!" Cuban Gardens, next to the North Kansas City dog track, billed itself as "a smart supper club for Kansas City's smart set." Dante's Inferno at 1104 Independence was famous—notorious, really—for its waitresses dressed as devils, complete with forked tails, who served "the finest of foods with refreshments." The Winnie Winkle Club advertised "Dine-Dance-Drink," and Aaron Brooks's Havana Inn, which billed itself as the "only Negro owned and operated tavern on 12th Street," offered "fine food, sandwiches, and fine bar-b-q" all night long.

The best clubs hosted jam sessions, "a Kansas City specialty, like crawdads and brain sandwiches. . . . They were scaled from pick up sessions at a place like Old Kentucky Bar-B-Que . . . to major league affairs at the Sunset, Subway, and Reno Clubs," wrote Russell.[44] Where jazz, food, and alcohol went together, the race lines could sometimes be crossed. The Pendergast era offered brief windows of opportunity for people inclined to mingle without having to judge fellow human beings exclusively through a color lens. Many clubs stretching from Twelfth up to Nineteenth Streets were Mob-controlled, and as Stanley Crouch put it in *Kansas City Lightning: The Rise and Times of Charlie Parker*, Italian gangsters "were so powerful that they did whatever they wanted and allowed whatever they felt like allowing," and interracial mixing was just one of those things.[45] Colloquially known as black and tan clubs, patrons of both races could eat, drink, and hear the music, although officially, the clubs might be billed as "white only" or "Negros only." "We could go there [to Scott's Club]," wrote John Dawson's father, reminiscing to his son about his "clubbing days," but "being white, we had to sit upstairs and look down over the railing."[46] Owners might also throw up makeshift walls or hang a curtain midway down the center. However, because "black" and "white" meant little when it came to actual skin color, the possibilities for inter-mixing were sometimes easy enough for those who wished to ignore the boundaries. Sometimes doormen broke the rules. The Orchid Room at 1519 East Twelfth Street billed itself as "the place where friends meet," and when white teenage boys craved its music, the kindly doorman at this club would put them up near stage and look the other way when the waiter served them beer. Ears—and eyes—were on the musicians.[47]

The best opportunity for racial intermixing took place after hours at "spook breakfasts," a Kansas City custom. At a different club each week, between four or five o'clock in the morning until noon, white and black musicians and patrons would meet. The food would be quick and fill-ing—hot dogs, hamburgers, chili—and while people ate, white musicians would try out their talents alongside black musicians, and race was mo-mentarily forgotten, shoved aside to make room for other considerations, music and appetite, both physical and sexual, among them.[48]

While the clubs along Twelfth and Eighteenth were sometimes black and tan, most Kansas City restaurants forbade African American patrons, or they forced them to order and take the food away. This was likewise the situation at coffee shops, luncheonettes, cafeterias, cafés, and department store eateries. Thus, the Eighteenth and Vine district had to meet many of the alimentary needs of African Americans. John Jordan "Buck" O'Neil summed up the ambivalence that African Americans felt about such limi-tations and restrictions in Jim Crow–Kansas City: It "was a horrible thing, but a bittersweet thing. We owned the Streets Hotel. We owned Elnora's Restaurant. The Kansas City Monarchs were our team. The money we made in the community, stayed in the community."[49] Given the density of the African American population in the Eighteenth and Vine district, it makes sense that an unusually high number of businesses in some fashion involved food. Candy kitchens, bakeries, fishmongers, produce stands, a dozen or more groceries, drugstore soda fountains, cafeterias, and take-aways were everywhere. Of the numerous sit-down restaurants, nothing surpassed Elnora's Café or the Rose Room at the Streets (sometimes called the Street or Street's) Hotel for sophistication and fine cuisine.

As with most African American restaurateurs, Reuben Street (1878–1956) spent time working in other people's kitchens and cafés before he went into business for himself.[50] After marrying Ella Davidson in India-napolis in 1900, Reuben decided to return to Kansas City, having grown up in the Armourdale District of Kansas City, Kansas. Reuben and Ella began modestly, operating a small restaurant at Eighteenth and Troost in Kansas City, Missouri. To supplement his earnings, Reuben continued working as a railway chef while Ella managed the restaurant. The Streets prospered, moving to various larger locations as their profits grew. By 1920, with a thriving restaurant at Eighteenth and the Paseo, the Streets were ready to take a significant risk. With financing from Theron B. and John Watkins, owners of the nearby Watkins Brothers Funeral Home, the Streets bought the building that housed their restaurant and started Kansas City's finest African American hotel.[51] Its sophisticated Blue Room featured the Bennie Moten Orchestra as one of its house bands; the Rose Room across the lobby could seat 125 diners at linen-clothed tables replete with crystal and silver.

"Imagine what it would be like staying in a fine New York City hotel, like the Waldorf-Astoria, and coming down every morning to breakfast, nodding hello to Frank Sinatra or Doris Day or Fred Astaire as you pass by their tables," Buck O'Neil explained. "Well, that's what it felt like for me, playing for the Kansas City Monarchs in the late thirties and early forties, staying in the Streets Hotel at 18th and Paseo, and coming down to the dining room where Cab Calloway and Billie Holiday and Bojangles Robinson often ate."[52] The Rose Room took some sting out of segregation by offering patrons the service and luxuries that white patrons expected at the Baltimore or Muehlebach. The Rose Room's window drapes muffled street noise, and its state-of-the art asphalt tiles deadened noise within.

Its grilled Kansas City strip steaks were sometimes prepared and presented by Reuben Street himself, and when he was busy, the expert service was carried out by a trained waitstaff. The à la carte menu featured the same fare found at other upscale Kansas City restaurants, including a variety of chops and steaks, chicken, fish, and seafood. Equally important, the Rose Room offered families and organizations a formal banquet room and catering for private celebrations. At the height of its popularity, John R. Ross Jr., *chef de cuisine*, oversaw the Rose Room kitchen.[53]

Previously, Ross worked at Lelia Coates Johnson's Blue-Bird Cafeteria on the southwest corner of Eighteenth and the Paseo. As with most of its competitors, Blue-Bird offered a mix of Southern and Midwestern plate lunches including baked ham or roast pork with a wide array of vegetables, waffles with syrup, fried fish and fried chicken, chili, and numerous pies and cakes. *The Directory of Colored Residents: Kansas City Missouri, 1937–38* also included advertisements for Mack's Place at 2330 Vine, which offered "Shrimps Every Nite" along with fried chicken. Mrs. Pearl Ross McDaniel ran Just-A-Mere Eat Shop at 2407½ Vine, advertising "real bar-b-q, hot fish, fried chicken, fried pies" as well as "good 20c meals." Harris' Snack Shop, run by Mrs. Lillian Harris, also advertised fried chicken, bar-b-q, chili, and "pastry baked in our own oven," with special Sunday dinners.[54]

Be it a takeaway, a restaurant, a tavern, or a cafeteria in Kansas City's African American commercial districts, barbecue reigned supreme for its flavor and its price. It could also be, like the jazz and blues that often accompanied it, a great equalizer. Although forgotten today, Ollie Harris's Barbecue at 1707 East Twelfth Street was considered by many to be the best available, and "whatever the barriers were at that time, if [white people] wanted good barbecue . . . they had to go to Ollie Harris's," stated local African American historian Sonny Gibson. Henry Perry had also observed with pride that his trade was "about equally divided between white and black." He served "both high and low. Swanky limousines gleaming with nickel and glossy black rub shoulders at the curb outside the Perry stand with pre-historic Model T Fords."[55]

The era right after World War II showed no letup in the public's love of slow-smoked meat, and barbecue as a serious commercial business attracted more practitioners, making the art no longer limited—or relegated—to African Americans. Currently, Kansas City is home to over one hundred barbecue restaurants, including not only Bryant's and Gates & Sons, but the almost-as-iconic Danny Edwards (what was previously Lil' Jake's Eat It and Beat It), Rosedale Barbecue, LC's, Snead's, Woodyard, and Joe's KC (formerly Oklahoma Joe's).[56]

1950s AND 1960s DESEGREGATION
OF KANSAS CITY RESTAURANTS

"I . . . get a bittersweet feeling because I remember that a lot of people lost their whole way of life," said Buck O'Neil, again referring to Kansas City's Jim Crow era. Segregation's legal end resulted in "another one of those ironies, the hardest one. Not only did a black business die, other black businesses did, too, the ones that were dependent on black base-ball and black entertainment. The Streets Hotel had to close because it couldn't compete with the Muehlebach Hotel downtown."[57]

O'Neil's reflections of "bittersweet" times might be applied as well to the way that Kansas City experienced the end of Pendergast machine politics decades before the end of segregation. In 1939, a coalition of businessmen, politicians, and suburbanites indicted Tom Pendergast on tax evasion, and during the early 1940s, numerous Kansas City restaurants and clubs cleaned up or shut down. Reformers turned "an agriculturally-grounded sin city into an urban amusement park of a different kind—a fantasy land for the aspirations of the middle class," as Thomas Frank acerbically described what happened to his hometown after World War II. Adjectives such as "white-washed," "white bread," "square," and perhaps most memorably, "Cupcake Land" (after Kansas City native Richard Rhodes termed it as such in 1987), characterized Kansas City, or more ac-curately, its white suburbs.[58] When jazz went away, the restaurant culture became increasingly homogeneous, either at pains to be as conventional in its *haute cuisine* as were fancy restaurants all over the United States, or eager to attract national franchises ranging from Denny's to Trader Vic's.

It can be easy, however, to forget that part of what was taking place in Kansas City after World War II had less to do with the quality of food and nightlife, and a great deal more to do with ensuring that all venues, includ-ing Denny's and Trader Vic's, were open to people of color. As was the case throughout the United States, stopping segregation legally could not stop de facto segregation, and yet eating together could be, as it had been briefly shown to be, a way to unite people. Again, barbecue restaurants were held up as an example of what peaceful coexistence could look like in other public venues.

Initial activists in the fight to end segregation were pacifists involved in the Fellowship of Reconciliation (FOR), a nationwide organization that saw race oppression and war as "twin evils." Joining FOR at the local level was the Penn Valley Meeting for the Religious Society of Friends, or Penn Valley Friends. The bombing of Pearl Harbor shifted the groups' focus exclusively to the home front and to developing strategies to bring peace to "the things that caused dissension and difficulties"; namely, racism. FOR members and Penn Valley Friends formed the Committee on the Practice of Democracy (COPOD) to target Kansas City's public facilities, chief among them eateries.[59] Each Saturday, COPOD members sent interracial teams to theaters, hotels, drugstore soda fountains, and restaurants to "determine the exact boundaries of segregation in public accommodation." When confronted with these interracial groups, the majority of managers were passive-aggressive. They politely refused the interracial groups service, or they seated them behind screens or in out-of-the-way corners; they overcharged them; or they seated them but refused to take their orders. Some managers explained that they were personally not prejudiced, but they did not wish to be the "first to break the ice" when it came to established customs.

By the 1950s, the Kansas City Chamber of Commerce recognized that if downtown restaurants and hotels refused to integrate, convention and tourism business would be adversely affected. The Human Relations Commission, the Greater Kansas City Restaurant Association, and the NAACP worked to ensure that by 1958, numerous restaurants had indeed quietly integrated. Others held out, even after a 1962 city ordinance made it illegal for Kansas City restaurants, motels, and hotels to discriminate. One case that received national attention occurred in June 1963. African American Richard Robinson, a veteran, went with his brother to the Peerless Café at 3115 Prospect. When owner Peter Karos refused service, the brothers left and returned at noon with nine friends. Again, they were refused service. Robinson indignantly pointed out to reporters that "you go in the service maybe to fight for someone like that. You come back, and he won't serve you." Karos responded by saying that tomorrow, he would serve African Americans on condition that they enter "one or two at a time" and were "nice-looking people." He also justified refusing Robinson service because he feared losing his white trade: "They don't want to sit with Negroes," he told reporters. Abruptly, Karos closed down for good.[60]

The most stubborn holdouts were downtown department store eateries. Store managers blamed their segregation policies on the Merchants Association; the Merchants Association blamed the policies on store managers. Finally, shoppers took direct action. Most important were the Twin Citians, an organization of professional African American women from both sides of the state line. In 1958, they allied with the pastors of black and white churches and their congregations to create the Community Committee for Social Action (CCSA). They organized a boycott and picket line for department stores refusing to allow a black shopper to sit down for a cup of coffee and sandwich.

The CCSA planned the protest to begin on December 19, 1958, in the midst of the holiday shopping season.[61] In spite of record-breaking cold, those walking the picket line were undeterred. The wind cut through Irene Marcus's thin coat, but Marcus refused to give up. "A lot of white people didn't even know what it was about," Marcus recalled. "They would ask, 'You mean you can't eat here?'"[62] Virtually all black shoppers and most white shoppers refused to cross the lines, and business was badly compromised. By February 1959, Peck and Macy's began to cave, followed in April by Emery, Bird, and Thayer and the Jones Store. In what historian Sherry Lamb Schirmer described as a "geography of avoidance," such victories were of little consequence, given the opening of far-flung suburban shopping centers, restaurants, and schools that made it possible for prosperous white people to avoid contact with people of color without any law or ordinance being broken. New freeways cut right through the heart of downtown as well as through African American communities, further exacerbating people's segregation, impoverishment, and the onset of urban blight.

The history of the Kansas City downtown decline and resurgence is complicated and multifaceted, well beyond the scope of this study's focus. Nonetheless, food and race have played a significant role in this history. The Kansas City of today projects a markedly different identity than it did just twenty years ago, and somewhat surprisingly, a nationwide food revolution that was triggered in part by Calvin Trillin is in part responsible.

"THE BEST RESTAURANTS ARE, OF COURSE, IN KANSAS CITY."

"The best restaurants are, of course, in Kansas City. Not all of them; only the top four or five," Calvin Trillin observed in his deceptively off-handed manner in the April 1972 issue of *Playboy* magazine.[63] While it might appear that Trillin had been infected with the same hollow boosterism that had infected many city officials around this time, Trillin's comment was an indictment of *haute* and *nouvelle cuisine*'s tyranny over the American palate. With its clichéd dishes, insistence on white tablecloths, and tuxedoed waiters, America's most heralded restaurants were more about answering to the narrow dictates of an elite group of gourmets than they were about offering up excellent food. Surrounded as he was by stale Continental restaurant fare, Trillin remembered the succulent ribs at Bryant's and the shattering crust of Southern pan-fried chicken from Stroud's; he also remembered that such places served their extraordinary food with no pretense, little aplomb. No matter the national hype that Trillin caused when he also commented that Bryant's Barbecue was likely the single *best* restaurant in the world, Arthur Bryant insisted that his establishment was a "grease house," no more, and no less.

Trillin's criticism of the state of American restaurants, however, did have a profound impact—"as much impact on American food culture as 'Call me Ishmael' had on American literature"—wrote John Mariani in his history of American restaurants, and nowhere was that more the case than in Kansas City.[64] In other words, Trillin busted open a paradigm. He offered people a radically different way to look at cuisine and more importantly, to appreciate regional specialties and the cultures of those who produced that food. He also made it acceptable to champion humble roadhouses, barbecue shacks, drive-ins, and cafeterias, all of which still had a strong presence in Kansas City in the early 1970s. Furthermore, African Americans, as slaves, freedmen, and migrants from the South, had played a significant role in cooking at and operating such eateries, just as they and white Southerners had had a profound influence on the flavor of the humble foods served therein. So excellent was Kansas City's cuisine that Trillin made scheduled trips back home just to eat, and his pilgrimages resulted in some of the nation's finest gastronomic literature, from *American Fried* to *Alice, Let's Eat*.

Some Kansas Citians at the time of Trillin's pronouncement were already looking for new inspiration and direction and were acting on their own impulses, irrespective of national culinary trends. Deeply troubled by the city's racist past and the challenges that desegregation brought with it, they remembered that the Pendergast era had resulted not only in corruption and criminal activity, but also in moments of racial cooperation, inevitably when music and food were involved. Black-and-tan supper clubs, barbecue establishments like Ol' Kentuck, and people congregating around a John Agnos lunch wagon all suggested that if good cooking and music could bring the races together at that point, was it not possible that it could bring them together in the here and now?

"Amazin'" Grace Harris, Roger Naber, and Lindsay and Jo Shannon all played notable, and noble, roles in answering this question, even if they did not explicitly set out to do so. In 1985, Roger Naber started the Grand Emporium, a phenomenally popular live-music venue that featured Grace Harris's distinctly Southern, soul-infused cooking. "Gracie had The Franchise on the food!!" declared Phil Mullin, recalling the magic that was the Grand Emporium.[65] Everyone—all races—lined up at the counter to order Grace's barbecue and her other specialties (particularly one of her special barbecue sauces), and they sat down to eat, party, and listen to live blues, root music, and jazz. The Grand Emporium was like a reincarnated supper club that helped people forget about skin color by bringing them together for food and music.

Naber went on to help organize a citywide Blues and Jazz Festival and sold his Grand Emporium, and "Amazin'" Grace likewise retired. Nonetheless, the philosophies that drove her cooking and Naber's love of blues and jazz are now manifest at Lindsay and Jo Shannon's BB's Lawnside Barbecue, in operation since 1990. Lindsay, a graduate of Southwest High School, paid homage to Kansas City's blues and jazz heritage by hosting a popular radio show in 1977. Constant memories of his listeners about barbecue and blues led him to launch a venture that combined the two. Like the Grand Emporium, BB's offers people of all races a space where they can mutually celebrate and take pride in the best of Kansas City's heritage.

What has been happening in Kansas City since the 1970s suggests how food can help heal racial wounds and also help residents accept the past for what it was, including the ugly scars. That past has also become the inspiration for a culinary renaissance. Distilleries, breweries, markets, and restaurants explicitly hearken back to the city's origins in the 1820s and 1830s, when waves of Southerners, black and white, arrived and immediately began cooking. Menu specialties such as fried chicken and catfish, grits and shrimp, sweet potato pie, peach cobbler, buttermilk biscuits slathered with sorghum and accompanied by country ham, and corn bread and beans are all prepared by old and new generations of restaurateurs paying homage to Kansas City's African American and Southern roots. Irrespective of their skin color, residents can not only peacefully commingle, but they can rightly claim a stake in the culinary legacy that has put their city "back on the map."

Chapter Six

Kansas City Markets and Groceries

Kansas City's provisions economy began in earnest when several Native American tribes were forcibly moved to Indian Territory and entrepreneurs saw an opportunity to open markets in their vicinity. Although fur remained important in the 1830s, the animals and subsequently the demand for their pelts dwindled; increasingly, food, livestock, and farming equipment became more important for trade. John Calvin McCoy's Westport settlement was initially created to do business with the Shawnee villages just over the Missouri border, and ledgers from McCoy's own border emporium indicated that he did brisk business selling food staples, including salt beef and corn (both as seed and as meal), as well as fishing and hunting equipment, and alcohol. Brandy sold for $1.75 a gallon.[1] It was illegal during this time to sell Native Americans alcohol, but if McCoy honored the law, plenty of his Westport competitors felt no such compunction.

"For whatever it's worth as a comment on the value of things social or economic, spiritual or architectural, the oldest continuously occupied building in Kansas City is a saloon," wrote Jim Lapham in regard to Kelly's Westport Inn, in business since 1947. When McCoy sold that particular lot on the northwest corner of Pennsylvania Avenue and Westport Road back in 1836, "saloon" and "grocery store" were synonyms, and a long line of grocers who operated at that location dealt in both groceries and liquor. Among the more colorful, or notorious, early proprietors was Samuel C. Roby, characterized by William A. Goff as a "likable rogue" tolerated by Native Americans "even when he was picking their pockets." Roby was one of the few traders to have his license revoked for selling alcohol to Native Americans. He was undeterred and eventually sold his business to George W. Ewing in 1848 for $1,500 to start another grocery/ saloon on the southeast corner of Mill and Westport Road.[2] George W. Ewing and his brother William were also Indian traders who ran their store from 1848 to 1859. The Ewings had a "somewhat unsavory reputation," Goff wrote, but they were mistrusted by their customers because they were "not 'home talent'" like Roby was.[3]

Albert Gallatin Boone, one of Daniel Boone's grandchildren, was the building's most famous owner. From 1854 to 1859, Boone enhanced the property significantly and operated a large trading post while selling slaves on the side. The Boone Trading Post, as it was called, was a secessionist holdout during the Border and Civil Wars. Along with the Harris House, it served as the main gathering place not only for political and military conversation, but also for social occasions. Boone sold the property to Robert Campbell for $7,000 when new job prospects involving the Santa Fe trade took him to Colorado. Throughout the rest of the nineteenth and early twentieth centuries, grocery stores continued to operate out of the Ewing-Boone Building, including those owned by Henry Rieger, David Meriwether, and before Randal Kelly purchased it and transformed it strictly into Kansas City's most popular saloon, John F. and Jake E. Wiedenmann, brothers in the grocery business whose family operated a store up through the mid-1940s.

Although Westport commerce was initially based on Native American trade, the Santa Fe Trail had a profound effect on Westport's development and shortly thereafter, on the Town of Kansas. McCoy sold his emporium in 1836 to William Miles Chick (McCoy's future father-in-law) because he wanted to invest in real estate ventures on the levy. The Town of Kansas Company was formed to improve the Westport, or the Town of Kansas, Landing, and to sell plats to prospective merchants. One was Charles E. Kearney, or "Mr. Grocery," as he was nicknamed.

Kearney was born in Galway, Ireland, and came to the United States after his parents died. He left clerking for the dry goods business in Mobile, Alabama, and New Orleans to join the U.S. military in its war with Mexico, signing up in 1846 with Samuel H. Walker's Texas Ranger regiment, under the command of General Zachary Taylor. Kearney's keen knowledge of the Southwest combined with his past experience in dry goods led to his decision to become a Santa Fe outfitter. Initially he worked out of Independence and then out of Westport. In 1854, Kearney

Boone's Trading Post (Wiedenmann Brothers Grocery); now the location of the enduringly popular Kelley's Westport Inn.
Missouri Valley Special Collections, Kansas City Public Library, Kansas City, Missouri

formed a partnership with William R. Bernard, and the firm of Kearney & Bernard became one of the most prosperous Town of Kansas businesses. In 1854 Kearney & Bernard sent eight hundred wagons of merchandise to Santa Fe, and in 1855, 1,217. Meanwhile, Kearney's riverfront wholesale grocery business was also thriving. Kearney was responsible for bringing into Kansas City from the East Coast many exotic, expensive foodstuffs, including oranges, citrons, and cranberries.[4]

Most coveted among early Kansas Citians were oysters, more so than citrus fruits and cranberries. They were sold by the barrel to grocers and tavern owners, and by the dozen to customers. Writing in 1859, Robert T. Van Horn noted that oysters were the greatest luxury on the market and that a "tip top Christmas and Steamboat dinner cannot well be got up without drawing on Baltimore for some of her fresh bivalves."[5] Kearney played a role in importing the oysters; however, Arthur Stilwell, a New Yorker who arrived in Kansas City in 1879 (purportedly because

voices in his head urged him to go West and create a railroad empire),
was more critical. Along with founding six railroads and forty towns,
Stilwell invented an oyster car for his Kansas City, Pittsburg, and Gulf
Railroad whose primary purpose was to ensure that customers in Kansas
City would have access to the freshest oysters possible. Stilwell built the
KCP&G Railroad from Kansas City and Pittsburg, Kansas, all the way to
Port Arthur, Texas (named after him). With the help of the Pullman Car
Company, Stilwell designed an oyster rail car to ensure that the bivalves
arrived in Kansas City alive. Eight feet wide and four feet high, the oyster
car was divided into four compartments complete with ventilators in the
top through which the oysters were loaded. Eight thousand two hundred
gallons of saltwater were also added. Painted an attractive dark blue with
THE STILWELL OYSTER CAR in silver, Kansas City customers could
easily see when fresh oysters were ready for delivery to the City Market.[6]

THE CITY MARKET

Well into the twentieth century, the City Market sold much of Kansas
City's fresh foods via wholesale and retail. It remains the oldest and largest farmers' market currently operating in Kansas City. The first road in
Kansas City was initially called Market Street, an explicit acknowledg-
ment of the importance of provisions to Kansas City's growing economy.
The road's peculiar angle, veering southwest rather than following the
straight north-south street grid that McCoy had sketched out, was the result of Kansas City's formidable geography; it was the one sizable breach
in the bluffs that allowed McCoy to move between the river landing where
a steamboat dropped off his supplies and his emporium four miles away.[7]
When McCoy organized the Town of Kansas Company, the land he and
the thirteen other investors bid on included both the Westport Landing and
the area around it that would quickly become City Market. As the difficult
work of excavating the cliffs began and Market Street was widened and
enhanced, it is no wonder that its name was changed to Grand Boulevard
to signify its literal as well as its symbolic significance.

Bringing food to the City Market in the early days involved several
strategies, one of which was train deliveries of foodstuffs into Union
Depot in the West Bottoms, and also by ferrying Clay County farmers

and their produce across the Missouri River. Clay County, along with six other counties, composed Missouri's "Little Dixie" or "Black Belt." Predominantly agricultural, these counties initially relied partly on slave labor to produce both food and tobacco. The Pike Road (remaining portions are now called Old Pike Road) started at Harlem on the north levee of the Missouri River facing Kansas City, and it ran north through miles of farmland to the Town of Barry. Colloquially known as the "fruit and vegetable highway," farmers came down the Pike Road, boarded the ferry at Harlem, arrived at Westport Landing, and made their way to the junction of Market and Main. Writing in 1857, Charles C. Spalding explained that from Clay County "we get a much larger trade than from Jackson." They "sell to our merchants largely of their home fabrics, farm products, and table supplies. This is an every day trade, and is one that keeps money constantly in circulation among our retail dealers. The yearly amount of this trade is estimated to be about $750,000."[8]

In 1888, the City Market was enhanced when a substantial red brick building including fifty-six stalls was built along Walnut near Fifth Street.[9] The growing stockyards, grain elevators, sophisticated cold storage systems, and the advent of refrigerated rail cars warranted even more expansion of the City Market, and it doubled in size in 1910, adding land between Third and Fourth Streets. While it continued to serve local farmers and individual customers, the wholesale grocery business grew rapidly, given City Market's proximity to the railroads and the provisions industries in the West Bottoms.[10] While increasingly integral to Kansas City's role as a nationwide distribution and storage center, the City Market saw its retail business decline in the interwar years because neighborhood grocery stores, especially in the new suburbs, were by then siphoning local shoppers away.

FAMILY-OWNED GROCERIES AND MARKETS

E. Whyte Grocery, Fruit & Wine Co.

One of the earliest successful retail grocers to expand and eventually operate Kansas City's first grocery chain store was E. Whyte Grocery, Fruit & Wine Co. Ebenezer Whyte Sr., a Scottish immigrant who came to Kansas City in 1877, opened a store at 912 Main. He was famously autocratic and proper, managing his store and employees, especially his four sons, with the proverbial iron fist. He dressed like the very successful merchant he was, sending all his collars to Troy, New York, weekly to be laundered, ironed, and starched, and he secured his collars around his neck with a gold and diamond pin rather than the usual necktie. When he died in 1901, he had trained his sons, William, Ebenezer Jr., George, and Frank Whyte, to take over his store, keep it prosperous, and expand it. Sophia Pritchard Whyte, Ebenezer's widow, became the company president.

At some point in the early 1900s, Whyte Grocery moved to 1121 Walnut and advertised with the jingle "Upon food and drink depend your health. 'Tis what you save that brings you wealth." As was traditional at the time, sides and quarters of beef, pork, and lamb hung from metal hooks outside the storefront, and chops and steaks were cut at the counter by expert butchers. Whyte Grocery, however, went against the trend when it moved in 1908 to even larger quarters at 1115 McGee. Two stories, seventy-five feet wide, and half a block deep, the new store was now large enough for the brothers to install on the ground floor a state-of-the-art refrigeration system to dry-age its beef and store its perishables. The unsightly look of carcasses swinging outside the entrance disappeared and was replaced by a large store-window display of attractively arranged chops, steaks, roasts, and dressed poultry. Adjoining the meat department was a large walk-in refrigerator. The store basement housed in pens turkeys, ducks, and chickens that farmers delivered early in the morning for the butchers to kill and dress for that day's orders. The large second floor of the grocery contained a bakery that produced a prodigious array of breads, cakes, pastries, cookies, and pies. A custom-made coffee roaster sent the aroma of beans wafting through nearby streets, itself an effective form of advertisement.

By 1912, Whyte Grocery supplied not only individual customers, offering them home delivery as well as personal attention within the store, but it also supplied area hotels and restaurants, including some in Excelsior Springs. At this point, the brothers were wealthy enough to make their next move: the Whyco chain store. They opened the first in 1915 at 2630 Prospect; the second followed shortly afterward at Thirty-Third and Troost, and a third opened at Thirty-First and Brooklyn. By 1925, fifty Whyco stores dotted the city, including two in Kansas City, Kansas. These were small operations that dealt primarily in canned goods and other shelf-stable products. Whyco advertisements in the *Kansas City*

Times called out to "Mrs. Housewife," asking her to "observe the remarkably low price of Del Monte or Sunkist Fruits," along with other items that routinely fill store shelves today, everything from cling peaches to Marshmallow Crème and Sun-Maid California Raisins. Shop boys pulled Whyco wagons loaded with orders up to customers' houses.

In 1927, Whyco was a prosperous company that competed effectively against other area grocers. A large national grocery chain wished to purchase the company, but the Whyte family turned down the offer, likely a decision it regretted. The 1929 stock market crash ruined the company, and by 1932, the chain was bankrupt. The last Whyco closed for good that year.[11] Such tragedy was not the case, however, for Whyte's main competitor, Wolferman's. This was in part because at the time, Wolferman's was strictly an upscale grocery with fewer stores and a customer base that largely withstood the worst effects of the Depression.

Wolferman's Grocery

While both the Whyte Grocery and its Whyco stores offered customized home delivery, Wolferman's is considered by historians to have been the first to introduce this service in Kansas City, in large part because of a father and son's desperation to stand out in a very crowded, competitive business arena. Wolferman's was founded in 1888 by Louis Wolferman, who owned a struggling vinegar plant. He made a gamble, mortgaging his family's home at 1521 Charlotte in order to purchase a bankrupt grocery store. His seventeen-year-old son, Frank, initially showed no interest in the grocery or vinegar business, but he decided to give up on his own dream of law or medicine to help his father. By age twenty-one, Frank was so successful that his father gave over the management of the store to him. Frank maintained an exceptional work ethic and ability to exceed his customers' expectations. When Louis opened the first Wolferman's store at Ninth and Oak in 1888, Frank rose early every morning to visit the City Market before the competition arrived. He bought only the best produce, meat, and fish and took the wares back to the store before setting out with his horse-drawn wagon to call on all his customers for their orders. By midmorning, Frank was back at the store filling orders. That afternoon he returned to everyone's house to drop off the groceries. His persistence, charm, and excellent understanding of good flavors and tastes paid off quickly.

Wolferman's Walnut Street Grocery, home of its fashionable Tiffin Room.
Missouri Valley Special Collections, Kansas City Public Library, Kansas City, Missouri

By 1895, Frank and Louis were able to purchase a larger building at 1108 Walnut, likely some years before the Whyte Grocery made a similar move to Walnut. Frank added a delicatessen, bakery, candy shop, and liquor department, and he personally taste-tested all items to ensure their quality. He loved good food enough to develop and patent the store's recipes. Not satisfied with the need to rely so much on vendors in general, Frank and his father decided in 1908 to purchase a farm at Ninety-Seventh and Holmes Road. This allowed them to source their own milk, butter, eggs, turkeys, and chickens. While Louis remained in charge of the farm, Frank focused on expanding the grocery business.

While a large store fire in 1909 might have seemed like a tragic occurrence for Wolferman's Grocery, it actually gave Frank the excuse to entirely remodel the store's layout and design. He added an elegant staircase, an indoor balcony, and the famous Wolferman Tiffin Room, the most elegant tearoom in the heart of Kansas City's shopping district. The Tiffin Room specialized in an array of cakes, pastries, and pies as well as luncheon entrées. Its salads were filled with expensive, often imported cheeses and meats and topped with house-made dressings, but its real call to distinction was the salads' accompanying English muffins, what the company is still known for today. Created in 1910 when the Tiffin Room opened, the muffin would seem basic enough. Bakers created a predictable blend of flour, yeast, water, and salt, but they bested the competition by making the muffins enormous, pouring the batter into tuna cans that had their tops and bottom removed. Equally important, they would put the filled molds directly over a grill in an oven to give it a distinctive, slightly smoky flavor.

Along with "Good Things to Eat" (the company slogan) and excellent customer service, Frank Wolferman had an uncanny understanding of real estate. He anticipated the direction of suburban development and prospered because he bought affordable land seemingly "in the middle of nowhere," built a Wolferman's store, and then watched as trolley and streetcar tracks were laid and housing developments sprang up. Such was the case with his Fifty-Ninth and Brookside Boulevard location as well as his store and tearoom on the new Country Club Plaza. Meanwhile, Wolferman continued to open more stores in Kansas City's Midtown, always near a trolley or streetcar stop to make it convenient for people out doing their own shopping.

By the time Frank Wolferman passed away in 1955, the company owned eight grocery stores and employed five hundred workers. Frank Wolferman Jr. took over the business from his father, but by the 1960s, the stores began to decline as larger chain stores began stocking gourmet foods, and as cheaper mass-produced food in general also competed effectively with the gourmet market. In 1984, the last Wolferman's Grocery closed, but the company continued a robust mail order business that specialized in Wolferman's English Muffins, other bakery items, canned goods, wines, and spirits. Currently, Wolferman's English Muffins are owned and distributed by Harry and David via mail order nationwide, and Wolferman's English Muffins are still stocked in many Kansas City grocery stores.[12]

McGonigle's Market

While Wolferman's became famous for its gourmet, house-made products, McGonigle's Market competed best in its meat department and continues to do so. McGonigle's family history dates back to 1881–1882 when Mike McGonigle's great-grandfather, Gerald McGonigle, married Florence Burnett, whose father owned Burnett's Meat Company in the West Bottoms. Burnett and his family lived over the shop. He purchased his meat directly from the stockyards, fabricated and aged it, and sold primarily to area restaurants and hotels. Gerald and Florence had three children, Gerald Jr., William (Bill), and Marjorie, and Bill would become integral to continuing the family business.

The 1903 Flood destroyed much of the West Bottoms, including the Union Depot and Burnett's Meat Market and warehouse, but the family recovered and at that point moved to Fifth and Main and entered the retail trade. Bill McGonigle showed aptitude and was interested in joining Grandfather Burnett's business, but World War II started, and Bill joined the military instead. After the war ended, Bill still had an interest in carrying on the business. He learned the craft from his grandfather, and when he took over, he moved the store to its current location at Seventy-Ninth Street and Ward Parkway in 1951, changing the name to McGonigle's Market. From there, Bill developed an expertise in steak. When Bill retired in 1986, his son, Mike, inherited the business.

The 1980s and 1990s exacerbated fierce competition in what had always been "an oversaturated and very aggressive grocery market," as

David Ball, executive director of Ball's Food Stores characterized the industry. For family-owned groceries to profit, they had to target often fairly narrow demographics. Mike McGonigle learned from his father the business of sourcing and fabricating meat, but he also understood what other grocers were doing and followed the best practices. Frank Wolferman Jr., for example, started Wolferman's successful mail-order business, and Mike McGonigle decided to start McGonigle's Nation-wide Steak Shipping Company. This lucrative sidearm of McGonigle's Market packs and ships grass-fed, grain-finished beef to customers and small markets. At his own store, Mike became increasingly involved in barbecue. McGonigle's stocks over one hundred different barbecue sauces, including most locally produced names, and McGonigle's Market also supplies meat to barbecue teams that compete in the American Royal, the Great Lenexa BBQ Battle, and other competitions. McGonigle's Market itself also enters barbecue competitions, and while the store remains a busy butcher shop, it also offers some of the finest take-out barbecue in Kansas City.[13]

Ball's Food Stores and Hen House Market

Kansas City's substantial role in nationwide food production and distribution led in 1924 to the Associated Grocers of Kansas City and from there, the Associated Wholesale Grocers (AWG), the second-largest retailer-owned grocery wholesaler in the United States. Many of Kansas City's grocery families were and remain a part of the AWG, and the strength of its distribution network explains in some part why Kansas City can continue to support many locally owned grocery stores. Fundamental to this story are Sidney and Mollie Ball of Kansas City, Kansas, and Harold and Mary Hinson of Kansas City, Missouri.

In 1923, Sidney and Mollie Ball opened a small grocery in Kansas City, Kansas, at Sixteenth Street and Stewart. In their early days, the Balls relied on the City Market and increasingly their own garden to stock the store's produce. From this small corner business, the Balls created the Ball's Food Stores Company and began to expand their number of groceries. Fred Ball took over the company from his parents and began strategizing how to respond to two developments occurring in the 1980s: grocery warehouse stores that could keep prices low by capitalizing on volume sales, and large national supermarket chains such as Safeway that were beginning to compete more aggressively in the Kansas City Metro. Around this time, Harold W. "Buck" Hinson and his wife, Mary Hinson, were ready to retire. Since 1936, Buck had operated two successful Hen House Markets. "I started out with a coop of chickens and a crate of eggs," Hinson recalled when he made his first foray into the grocery business in 1936. Hinson's decision to specialize in fresh poultry probably had to do with cheaper start-up costs and the fact that poultry was a more affordable protein for consumers during the Great Depression. When World War II broke out, it was more available than beef.

The quality of Hinson's poultry led to profits, and Hen House moved from Seventy-Ninth Terrace and Wornall Road into a larger building at Eighty-Second and Wornall. Hinson opened a second Hen House Market at 9550 Blue Ridge Boulevard in 1961. What made Hen House stand out was its attention to fresh poultry, eggs, and seafood. Thanksgiving was a booming time of year for Hen House, given that as late as the 1980s, it was the one grocery store where customers could count on fresh rather than frozen turkeys. People reserved their birds in advance, specifying the weight and size, and in the two days before Thanksgiving, they drove in from all over the Metro to pick up their orders and complete the rest of their Thanksgiving shopping. By focusing on fresh poultry rather than frozen, Hinson built his reputation as Kansas City's poultry man.

By the time he turned eighty, however, Hinson and his wife were ready to retire. They had been in the business for fifty-four years when in 1989 they sold the two Hen House Markets to Ball's Food Stores. It was the case of one highly successful family grocer giving over its legacy and future to another successful family grocer. Fred Ball was interested in Hen House's established reputation in poultry. He understood that to remain viable, it was best for his company to create two distinct concepts: markets such as Hen House that focused on smaller store spaces, fresh produce, and custom meats that catered to a more affluent demographic; and warehouse stores that maintained low prices by buying in volume, keeping down overhead costs, and relying on customers to do their own sacking. When Ball's Food Stores acquired Hen House, the company had already made successful inroads into the warehouse grocery store concept with its Price Chopper chain. Fred Ball oversaw six Price Choppers and three Ball's Super Food Stores. His intention was to continue growing that concept while keeping Hen House Market as the specialty store it already was, but also adding a cheese department, bakery, and full-service deli.

Fred Ball moved quickly. The third Hen House Market and the first in Johnson County, Kansas, opened in 1990 at Eighty-Seventh and Lackman in Lenexa. It fulfilled Fred Ball's expectations and became the model for future Hen House Markets: focus on fresh meat with a specialty in poultry. When Ball's Super Foods celebrated its seventy-fifth anniversary in 1998, it owned eleven Hen House Markets and twelve Price Choppers in the Kansas City Metro, and it continued to remain innovative, this time going head-to-head with national chains that dealt primarily in organic food.

Given the Ball family's long history of relying on their own garden to stock the freshest produce, it made sense for Ball's Super Foods to start its "Buy Fresh Buy Local" program as a way to support some 150 family farms that sourced much of Hen House's produce, meat, dairy, eggs, honey, and various sundries such as preserves and pickles. Added to this consortium of family farmers are many area manufacturers whose products fill both Price Chopper's and Hen House's store shelves. In this way, Ball's Food Stores, now under the leadership of Fred's son, David, maintains traditions that trace back to his own grandparents but that also echo the strategies that had been used by Wolferman's and Whyte's Groceries. Ball's Food Stores has now entered its ninety-second year, thus making it Kansas City's oldest operating independent grocery company.[14]

Price Chopper

Price Chopper in Missouri, Kansas, and Iowa was a brand created in 1979 to unify the buying power and strength of five separate grocery families from the Kansas City Metro (Price Chopper in this region is unaffiliated with Price Chopper in the eastern United States or in Canada). Along with the Ball family, the Cosentino family also operates several local Price Chopper grocery stores and has well-established local roots in the business, including the AWG. Cosentino's Food Stores Company began modestly in 1948 when two brothers, Jim and Jerry Cosentino, opened their first store on Blue Ridge Boulevard. Jerry remembered it as roughly "forty feet wide and sixty feet deep," and the brothers' main motivation to succeed was fear of their parents ending up on the streets after they had mortgaged their house to help the boys' business. When local bankers ignored the brothers' request for a loan, and after they were turned down for a federally backed small business loan, a family friend lent them $5,000, merely asking them to pay it back when they could. When a local supplier made a similar gesture, the boys, now joined by their younger brother and their sisters, were able to gain a foothold in the grocery business and begin to prosper. Also important to the Price Chopper brand are relative newcomers. The Queen family started in 1974 and operates five area stores in Wyandotte and Johnson County, and the McKeever family, which founded McKeever Enterprises in 1976, currently operates nine stores, in Independence and the Northland as well as Johnson County.

CONFECTIONERY

Kansas City has many ties to the confectionery industry, including the Whyte brothers and Wolferman's, as well as earlier manufacturers. Adam Long started a confectionery and grocery business in 1854, and the "Jobbers of Teas, Fruits, Fancy Groceries and Confectioneries"—J. P. Campbell, W. C. Jameson, and C. A. Brown—established a business in 1869. In the 1940s, Kansas City's fourth largest industry was confectionery, including the Price Candy Company (which started operations in 1913 in the basement of the downtown Jones Department Store), the Hill Candy Company, Dye Candy Company, Missouri Candy Company, and Crane Chocolate Company. The best known are Russell Stover Candies, and to Kansas Citians at least, Russell Sifers Candy Company.

Russell Stover Candies

Clara and Russell Stover were not Kansas City natives. They initially operated their company, Mrs. Stover's Bungalow Candies, in Denver, and in the mid-1920s they built their second factory in Kansas City. To try to save their stores and factories when the Great Depression began to jeopardize their business, the Stovers moved their corporation to Kansas City, and along with selling candy, their remaining company stores also sold ice cream and cakes. The move to Kansas City proved to be successful.

Russell Stover was born near Alton, Kansas, in 1888 but grew up on his grandfather's farm in Iowa. He met his business partner and wife, Clara Lewis, while the two were studying at the Iowa City Academy; however, they did not marry until some time later, when they again met up. Russell studied chemistry at the University of Iowa, and after he and Clara married in 1911, they moved to Saskatchewan and attempted to farm before floods ruined their enterprise. Russell found work in Winnipeg working for a candy company, and he and Clara together made candy at home, selling their wares to local pharmacies. They continued this homegrown enterprise after returning to the United States.

Russell's first breakthrough came when he created an ice cream that did not melt if it was dipped in a hot chocolate coating. He patented his Eskimo Pie in 1921, and it created an immediate national sensation. In the chaos that ensued, the Stovers were eventually forced to sell the manufacturing rights for what was considered a pittance—$30,000. Nonetheless, the couple used that as seed money to start Mrs. Stover's Bungalow Candies, incorporated in 1925. Clara was president and secretary and Russell vice president and treasurer. Until the Great Depression, the couple did a robust business, and after regrouping and coming to Kansas City, they endured the Depression and saw their company's sales and profits begin to soar in the 1940s. In 1943, the company name was changed to Russell Stover Candies, and Russell became president. Its headquarters again moved to Denver, although the Stovers bought a home in Mission Hills, Kansas, and divided their time between there and a second home in Miami. At the time of Russell's death in 1954, the company owned forty stores while stocking its candy at two thousand pharmacies and department stores as well. Clara remained in Kansas City until her death in 1975. While the Russell Stover corporate headquarters is now located at 4900 Oak Street in Kansas City, the company is part of Lindt & Sprüngli.[15]

Russell Sifers Candy Company

Sifers Confection Company (now Russell Sifers Candy Company) has had a long presence in the Midwest and in Kansas City as well. It was started in Iola, Kansas, in 1903 by Samuel Sifers; was taken over by his son, Harry; and is now in its fifth generation, run by Russell Sifers and his son Dave. Around 1916, the company moved to Kansas City, operating out of a factory at Twentieth and Main. The most enduring and last remaining candy produced by Sifers is Valomilk, a marshmallow cream confection contained in a milk chocolate cup. It is currently produced by a small team of dedicated candy makers who work out of a factory in Johnson County.[16]

Valomilk was a relatively late creation in the Sifers Confection lineup, created in 1931 by accident when an employee added too much vanilla extract to a batch of marshmallows, creating an oozing semiliquid mixture that did not solidify. Harry Sifers, who Russell thought to be the most imaginative candy maker in the family, decided to contain the runny marshmallow in chocolate cups, and Valomilk was born. The current company tempers chocolate by hand, because as Steve Almond put it in *Candyfreak: A Journey through the Chocolate Underbelly of America*, Russell Sifers is "attractively fanatical" when it comes to making candy. Sifers uses pure cane sugar, Madagascar vanilla, and pan-dried egg whites that are rehydrated with distilled water and whipped into a snow-white meringue. The Hobart mixer used in this process dates back, as does much of Sifers's equipment, to the old factory on Main Street.

In 1971, a larger national candy company, Hoffman, purchased Sifers Confection Company, and by 1981, Hoffman had shut down the Sifers Kansas City plant, making Valomilk obsolete. Working on the assembly line at GM, Russell Sifers determined that it would be better to quit that job, clean out the old candy factory on Main and refurbish the equipment, secure the rights to the Sifers Valomilk name, and start the company afresh. He accomplished all four tasks. The small size of the operation, the use of premium ingredients, a small budget for transporting the candy, and the fragile nature of Valomilk itself all keep Sifers from wide-scale distribution. Even altitudes can interfere with the candy's quality and hence, distribution. Sifers explained to Steve Almond: "Well, they don't explode exactly, . . . I just use that word to make it sound dramatic. But the filling does expand and they leak. The ones that don't have a leak already become little leakers and the little leakers become super leakers. You can't take them over the Rockies, or on a plane." Because candy was Russell Sifers's calling, as it were, these logistics and barriers to a larger customer base do not disturb him. As it is, the candy remains popular and integral to Kansas City's confectionery heritage.[17]

THE REVITALIZATION OF THE CITY MARKET
AND OTHER AREA FARMERS' MARKETS

The revitalization of the City Market is due to numerous factors, chief among them nationwide trends that support the return of locally grown produce and the farmers who grow it, as well as the efforts spearheaded by Mel Mallin, a local businessman who saw the potential of reinvigorating the River Market neighborhood, doing what had been done in New York City's SoHo district. When the City Market was placed on the National Register of Historic Places in 1978, it brought wider attention to the importance of the area's architectural and cultural heritage. In conjunction with tax incentives and grants for developers, the City Market infrastructure was improved, as were the streets around it. Abandoned warehouses and old cold-storage units were made into loft apartments and condominiums, independent restaurants began to move in, and the demand for fresh produce and other locally made products grew quickly. While numerous Italian immigrants found their economic livelihood by working out of the City Market in the early twentieth century, many Asian immigrants who moved to the area in the 1970s and 1980s likewise found their own foothold in the produce and fish business. At present, the City Market operates 180 outdoor stalls as well as glass walkways in the east building to protect vendors and shoppers from inclement weather.[18]

Rather than merely fulfilling a weekend entertainment need for occasional market-goers, the City Market is a vital enterprise that connects thousands of people to high-quality produce and meat. It is joined by numerous area farmers' markets, many of which have enjoyed increased patronage over the past decades. Many of the smaller markets fill special niches. Brookside Farmers' Market, a decade old, specializes in organic produce and cruelty-free meat. Its vendors are also coming from no more than one hundred miles away. Niles Garden Market at Thirteenth and Highland is an educational garden site as well as a market. It uses organic no-till practices and serves as a model and outdoor classroom for beginning gardeners who are learning about sustainable urban farming. Along with the Troostwood Youth Garden Market at 5142 Paseo, Niles Garden Market sells produce and uses proceeds to support community youth working in the garden. The Overland Park Farmers Market in downtown Overland Park is Johnson County's largest outdoor, seasonal market and has been in operation for more than thirty years. It serves as an important community gathering place, sponsoring concerts and cooking demonstrations, as well as a full array of educational activities designed for children and adults alike. Its popularity keeps downtown Overland Park economically viable, attracting and supporting a plethora of small food stores, restaurants, a culinary school, and bakeries that likewise promote local farmers and producers.

Chapter Seven

"Kansas City, Here I Come"

*Historic Restaurants at
America's Crossroads, 1860s–1970s*

Kansas City has always been a restaurant town. Even more than needing a place to sleep, thousands of people hurrying through needed a meal, and thus many residents made their living by feeding others. Several of the city's historic restaurants were built primarily to satisfy the needs of travelers first and residents second. They were located inside hotels, in train stations or near them, on the old "blue highways" edging the Metro, even in the airport. Accessibility was critical, and so was the restaurateur's skill at catching the eye of a hungry traveler. As Kansas City's adopted son, Fred Harvey, sagely put it: "Travel follows good food routes." Kansas Citians benefited from that truth as much as travelers; good food of nearly every description, at every price, was for sale. It might be said that restaurants have been a part of Kansas City culture for so long that *eating in* was something special; *eating out* was the norm.

HOTELS, THEATERS, AND EXCURSION PACKAGES

While earlier chapters in this book covered how Emily Fisher's Hotel in Independence and the Harris House in Westport fed pioneers and traders, the most important restaurant in early Kansas City was the Broadway Hotel, or what soon took the name of its owner, the Coates House Hotel, or Coates House. From its opening in 1868 up through the 1880s, the Coates House was known for exceptional cuisine and its ability to meet patrons' high expectations for dining, not merely for eating. Kersey Coates came west initially to join abolitionists settling in Kansas Territory, but he and his wife, Sarah, saw potential in Kansas City, Missouri, and decided to

123

settle there instead. The Civil War stopped most construction and commercial development, and the newly dug foundation of the Coates House was covered up and used for Union Army equipment and horse stables. After the war, its construction quickly resumed.

The Coates House checked in its first visitors a year or so before the Hannibal Bridge opened, and from 1869 on, tens of thousands of travelers passed through Kansas City via rail. Coates knew that if given a reason, travelers might linger awhile, so he built the Coates Opera House diagonally across the street from his hotel at Tenth and Broadway. After arriving at the Union Depot in the West Bottoms, passengers took the Ninth Street Incline (a cable car) up to the city center—within a block of the Coates House. Excursion packages enticed people in neighboring states to pay one price for rail and opera tickets, a stay at the Coates House, and meals in its elegant dining room.[1] The Coates House was popular enough in the 1880s to warrant expansion and remodeling, and its dining room was enhanced.

Men and women attending a Knights of Columbus banquet at the Coates House Hotel, 1906.
Missouri Valley Special Collections, Kansas City Public Library, Kansas City, Missouri

The food was highly praised. Laura Reed Yaggy, the Coates's grand-daughter, recounted that the kitchen staff killed and butchered animals and prepared food to order. "They got things live then. If they wanted to make turtle soup, they would get a big live turtle." The Coates's children rode around on its back before it was destined for the pot.[2] Costly and difficult to prepare, turtle soup was a staple dish among the Victorian elite, and the Coates's meals met such standards of taste. An October 1897 Sons of the American Revolution banquet is indicative. The meal complied with the order of courses that defined late-Victorian-era fashions, beginning with Blue Point oysters as the hors d'oeuvre, followed by the soup, a clear consommé. Oregon salmon with cucumbers and a palate cleanser or punch course came next. The *pièce de résistance*, calf sweetbreads, was accompanied by potato croquettes and peas. Roast quail with Saratoga chips (homemade potato chips) followed. The sweets course was Nes-selrode pudding, a confection of custard mixed with chestnut puree and Maraschino liquor frozen in an elaborate mold. Fruit, cheeses and crack-ers, coffee, and liquors rounded out the repast. A similar banquet for Uni-versity of Michigan alumni earlier that decade offered the common refrain after such Coates House affairs: The courses were "of a sort to transport an epicure into the seventh heaven of gustatory ecstasy."[3]

The Coates House's ability to deliver patrons elegant accommodation, fine food, and nearby entertainment set a precedent, and by the early twentieth century, it was competing with other successful hotel-theater-restaurant enterprises, most importantly, the Hotel Baltimore and Willis Wood Theater. Hotel Baltimore opened its first unit on the corner of Eleventh and Baltimore in 1899 and continued to expand until by 1908 it was an imposing twelve stories. The grand Willis Wood Theater, which opened in 1902, was connected to Hotel Baltimore by underground tunnel, colloquially known as Highball Alley. The ease of moving from dinner to theater with no need to bother with outerwear clearly delighted patrons.[4]

The hotel's Pompeian Room was strikingly beautiful. Its white inte-rior was accented in "Pompeian" red, green onyx, and gold leaf. When air-conditioning was installed in 1915, fine dining in summer could take place in comfort, a luxury that no other Kansas City hotel offered at that time.[5] Equally important to the Pompeian Room's reputation was Chef Adrian Delvaux, whose signature dishes included Lobster Baltimore, a lobster sautéed with mushrooms, brandy, tomatoes, and demi-glace before being finished off with a French Boudreaux reduction and garnish of brilliant green minced chives. *Hors d'oeuvre Baltimore* showcased the chef's whimsy. Buttered toast triangles were spread with caviar and crowned with a stuffed olive, itself encased by teeny pearl onions. The canapé was decorated with "yellow decorating butter" consisting of mashed hard-boiled egg yolks, butter, lemon juice, and seasonings. These recipes were popularized in the International Cooking Library's 1913 series featuring celebrity chefs.[6]

The Coates House specialized in Victorian cuisine, and although its food was lavish by today's standards, the Pompeian Room outdid it with Gilded Age decadence. The à la carte menu was a leather-bound, gilt-embossed affair containing some 379 selections, among them thirteen lobster specialties; forty-three steak selections took up a bulk of the menu, including the extra-large porterhouse steak with mushrooms for $3.75.[7] When a Kansas City meatpacker made a weekly wage of $10 and a schoolteacher a yearly salary of $450, the idea of spending $3.75 on just one course put this cuisine beyond the reach of ordinary people. Nonetheless, Hotel Baltimore, the Coates House Hotel, the Midland, and the Centropolis Hotel made Kansas City competitive when it came to indulging well-heeled travelers.

GRILLROOMS, CABARETS, AND SUPPER CLUBS

Businessmen often appreciated something more understated but with the same comforts and fine food as the grand hotels. One that particularly appealed to them was the Savoy at Ninth and Central, built by John and Charles Arbuckle in 1888. Its location ensured that when passengers disembarked at Union Depot, the Savoy would be the first fine lodging option they saw. In 1903, the Savoy was remodeled and added a west wing; it also opened what is Kansas City's oldest surviving restaurant, the Savoy Grill. Its name evoked the exclusive London Savoy Hotel Grill Room that opened in 1889, a bastion of privilege where London gentlemen could drink whiskey, smoke cigars, swear, tell lewd jokes, and conduct business without the fear of offending ladies or having to cater to their needs. Kansas City's Savoy Grill likewise excluded women, and its décor was "muscular." Art Nouveau stained glass allowed in outside light, but dimly. Edward Holslag's Westport Landing murals were a medley of tans, browns, and golds. The oak-carved bar was lined with square bottles of bourbon, rum, gin, and liquors. In high-backed green leather booths spotlit by electric lanterns, powerful men "wheeled and dealed" over steaks. Silent, expertly attentive waiters hovered just beyond earshot to refill cocktails and whisk away plates.

The Savoy Grill opened around the time that men and women began challenging Victorian-era rules of morality and conduct. London and Paris had their *fin de siècle*, with voyeurs and *flâneurs*, dandies and bohemians, all of whom pushed at and tore down walls that kept ladies and gentlemen from commingling. Kansas City had the Pendergasts, Joe Donegan, and ragtime, all of which pushed at and tore down those same walls. The Savoy Grill dropped its males-only policy shortly after it opened, likely because it felt the financial pressure of remaining an old-fashioned Victorian holdout to a good time. Three blocks away on Twelfth and Central stood what is now the Folly Theater but what was then called the Century; it was adjacent to the Hotel Edward. Managed by "the King of Twelfth Street," Joe Donegan, both the theater and hotel were hugely popular, not only for the Century's Empire burlesque circuit shows, but also for Donegan's Edward Cabaret in the hotel's basement grillroom.[8]

Donegan was a generous-hearted Irishman who loved a good time. He not only allowed women into the grillroom, he encouraged them, especially showgirls who needed supper and a long draw of beer after their performances. As former *Kansas City Star* editor William M. Reddig gamely observed, Donegan's operation was disturbing because "it provided a popular way to circumvent the old social taboo and law which imposed on women the awful indignity of not being allowed to get tight with their men in public, and it also gave encouragement to the dance craze which alarmed the puritans in the years before the First World War."[9] Donegan, in other words, was not only allowing women into the establishment but he was also supplying music and allowing people to dance. Other cabarets were opening in the vicinity, including Tom Pendergast's Jefferson Hotel Cabaret and Grill Room. This one, along with the Hotel Edward, were probably the main reason the Savoy Grill abandoned its exclusionary policies. When the Savoy joined the new rage, women in their shockingly short skirts and bare shoulders smoked cigarettes and even cigars alongside their beaus, daringly swigging bourbon and dancing to ragtime.

By the 1920s, downtown was awash with electric lights pointing the way to numerous supper clubs where people ate, drank (in spite of Prohibition), and danced. As a previous chapter on African Americans detailed, the Vine Street corridor, starting at Twelfth and moving tantalizingly up to Eighteenth, was the epicenter of "Paris of the Plains." To compete with the supper clubs, hotels offered patrons restaurants that combined eating with dancing. At one end of the corridor was the Streets Rose Room and Blue Room with the Bennie Moten Orchestra, and at the other end was the Muehlebach Hotel Plantation Grill with the Carleton Coon and Joseph Sanders' Novelty Orchestra.

The Muehlebach opened to great fanfare in May 1915 at the corner of Twelfth and Baltimore, replacing the Hotel Baltimore as the city's most exclusive accommodation. President Harry S. Truman used the Muehlebach as his summer headquarters, and well into the 1970s visiting celebrities and dignitaries relied on it as well. Adding early on to the Muehlebach's reputation was its decision to broadcast live from the Plantation Grill over the WDAF radio station. In December 1922, Coon-Sanders had formally concluded its midnight radio program, but announcer Leo Fitzpatrick casually remarked into a live mic that "anyone who'd stay up *this* late to hear us would have to be a real nighthawk." The next week, five thousand listeners from as far away as Mexico wrote in to confirm that yes, they were nighthawks. From that point, the band became the Coon-Sanders Original Nighthawk Orchestra, and its theme song, "Nighthawk Blues," became famous.[10] People from across the nation made a point of visiting the Plantation Grill Room if they were passing through Kansas City.

At the onset of the Great Depression, Barney L. Allis took over Muehlebach management and eventually purchased the hotel. The son of Polish Jewish immigrants, Allis has gone down in Kansas City history as the most talented and demanding of all hoteliers; his legacy lives on in a downtown plaza area near the Muehlebach that is named after him. He knew his staff by name, he knew his guests by name, and he managed to turn profits even as the Depression dragged on. Early in his tenure, Allis oversaw the Plantation Grill's remodeling, and it opened as the Terrace Grill in 1936. Replacing the cool whites and wickerwork with mirrored pillars, red wallpaper, and elaborate sconces, Allis gave the space a swank new feel. He kept the Plantation Grill's spirit, however, attracting new generations of dance bands and crooners, among them Guy Lombardo,

Buddy Rogers, and Ted Lewis. The WHB radio station broadcast live from the Terrace Grill three times a day in 1938.[11]

In some cases, hotel grillrooms and supper clubs offered homegrown talent a chance at stardom. Jazz greats such as Charlie "Yardbird" Parker and Julia Lee were just two famous jazz musicians to start in Kansas City, and in regard to the American Songbook tradition, some other names are also worth mentioning. Joe Donegan helped launch Edythe Baker's musical career. She left Kansas City for Broadway's Ziegfeld Follies, and from there, London, where she taught the Prince of Wales how to dance the Black Bottom.[12] Marilyn Maye received her break as a singer at the Ralph Gaines Colony Steak House, in the Ambassador Hotel at 3560 Broadway. Maye was singing one night when she was discovered by television personality Steve Allen, guest host of *Arthur Godfrey's Talent Scouts*. While Maye went on to become a popular performer on Johnny Carson's *Tonight Show* (along with other venues), Gaines achieved fame as a restaurateur, and in a restaurant city, that can be difficult to do.

Marilyn Maye and the Sammy Tucker Trio, performing in the lounge at Ralph Gaines Colony Steak House.
Personal collection of Karen Gaines

Ralph Gaines moved to Kansas City from Chicago in 1951 when Jay Dillingham hired him as general manager of The Golden Ox, Dillingham's new upscale steakhouse in the West Bottoms. Recognizing the lucrativeness of Kansas City's downtown hotel scene, Gaines started his own rival steakhouse-supper club, the Colony, in 1953. His success, Maye recalled, was "all about serving food and making sure his patrons got the best service."[13] The Colony's bar lounge was on the ground floor where diners could eat their meals, or they could descend to the basement dining room where oftentimes Gaines was waiting to lead them to their tables—and wait on them and bus their tables if the restaurant was extremely busy. Gaines was also very much a "steak man," his daughter Karen noted. He oversaw the dry-aging and fabrication of his steaks, becoming particularly regarded for his signature coulotte steak, a beefy but tender cut from the sirloin.[14]

OTHER DOWNTOWN RESTAURANTS

Italian Gardens

Supper clubs, hotels, and grillrooms were by no means the only options when it came to downtown. Alongside them were restaurants that people today refer to as institutions. While these are no longer in operation, their importance to Kansas City's food heritage is significant; they testify to Kansas City's vibrant crossroads hospitality in the twentieth century, and they point to directions that current restaurateurs consider as they work to revitalize the downtown. Among these institutions was the Italian Gardens. Its closure in December 2003 was not met with indifference, but rather with a keen sense that the city had lost a piece of itself.

The restaurant began in 1925 as Il Trovatore at 1300 Walnut. It was created by Johnny Bondon, his older sister, Teresa, and shortly afterward, Johnny's nephew, Frank Lipari. As chief cook, Teresa used her family's Southern Italian recipes to produce cheese ravioli, Veal Potenza, sugo, and other staples.[15] Italian Gardens' popularity was also due to the energy and hospitality of its main restaurateur, Carl J. DiCapo. He began his career at The Gardens (as the restaurant was colloquially known) when his brother-in-law, Ralph Bondon, called him to fill in one night. It was 1953, and DiCapo was working for the IRS. He never went back to his desk job.

For most of its life, Italian Gardens was at 1110 Baltimore, in the middle of "Hotel Row," with the Muehlebach across the street. "Investing in all that real estate on Baltimore Avenue was the best business decision my Uncles ever made," wrote DiCapo. "It was Baltimore—not Grand or Main—that was the real avenue of influence in Kansas City." While it catered to celebrities, many of whom called the restaurant for a delivery order as soon as they checked into the Muehlebach, Italian Gardens' fame also came from DiCapo's work to make it "Everyman's Club," which he differentiated from the private University Club a few blocks away. On Thursday nights and weekends, people crowded downtown to shop and catch a show, and hundreds made lunch or dinner at The Gardens part of the ritual. It was one of the first downtown restaurants to desegregate, and even during the height of Jim Crow, the restaurant would quietly disregard the "whites only" rule, tested one evening when a business manager called Frank Lipari from the airport to explain that he was bringing into town twelve managers "from all over the world . . . and one of them is black." Frank responded simply, "Well, bring 'em along." When the man asked for clarification, "You mean, I can feed him in there with us?" Frank again responded simply, "Is he hungry?" The food was excellent, but what

Looking south on Baltimore Avenue, with Italian Gardens' iconic sign prominent, 1999.
Missouri Valley Special Collections, Kansas City Public Library, Kansas City, Missouri

keeps alive memories of the Italian Gardens was illustrated in Lipari's straightforward response to an anxious businessman, and Lipari's cordiality to an African patron. Owners and waitstaff treated patrons as "guests" long before the term became established in the catering industry. Truckers, ex-cons, nightclub singers, theatrical troupes, families in from the suburbs, welterweight boxers, workers coming off their shifts, prom dates, and Gray Line tourists remember the Italian Gardens and the vibrancy of downtown when downtown was the nation's crossroads.

The Forum Cafeteria

The cafeterias offered even more of an everyman invitation than Italian Gardens. John Mariani suggested that the cafeteria ritual, where people politely lined up, took a tray, and then moved along picking from an array of selections, was "American eating in its most fundamental, democratic form."[16] Convenience, cleanliness, pleasing interiors, and fair prices made them attractive to many segments of society. The concept originated at the 1893 World's Columbian Exposition in Chicago, where John Kruger began a self-service eatery patterned after the Swedish smorgasbord, although he called his eatery a "cafeteria" after the Spanish word for coffee shop. Cafeterias were especially popular during Prohibition, when fine dining declined due to restaurants' dependency on liquor sales to stay viable. The selections of wholesome, unpretentious food that cafeterias served up often paired better with iced tea or coffee than with Bordeaux and martinis. The Great Depression and wartime economy perpetuated the cafeteria's popularity because these operations bought in bulk at significant discounts and utilized everything. Leftover roasts became savory hashes while leftover baked ham became a tasty ham salad; vegetable scraps and bones created soups.[17]

Many cafeteria options existed in Kansas City, including at various times and locations the Colonial Cafeteria, Char-Mont, Valerius, R. S. McClintock's, and Putsch's. Two cafeterias are firmly rooted in people's recent memory: Myron Green's (which will be discussed in chapter 9) and Clarence Hayman's Forum Cafeteria. After working as a line chef in various hotels throughout the region, Hayman opened a restaurant at 619 East Twelfth Street in 1911. Shortly thereafter, he established the Forum Lunch at 707 East Twelfth, and success with this small enterprise convinced Hayman to expand the concept. The first Forum Cafeteria was a large, ground-floor operation that opened in 1921 at 1220 Grand Avenue. Shortly thereafter, Hayman opened others, including one at 2016 Main. Ultimately, Hayman oversaw a chain of regional Forum Cafeterias.[18]

Kansas City children growing up in the early to mid-twentieth century often experienced their first meals out at cafeterias, where parents and grandparents could afford to indulge them in a wonderland of colors, sounds, aromas, and flavors. "ABSOLUTELY every Saturday night when I was young [we went] with the grandparents" to the Forum, recalled Rick Greenberg. "Deep-fried fish, whole whiting, then a movie at the Midland down the street." Valorie Montavy remembered that the Forum was a once-a-week excursion she took with her mother. "I loved the smells, pushing the trays along and getting to pick out what I wanted to eat. I think I became a mashed potato fan at that place." Judith Cammack recalled the "Tiffany-like lighting fixtures at the downtown Forum. . . . I always had the meatloaf and mac & cheese, green beans and cherry pie. It was wonderful."[19]

"I MIGHT TAKE A TRAIN": FRED HARVEY, UNION STATION, AND THE RAILROAD

Train passengers converged with the locals to take full advantage of downtown eateries, entertainment, and shopping, particularly after the Union Depot closed and Union Station opened in 1914. For thousands coming through, the first meal options to greet them were Fred Harvey's Lunchroom and Restaurant. Historically, Kansas City has managed dueling impulses: meet the expectations of sophisticated travelers looking for superb cuisine, and look after more modest travelers seeking the security of home through meals. For obvious reasons, fulfilling such divergent expectations was a daunting task for restaurateurs, and few attempted it, instead choosing to focus on one clientele or the other. The Fred Harvey Company was the exception. Its Union Station Restaurant catered to gourmets who had exacting tastes and the requisite evening attire, while the Lunchroom (which was actually a twenty-four-hour operation) offered patrons a comforting bowl of chili, grilled cheese, hot apple pie, and a cup of coffee.

The founder of the company, Frederick Henry Harvey, was not a Kansas City native, but he eventually made Kansas City the company's corporate headquarters, and his son, Ford, made Kansas City his residence. Fred Harvey came to the United States from England in 1853 and worked at Smith and McNell's, a New York City restaurant. He washed dishes, bused tables, and rapidly worked his way up to line cook. Taking his skills with him, Harvey spent some formative years cooking in New Orleans. When he moved west, he took various jobs, including one as a freight rail agent in Leavenworth. Over time, Harvey developed a keen understanding of the travel industry, noting weaknesses in the food supply chain and how rail passengers were often forced to eat subpar meals at filthy depot restaurants. Harvey revolutionized the industry by providing travelers with clean dining rooms that served excellent food at fair prices, from steak dinners to chicken pot pie.

It made sense that the company moved operations to Kansas City. It was, as Harvey biographer Stephen Fried put it, "the dead center of the United States, the middle of the middle of America." Union Station "would lay claim to the nation's crossroads as well."[20] When it opened in 1914, Union Station was a visual testimony to the Fred Harvey ideals of beautiful spaces that catered to travelers' needs. The Lunch Room seated two hundred patrons at tables or in swiveling cane-backed chairs along its marble counter. Tiffany silver urns reflected the electric lights, making the place a beacon, particularly during late nights when tired diners sought the comfort of a well-cooked meal. For thirty-five cents, a midrange price, one could order a substantial breakfast of pancakes, steak and eggs, hash browns, apple pie, and coffee. Lunch and dinner entrées ranged from stuffed green peppers with Creole sauce and buttered yellow rice to grilled chopped beef with Bordelaise sauce and two freshly made sides.[21]

The Restaurant, next door to the Lunch Room, was elegant and posh. During the Great Depression, it was one of Kansas City's few fine-dining options, competing with the best hotel restaurants. The layout and design were overseen by architect Mary Coulter, who blended elements of the Arts and Crafts Movement with Spanish Colonial Revivalist architecture. The high-ceilinged Restaurant allowed 152 diners space to take their meals in leisure. Harvey recruited the best chefs, often from Germany, Italy, and France, who took pride in their work and shared recipes with colleagues along the Harvey line. In Kansas City, Frederick Sommers commanded the Restaurant kitchen, and over its life span, so too did Roy Miller and Joseph Amherd.[22]

Between 1936 and 1937, Coulter updated the interiors and the Restaurant was renamed the Westport Room. The space became more intimate due to a lowered ceiling and refurbishing to make it resemble the dining saloon aboard a Missouri River steamboat, complete with brass pillars, old-fashioned lighting fixtures, heavy red brocades, and a thick patterned carpet. Coulter also commissioned Hildreth Meière to paint a mural depicting life along Westport Landing during pioneer days, a theme that artist Edward Holslag had also used with great effect at the Savoy. To compete with the downtown hotels, Coulter also added a cocktail lounge to the Westport Room.[23]

At its peak during World War II, Fred Harvey eateries supplied meals to roughly sixty thousand people a day nationwide, with thousands of them pouring into Kansas City's Union Station. The end of the war brought about a relatively fast decline in train traffic, however, as commercial airlines and the interstate highway system replaced the rails. Inevitably, the Harvey concept likewise began to suffer. The Westport Room responded by modernizing the menu and capturing in its final decade the loyalty of many influential locals. Again, the restaurant was remodeled and to celebrate its new opening on October 16, 1958, it published a souvenir menu. Some entrées recalled Kansas City's own Creole-Southern heritage, including red snapper throats and a Louisiana shrimp platter. More elaborate entrées included Baked Gondola of Lobster Newburg.

The 1950s- and 1960s-era restaurants were about more than just the meal; they were also about the occasion. People who could afford to dress up and visit the Terrace Grill, Ned Eddy's Restaurant (a swank supper club at Thirteenth and Baltimore), Golden Ox, Colony Steak House, or Bretton's were not merely looking for sustenance. They wanted something—or someone—to make that night out memorable. The Westport Room's greatest asset in this regard was maître d'hôtel Joe Maciel Sr. Maciel's beginnings resembled those of many Kansas City restaurateurs. He arrived to Kansas City in 1923, a seventeen-year-old immigrant from Ocotlan, Mexico. Three days working in the train yards convinced Maciel that there were better opportunities to be had in catering, and he was hired on as a Hotel Baltimore busboy. He moved to the Union Station Harvey Restaurant in 1935, where he worked his way up to maître

Dinner at Harvey's Westport Room, circa 1950s. Note the Harvey Girls in attendance. Joe Maciel is standing at strict attention to the far left of the photograph.
Personal collection of Rick Moehring

d'hôtel. Joe Maciel III remembered his grandfather as the man who knew how to "grab a room." Table-side cooking gave Maciel a chance to "work the audience," particularly with his signature specialty, Chicken Maciel, a chunked chicken breast sautéed in butter and blended into a curry-accented cream-sherry sauce. When a patron ordered it, which was frequent, Maciel finished the dish table side and presented it with the accompaniment of a gong, thus arresting everyone's attention. Pat Price, a *Kansas City Star* reporter, noted that Maciel was also a trusted confidant and that travelers passing through made an effort to go to the Westport Room to consult with him about their problems.[24]

While the Westport Room was not exclusively an upscale steakhouse like The Golden Ox or Colony, it nonetheless championed steak. The Flood of 1951 was partly responsible for the rise of the Kansas City steakhouse as a distinctive entity. In three harrowing days of rain and broken levies, the stockyards flooded, and the city lost a substantial source of its economy; its heritage and identity were likewise in jeopardy. While beef always figured heavily in the meals of wealthy Kansas Citians, it was often taken for granted the way one took for granted oysters on the half-shell, or roast duck. The expensive steakhouse, and equally important, the promotion of the Kansas City strip (a boneless strip loin) suggested that restaurateurs and patrons alike during this time period were holding on to something that was more and more elusive: the Kansas City beef industry. Steakhouses clinched their reputations by celebrating the grading, dry-aging, fabrication, and expert grilling of Hereford beef, even if more often than not, that beef was now from Chicago or elsewhere, particularly by the 1970s. The Westport Room menu was indicative of this trend at its inception: "Famous Kansas City Steaks" read the heading. "U.S. Prime beef selected by Fred Harvey and aged under our careful supervision to assure tenderness and flavor," the explanation assured diners.

"I MIGHT TAKE A PLANE": JOE GILBERT AND THE DOWNTOWN MUNICIPAL AIRPORT

Before the Westport Room closed for good and train traffic dwindled to a standstill, Freddy Harvey, heir to the company, had strategized on how the operation might cater to airports and airlines. When Ford, Freddy's father, died from influenza in 1928, Freddy was already investing money in the short-lived Transcontinental Air Transport, or TAT, which combined flight and rail to carry passengers from New York City to Los Angeles in a record three days. Kansas City's newly built airport, what became known as the Downtown Municipal Airport, was important to the TAT flight-rail route. Freddy knew that air travel was the future, and although he was correct, his own death in a plane crash ended Kansas City control over the Harvey Company (it was transferred to a Harvey heir in Chicago), and work on flight catering halted.

However, by the late 1930s, another young Kansas Citian, Joe Gilbert, was also exploring the feasibility of airline catering. He had demonstrated his talents as a restaurateur by taking his father-in-law's failing Fowler's Lunch at the Westgate Hotel and making it profitable. With no financial backing, but with the Kansas City mayor's assurance that the airport's concessions contract was his if he could finance the venture, Gilbert searched for investors. In the final hours before the bid expired, Gilbert received a call from Truman (True) Milleman, former manager of the Fred Harvey Union Station Restaurants. Milleman put up money for the airport concession, and he agreed to a fifty-fifty partnership with Gilbert. Milleman & Gilbert's Airport Restaurant opened in 1940 and was a successful enterprise, so much so that when Joseph William (Bill) Gilbert joined his father in 1945, he decided that the restaurant business was also his calling.[25] Ultimately, Milleman & Gilbert became the first caterers for the airline industry nationwide, and the Milleman & Gilbert Restaurant successfully incorporated many Harvey Fundamentals: most importantly, travel follows good food routes. Reminiscing about his love of Milleman & Gilbert, C. R. McAlister confirmed that truth when he wrote in *Flying Magazine* that he always longed for a Joe Gilbert hamburger when coming through the Municipal Airport, along with "that marvelous 'guaranteed five inches high' lemon meringue pie!"[26]

After True Milleman left the enterprise, the Gilberts changed the name to Four Winds and made it into a sophisticated restaurant-lounge on par with the Westport Room, albeit with a large terrace and windows from which one could watch planes taking off and landing. Again, steaks were a prominent feature on the menu, and they were grilled in full view of the patrons. A large fireplace added warmth and coziness on cold winter nights, but good weather brought in many locals who enjoyed the drama of eating meals while planes took off and landed. Prior to jet travel, transcontinental airplanes refueled and were serviced in Kansas City, and the restaurant was popular for celebrity spotting, as many travelers waited at the airport en route to the coasts. Having taken on the airline catering market with his father, Bill Gilbert would soon turn to opening restaurants that depended more on automobile traffic.

BYWAYS AND HIGHWAYS

By the 1950s, the Metro had been radically altered due to road construction. Expressways, flyovers, bridges, and the interstate highway system forged the Kansas City people recognize today; the Kansas City of the 1930s and 1940s would largely be foreign territory. The most important visionary in how cars would shape Kansas City's commercial and residential development was J. C. Nichols, who created the Country Club Plaza and the exclusive residential and commercial developments that surrounded it. People living in what Nichols called his Country Club District depended primarily on automobiles for transportation, and many restaurants in the mid- to late-twentieth century likewise catered to motorists. Importantly, two events dovetailed with the arrival of the auto, both of which also influenced Kansas City's restaurants: Prohibition and women's suffrage.

Grillrooms, supper clubs, and cabarets benefited from women and men who challenged Victorian codes of conduct, but women's suffrage and Prohibition offered women even more opportunities, this time as caterers. Fine-dining restaurants were male controlled, chefs were usually men, and restaurant profits depended on alcohol sales—what women had been prohibited from consuming in public, let alone selling (barmaids were an exception). Prohibition, even in Kansas City, posed significant challenges to restaurateurs who scrambled to make up for lost revenue from liquor sales. Their vulnerability and in some cases bankruptcy gave women an opening.

What Jan Whitaker called the "tearoom craze" resulted from women gaining the political and social agency to run their own catering businesses. A dry nation made tea and other soft drinks popular, and tearooms had never been set up to sell alcohol in the first place. The concept was already successful in luxury hotels and large department stores, and Prohibition simply made patrons and entrepreneurs alike more eager to frequent tearooms. The automobile also facilitated the tearoom craze because women with limited capital could turn a family dining room or refurbished outbuilding into a tearoom or teahouse. As a result, America's highways, including those in and out of Kansas City, saw a proliferation of restaurants and tearooms with women at the helm.[27] Although Prohibition was short-lived, tearooms and other such roadside establishments remained popular for many decades.

"Tea" can be a confusing word. While some establishments, such as Virginia McDonald's Tearoom in Gallatin, Missouri, and Libby Kriz-Fiorito's Castle Tea Room in Lawrence, Kansas, did offer light refreshments accompanied by pots of tea, many tearooms used the word "tea" as shorthand for no hard liquor. Mrs. Thatcher and Mrs. Bailey's Tea House by the Side of the Road on East Forty-Fifth Street, for example, served a family-style meal "presented in its proper setting—snowy linen, bright silver, bits of Spode—all sedate and genial, gently Victorian, and really very nice."[28] The word "inn" often promised similar food and homelike interiors, and by the later twentieth century, large homes that operated as restaurants, such as the Dinner Horn or Dolce's Highland View Farm in Kansas City's Northland, also advertised a wholesome atmosphere, even if wine and beer were back on the menu.

Kansas City's Southern hospitality and its Southern-inspired cuisine influenced many such roadside eateries. Pan-fried chicken, biscuits or rolls, relishes, mashed or fried potatoes and gravy, green beans, and pies were ubiquitous. Some offered ethnic specialties as well, and others featured steak or barbecue. Among the many, some stand out in Kansas City lore.

THE WISHBONE RESTAURANT

At Main and Forty-Fifth Street near the Country Club Plaza, Phil Sollomi and his mother Lena started the Wishbone Restaurant in 1945. The house had at one time been owned by a lumber magnate and sat well off the road on a shady estate. In a particularly evocative memory that captured the magic of both the automobile and the roadside restaurant, Linda Bureman recalled that her father's homecoming from military assignment in Korea warranted a family drive to the Wishbone, regardless of blizzard conditions. "Nothing would stop us. Not even the weather," wrote Bureman. "The four of us climbed into our 1956 red Ford and off we went—out of the garage and into the winter whiteness, a dot of color on the deserted Holmes Road." When the family finally pulled up to the restaurant, dismay gripped them, as there were no cars, and it appeared that the restaurant was closed. Nonetheless, they "trudged across the parking lot, heads down against the wind." Joy filled the family when indeed, the restaurant was open, and the host led them "into a beautiful room decorated in green. A fire was burning merrily in the corner. Antique tables were set with crystal goblets, shiny silverware, and white china." Soon waitresses carried platters of fried chicken and bowls of mashed potatoes out from the kitchen, and the meal was delicious, made more so by a father's homecoming.[29]

The Wishbone Restaurant, front view and driveway, at 4455 Main Street, August 1952.
Missouri Valley Special Collections, Kansas City Public Library, Kansas City, Missouri

Phil Sollomi sold the Wishbone Restaurant the year after he opened it to Dora and Joe Adelman, two restaurateurs who over the course of their career and marriage operated several local eateries, including a number of popular family-style fried chicken restaurants appropriately called the Drumstick, as well as Rugel's, a North Kansas City fried chicken house. Dora Adelman knew, in other words, how to fry chicken, Joe knew how to source them, and the entire Adelman family worked to make their restaurants successful. The Wishbone, given its beautiful location and homey feel, was the proverbial "jewel in the crown." In a tribute written after Dora Adelman's death in 2007, her daughter, Jackie Friedman, spoke of her mother's resolve. She "was a fixture [at the Wishbone]. She'd be up front, seating people. Mother's Day, Easter and Thanksgiving. We all worked at the Wishbone."[30]

While many stories circulate as to who created the famous Wish-Bone Salad Dressing, the most authoritative sources credit Lena and Phil

Sollomi, the original owners. Lena used her family's Sicilian recipe, a blend of piquant herbs and spices mixed with vinegar and oil, and demand for it led Phil to set up a small operation where he produced the salad dressing by the barrel. Although the dressing passed out of family hands years ago (it was purchased by Lipton and is currently owned by Pinnacle Foods), Wish-Bone dressing is still made in Independence, Missouri.[31] The Wishbone Restaurant itself remained in operation until 1978.

SANDY'S OAK RIDGE MANOR TEA HOUSE

Sandy's Oak Ridge Manor Tea House was just as popular as the Wishbone, but north of the river, in Clay County. It sat on land granted to David Hale in 1827. The original property consisted of two log cabins built close together. In 1844, one of Clay County's most prominent slaveholding families, James and Mary Ann Compton, purchased and built a ten-room home around (and including) the two original cabins, naming it Oak Ridge. The Comptoms epitomized Southern hospitality, as detailed in various places in this book. When Emma Compton, the last surviving family member living at Oak Ridge, sold the estate in 1954, Louise and Darwin Sandstrom purchased it. They wished to perpetuate the Comptons' reputation for hospitality while also preserving relics from Clay County's past. To do so, they opened a teahouse.[32] Although Darwin died of a stroke in 1959, Louise successfully ran the establishment on her own. She had come to the United States from Germany during World War I, and she specialized in sauerbraten so delicious that motorists made Sandy's a destination so they could order her roast beef drenched in spicy brown gravy. Louise also specialized in pan-fried chicken and homemade chicken and noodles. On weekends, the teahouse filled to capacity.[33]

STROUD'S PLACE

Sandy's Oak Ridge Manor remained in operation until the early 1980s. Most Kansas Citians today know that location as Stroud's North because the estate was sold in 1983 to Jim Hogan and Mike Donegan. They wanted to open another branch of Stroud's, Kansas City's most famous fried chicken restaurant. At that point in time, Louise Sandstrom's family-style restaurant fit in with Stroud's own service model, and so the transition from Sandy's to Stroud's made sense to patrons. However, when Stroud's was originally started, it was far from being a genteel, family-friendly establishment; its origins and success were grounded in another tradition, that of Pendergast machine politics and what we might today call "living on the edge."

Stroud's originally opened in 1933, and its location at 1015 East Eighty-Fifth Street put it just over the Kansas City border (at the time). The establishments already clustered along Eighty-Fifth Street were considered off limits by polite society. Many ostensibly operated as chicken farms but were probably bootleg liquor operations. "That's where Kansas Citians would drive out to buy their hooch," noted Chuck Haddix. [34] Black and tan clubs also operated along this corridor, beyond the purview of Jim Crow and various killjoys. Significantly, Lindsay and Jo Shannon's BB's Lawnside Barbecue, discussed in chapter 5, paid homage to those clubs when it opened in what had once been the Silver Moon Tavern and Barbecue. [35] Helen and Guy Stroud also contributed to the street's reputation when they opened a business guaranteed to net them easy revenue in the midst of the Depression: first a fireworks stand, and a bit later, a barbecue shack that sold liquor on Sundays, as it was right over the city border.

Stroud's, in other words, depended on motorists, but in its early days, it was more about carousing than iced tea and mother's cooking. When World War II rationing made beef expensive, Helen Stroud resourcefully turned to frying chicken. She was an excellent marketer of her product, among the first Kansas City entrepreneurs to make a substantial profit selling fried chicken to motorists, and indeed, making it increasingly viable for more genteel teahouses and inns (including Sandy's and the Wishbone) to promote fried chicken as a special occasion food, rather than just as a "yardbird." Helen boasted that her pan-fried chicken was the freshest available, carried into the kitchen on ice and fried within hours of delivery. With a cadence and authority that she might have learned from the king of self-promotors, Henry Perry, Helen intoned that the only way to fry chicken was in an iron skillet, that the chicken was to be lightly dredged in flour, and that no spice was to be added other than salt and pepper. In this stripped-down fashion (no deep-fat fryer, no buttermilk, no steam-fry contraption, no secret blend of herbs and

The original Stroud's Restaurant in 2006, shortly before it was demolished to widen Eighty-Fifth Street.
Missouri Valley Special Collections, Kansas City Public Library, Kansas City, Missouri

spices) cooks could not hide behind an inferior product or technique. Helen initially hired two Southern women to help her, and the roadhouse grew in popularity. In the 1950s and 1960s, her most talented cook was David Bragg, but when he died of a heart attack in 1963, Helen managed to find the staff and the means to keep her fried chicken consistently excellent, and the sides, particularly the cottage fries, cream gravy, and cinnamon rolls, excellent as well.[36]

By the 1960s, many roadside establishments were beginning to fold as franchises and chains also appealed directly to motorists; however, Kansas City's romance with Stroud's had only begun in earnest, especially as Kansas City boundaries engulfed and then moved past the little ramshackle building. Furthermore, "Helen" had become a tamer "Mrs. Stroud," and by this point, a respectable widow. Nonetheless, patrons did identify Stroud's with its past raciness, and after Wilbert Harrison's 1959 bluesy hit, "Kansas City," reached the top of the charts, the roadhouse fit into a past that had historically made Kansas City a magnet to people who lived on the edge. Suddenly vestiges of that past, including roadhouses on the "wrong side of town" like Stroud's, were bathed in a nostalgic light. Many families made Stroud's a destination, one with just enough liveliness to make it exciting, a place that gave children some sense of their Kansas City heritage.

For a brief time, however, there was no "Stroud's." In 1972–1973, Helen Stroud retired and turned the establishment over to Bob Ford, who changed the name to Bob Ford's Cantina Bar and Restaurant, although he kept the sign over the front that read "Home of Pan Fried Chicken." Helen Bess drummed the piano during this phase of the restaurant's history, but reviews of its food were inconsistent, and problems that did not happen under Helen's management (chicken allowed to sit at the pass and cool off, for example) compromised quality. When Mike Donegan and Jim Hogan bought Bob Ford's restaurant in 1977, they contacted Helen, asked for permission to use her name, asked her for her recipes, and brought Stroud's back to life.[37]

When Donegan and Hogan bought Sandy's Oak Ridge Manor in 1983 and opened Stroud's North, they saved a venerable Northland establishment and perpetuated Louise Sandstrom's hospitality and family-style meals. When in 2005 the city demolished the old original roadhouse to widen Eighty-Fifth Street, Donegan, who had bought out Jim Hogan's interest in the business, moved Stroud's to Fairway, Kansas, close to the Country Club Plaza. He saved the old lettering, just as Jim Ford did, and while the floor no longer slants, and the roof does not leak, both that Stroud's and Stroud's North thrive.

COUNTRY CLUB PLAZA:
JUSTUS PUTSCH, GILBERT-ROBINSON

Before Helen Stroud retired from frying chicken, her landlord, Miller Nichols, came for dinner. At that time, the area around Eighty-Fifth and U.S. 71 was owned by the J. C. Nichols Company. After finishing his meal, Miller Nichols sent Helen a note, which she hung by the roadhouse's door: "We counted the people in the restaurant with whom we were personally acquainted and concluded that we saw more of our friends at your restaurant than we would have seen had we gone to Putsch's 210 Restaurant. Surely your friends seemed to be enjoying themselves and the spirit of fun was surely evident."[38] Nichols was alluding to Kansas City's fanciest restaurant, and although Putsch's 210 was the antithesis of a roadhouse, the success of both these establishments was due largely to the automobile.

Miller Nichols, son of real estate developer J. C. Nichols, inherited an empire that included the Country Club Plaza, the nation's first shopping center designed exclusively for automobile traffic when it opened in 1923. Nichols allocated an unprecedented 46 percent of space on the Plaza for streets and parking lots.[39] While its Seville-inspired Spanish architecture remains as compelling a reason to visit the Plaza now as it was then, the plaza's convenience to increasing numbers of motorists was a chief reason for its success. By the 1970s, the Plaza had become a badge of pride to the city because so many residents had cars to reach it and share in its beauty.

In its earliest days, however, the Plaza was intended to satisfy the needs of the residential developments that surrounded it, a story covered in the next chapter. Interspersed with a grocery store, a bank, a bowling alley, a movie theater, a gas station, dress shops, department stores, and drugstores were many eateries, including several owned by Justus W. Putsch. Putsch's Cafeteria, Putsch's Coffee Shop, Putsch's Sidewalk Café (the first in Kansas City), and the very fashionable Putsch's 210 catered to a diversity of needs and tastes. In this regard, Putsch was as skillful a restaurateur as Fred Harvey had been a generation before him. Putsch's Cafeteria exemplified American egalitarianism like other cafeterias. People waited their turn in line and loaded trays with whatever dishes took their fancy. Putsch's Coffee Shop was also casual, and its hours catered to those craving a delicious breakfast of French toast or a late-night snack of hamburgers and a sundae. The Sidewalk Café invited shoppers to sit outside and enjoy the Plaza ambiance itself while sipping iced tea and eating cake. And Putsch's 210, with its table-side cooking, strolling violinist, candlelit tables, and stunning murals in deep reds and golds that depicted New Orleans Mardi Gras, became the destination for patrons who reserved a table there for the most special events in their lives. Subsequently, they cherished memories of dining at Putsch's 210 almost as much as the engagement rings or other special mementos attached to the occasion.

Missing from the Plaza and Kansas City in the 1960s and early 1970s, however, were medium-priced restaurants that could be stylish and affordable—less canteen-like than cafeterias, less casual than a drive-in burger joint, but something not limited to special occasions. Cars and freeways were making it possible for Kansas Citians to move around the Metro with ease, and restaurateurs with limited start-up budgets took advantage of affordable real estate in new suburban shopping centers. Just as Joe Gilbert had capitalized on the airline industry, his son, Joseph William (Bill) Gilbert, along with business partner Paul Robinson, were ready to take advantage of this new market. Their first restaurant, the Inn at the Landing, was a "suburban Golden Ox," noted Bill Gilbert.[40] Opened in 1961, the Inn was located at Sixty-Third and Troost at the Landing Shopping Center. While classy, it was not a traditional Continental restaurant. A young married couple could hire a babysitter and slip out for a nice meal, but at a price that did not demand a significant financial sacrifice. Although Gilbert and Robinson opened the restaurant with next to no financing, working out deals with the J. C. Nichols Company and a restaurant outfitter to equip the kitchen, the Inn at the Landing was immediately successful and started a new trend in Kansas City dining.

The Gilbert-Robinson team, which included Joe Gilbert when the Plaza III Steakhouse opened on the Plaza in 1963, reinvigorated Kansas City restaurant life. While cars were essential to most of the company's restaurant business, Gilbert-Robinson also understood the shifting cultural climate. Grillrooms and cabarets had challenged Victorian moral standards, but Gilbert-Robinson restaurants such as Annie's Santa Fe (a Mexican/Tex-Mex concept) and Houlihan's Old Place catered to a generation coming of age at a time of unprecedented postwar affluence and access to the birth control pill.

Located on the Country Club Plaza, both Annie's Santa Fe and Houlihan's Old Place focused on stylish good fun, large bars where singles could meet (many blind dates in the 1970s took place at these two restaurants), affordable prices, and food selections that were at the time whimsical, intriguing, and delicious. Tortilla pizzas, chimichangas, deep-fried zucchini sticks with ranch dipping sauce, quiches, and baked camembert with Black Forest ham were entirely unexpected, welcome foods in 1970s Kansas City, appealing not only to young couples but also to families with some disposable income and the desire for a delicious meal that did not demand dressing up. The welcome of patrons dressed in casual attire and concepts that promoted fun and festivity were hallmarks of the Gilbert-Robinson brand, ones that shared important similarities in service, sourcing, and consistency with Fred Harvey. Gilbert-Robinson ultimately helped create the casual dinner houses that Americans—not just Kansas Citians—now take for granted.

Kansas City has entered a new phase in its culinary development, one that increasingly witnesses travelers coming to Kansas City with the intention of eating more than sightseeing or merely passing through. Restaurateurs and chefs have made national names for themselves in part because they take into full account Kansas City's past heritage for their own inspiration and innovations. Since 1974, the American Restaurant at Westin Crown Center has continued the tradition of the very finest restaurants located in hotel complexes, in this case, a restaurant that celebrates not only the best of New American cuisine, but that in its first decades championed local flavors, from Missouri-cured ham to grandmother's wild greens. Meanwhile, Jess & Jim's Steak House in Martin City, praised by Calvin Trillin alongside Bryant's Barbecue as one of the best restaurants in the United States, attracts tourists and locals who appreciate the quality of the finest aged beef and chefs who refuse to dress it up or hide it under elaborate sauces and seasonings. As train traffic and streetcar traffic begin to increase, restaurants around Union Station in the Freight House District, the Power & Light District, and the Crossroads benefit. Most importantly, downtown as a whole has come back to life, with urban neighborhoods and hotels generating wide demand for eating options. While the cafeteria has not yet seen a resurgence, plenty of chef-owned restaurants, casual bars and grills, late-night greasy spoons, jazz supper clubs, and food trucks are paying homage to the city's crossroads identity and its enduring reputation for welcoming locals and visitors alike.

Chapter Eight

Kansas City Home Cooks and Homegrown Festivals

On the day Union Station opened, Harvey Girls served meals to over five thousand eager customers. While many were travelers, a surprising number were locals. The luxury of being served delicious food in such pleasing interiors was enticing and the convenience unbeatable, especially with the twenty-four-hour Lunchroom that could accommodate anyone's schedule and hunger pains. By the 1920s, it became customary for Kansas Citians to eat the most sacred meal of the week—their Sunday dinner—at a Harvey restaurant, long before that trend was established elsewhere in the United States, Stephen Fried noted.[1]

When a city largely caters to people passing through, it can be easier and cheaper for its residents to likewise eat away from home, to the point that dining out is taken for granted. After the Civil War, many types of food, at any price, and at any time, were available, often just blocks away from a family's home. Such convenience was as alluring then as now. Thus, home-cooked meals often stood for something better, something more civilized and special, no matter one's income, race, profession, or age. Along with satisfying one's hunger, dinner at home reinforced an immigrant's heritage and sense of self-worth, even if his employment dehumanized and defaced him. It offered family members time and space to express themselves as individuals, giving them a respite from the mind-numbing conformity that public life often demanded. Equally important, it allowed families the opportunity to offer guests generosity that was often more special than an invitation to eat out. While the same observations apply to family meals anywhere in the United States, it was Kansas City's industry and its history as a provider and crossroads that gave at-home meals a certain distinction. This chapter will detail how and why.

"UNE BANQUETTE SOMPTUESE":
HOSPITALITY AT KAWSMOUTH

Father Donnelly's first congregation near Westport Landing was indicative of how many early French inhabitants treated both guests and meals. When Donnelly first arrived at Kawsmouth, he boarded with parishioners and made long trips to his mission churches to administer the sacraments. Even if the food was scarce or simple, the French parishioners characterized their meals as "une banquette somptuese." Certainly that was Mons. Henri's description of a hard-won meal that he and Donnelly shared. After a long trek to visit a mission church, Donnelly returned to Mons. Henri's cabin where he boarded. He was understandably hungry and asked Mons. Henri, "Avezvous quelque a menger?" [Have you anything to eat?]. "Rien de tout," [Not a thing], Mons. Henri replied.

Not one to complain, the discouraged priest retired to his room, but shortly thereafter, Mons. Henri, by trade a basket maker, devised a plan. He left the cabin with two baskets and returned with one filled with new potatoes; the other he had traded to obtain the potatoes. Donnelly thought they "looked fine and palatable" and eagerly asked Mons. Henri what he had to put with them, to which Mons. Henri replied that he had "salt and pepper and a handful of corn meal, and if [Donnelly would] take Le Pere de Smidel's gun and shoot a chicken," he would cook up "une banquette somptuese." Donnelly took the gun and went to the graveyard that doubled as Mons. Henri's chicken yard. He fired and killed two plump birds with one shot. Sadly, it turned out that Donnelly had actually killed the "whole two of them!!! One was the rooster." Not discouraged, Mons. Henri simply went to work. His son Joe gathered "some cabbage sprouts and edible wild plants," and with the chicken and vegetables slowly stewing in a cornmeal roux, this family of men (Mons. Henri was a widower) tucked into their banquet.[2]

Although meals could be difficult to prepare, Mons. Henri's attitude and approach to dining helped set standards and customs that continue to characterize Kansas City foodways. Donnelly later recalled how on a long journey to Cass County, Missouri, to administer a funeral, he was returning home when it became too dark to continue. He spent the night as the guest of a party of young men who graciously offered the priest a "general invitation to supper. Our tables were pretty much the same as the Trojans had in their hasty tramp from the flames and ruins of Troy," Donnelly wrote. "The delicacies were flapjack cakes, cold ham, squirrel, rabbit, prairie chicken, dried buffalo, hot coffee without cream or sugar and all safely stowed away in stomachs whose digestive capacities were considerably aided by temperate stimulants of genuine bourbon whiskey with which a little water from the Blue [River] had been mingled." Donnelly offered such detail of a meal more than thirty years after its occurrence because he had been filled with good food and was grateful.[3]

In spite of hardship and deprivation, a persistent *joie de vivre* characterized French society in Missouri Territory. At Kawsmouth "floors and dancing, wine, and gatherings, and telling tales together" were planned-out events lest society become too dull and people fixated on toil at the expense of pleasure.[4] Holidays offered the best reason for food and festivity. Young ladies gathered on the eve of the Epiphany to fry pancakes for their gentlemen callers.[5] Mothers and daughters prepared large batches of *croquignoles* to distribute to visitors on New Year's Day and for any large gathering. Made by mixing flour and egg yolks with brown sugar, butter, milk, nutmeg, and leavening, the dough rested overnight before being rolled into thin circles, slashed in strips starting at the center, then twisted and fried in deep fat. They were often served with cherry bounce and ratafia, which enhanced frivolity and good cheer.[6]

The difficulty of transportation meant that people had to be resourceful when it came to food and supplies. A chicken gumbo was evidence that a farmer had successfully warded off constant predators after his flock. Gooseberry wine resulted from a housewife's industry. Narrow yards were given over to grape arbors, vegetable gardens, and fruit trees. St. Louis merchants advertised French imported "cabbage seeds of all kinds. Collyflower, Brocolie of divers kinds, with a choice selection of herb seeds."[7] These precious packets made their way, along with Carolina rice, spices, sugar, spirits, and other delicacies up the Missouri River by keelboat in the summer and fall months. Their price and rarity meant that most people had to ration them.

Lettuce salads were popular, and women created an ersatz olive oil by clarifying bear's oil with slippery elm bark.[8] Fricassees of plovers, bear, turkey, bison, prairie chicken, whatever fresh game was available, were common. Fridays were fasting days, and hence catfish chowder was popular. On special occasions, the French used their precious rice stores to make *jambolail* (spelled *jambalaya* in Louisiana). They cut up an old hen, seasoned it liberally with salt and pepper, and browned it with onions. A roux of flour and fat was darkened, water added, and last, a cup of washed rice was added. The whole pot was transferred to a wood-burning oven to be slowly baked.[9] Equally precious were chocolate, coffee, and tea. In St. Louis, coffee sold for the (then) exorbitant price of 62 to 75 cents a pound. By the time it reached Chouteau's Landing, it cost twice or thrice that. As such, "coffee was so special it was reserved for the master of the house and only for his breakfast," wrote historian Jerena East Giffen.[10] Tea was never consumed at meals but reserved for special social occasions.[11] Chocolate was most likely reserved for holidays.

Before John Calvin McCoy arrived in 1833 to establish his border emporium, Americans of English, Scotch-Irish, and German descent had already begun to arrive from the South. Their food customs blended with those of the French, but like everyone else, they too relied heavily on Native flora and fauna. All frontier families had a hominy block, as critical to their homestead as a rain barrel and a fireplace. To create what was in essence a corn mill, the family looked for two trees positioned so that the supple limb of one hung over the trunk of the other. One tree became the block, cut so that the stump stood roughly four feet high. From there, its inside was hollowed out. A large, heavy wooden pestle was created with handholds on each side. This was attached to the limb of the neighboring tree with a strong rope. The person whose job it was to crack the corn soaked and drained it, poured it into the hollowed block, grasped the pestle, and pounded. The springing action of the limb pulled the pestle back up from each pounding, thus reducing human labor and helping to pound the corn into grits or samp.[12]

Honey was also essential to good cooking and preserving, given the rarity of cane sugar. First one located bees by attracting them to a fire that included in it a bit of honeycomb. As the wax melted, bees scented honey and arrived. From there, the settler followed the bees back to their hive. If triumphant, the settler "blazed" the tree, which meant that no one was allowed to claim its honey. When honey was unavailable, tree sap often sufficed. A treat for children was "hickory goody," made by taking green hickory logs and putting them in the fire so that the sweetish sap oozed out of the chopped ends.[13]

"Those who followed the pioneers," wrote Carrie Westlake Whitney, "found the life less arduous. They brought their habits and customs from 'home,' back in 'ole Virginny' or 'Kaintuck,' along with the family mahogany, silver, feather beds, horses and slaves." They also brought their love of outdoor entertaining, including barbecues and fish fries. Kansas City's communities coalesced around Chouteau's Landing, the Westport Landing, Westport itself, Liberty, and Independence; the wealthy had leisure for long-term visits as their chief means of entertainment.[14] Dr. James Howard and Mary Ann Compton, whose Clay County farm would become Sandy's Oak Ridge Manor and later Stroud's North, stored away sixteen feather ticks so that when visitors arrived for Christmas, they would be inclined to stay for days. Slaves hurried back and forth from the fireplace, where they roasted venison and pork and baked pies and biscuits to feed guests.[15]

After the 1844 flood destroyed the Chouteau warehouse and home, Madame Berenice, then a widow, built her new home on the bluffs along Pearl Street. Her two-story colonial house with its wide center halls, long verandas, and French windows was surrounded by a manicured yard. The layout lent itself to al fresco dining during much of the year, and a formal dining room sufficed during the winter.[16] As Westport settlers grew rich, many also moved to the Town of Kansas and joined Madame Chouteau on Pearl Street. William Miles Chick settled between Second and Pearl, and John Calvin McCoy and his family built close by, as did John Calvin's widowed mother, Mrs. Isaac McCoy.[17] Along with the Jarboes, Campbells, and Riddlesbargers, these families formed a close-knit community where Madame Chouteau became accepted as "the file-leader of the vanguard of the civilization that has since, like a great tidal-wave, swept across more than half of our great continent"; this is how she was eulogized by John Calvin McCoy when she passed away in 1888.[18]

BOARDINGHOUSE REACH

By the 1840s and 1850s, "at-home" meals for thousands of Kansas Citians actually took place in a boardinghouse, and the proprietors of the best ones made boarders feel like family. Often unaccompanied by spouses and children, many immigrants in particular had no choice but to rely on a hired cook to appease their hunger. The common use of the word "house" for "hotel" in the nineteenth century was not by accident. Particularly in early Kansas City, where housing options were scanty, many people boarded at a hotel that provided the "American plan": room and meals on a weekly basis. Oftentimes, boarders hesitated to bring loved ones to Kansas City until they had accumulated enough savings to build a house, or they only wished to stay long enough to earn money and continue west. A family in Belgium, Ireland, or Germany might send their oldest daughter to Kansas City because it would be easy for her to find work as a servant. She would save money and pay for the passage of her brother, and the rest of the family would slowly follow as the children became established. This type of immigration pattern made boardinghouses essential.

Mr. Thompson McDaniel's Hotel, established in 1846, was one of the earliest. Located on the southwest corner of Main and the Levee, it contained only a living room, dining room, and bar on the ground floor. Above were McDaniel's office and the lodgers' rooms.[19] Mr. McDaniel's success quickly led to competitors, given that many people disembarking from the steamboats were interested in temporary housing while they looked into possible job prospects. The three hundred Irishmen who arrived at Father Bernard Donnelly's request are illustrative of that need. As discussed earlier in this study, Donnelly relied on two Catholic families to run some boardinghouses in "Connaught Town." Irish immigrants also boarded closer to the West Bottoms near their employment. Patrick Shannon's Hotel is well remembered. It boasted of being equipped "with every facility necessary to the most perfect comfort" and was "prepared to receive boarders at the very lowest customary rates. [Patrick Shannon] promises that no pains should be spared to contribute to the comfort of those who shall be so kind as to bestow upon him the favor of their patronage and good will." This 1855 advertisement called special attention to Shannon's tavern for meals and its saloon "with the most superior quality of liquors of every description."[20] Dinnertime was crowded. Lodgers passed platters of fried pork and potatoes, baskets of corn bread or biscuits, pitchers of thick gravy, and bowls heaped with boiled greens drowning in vinegar. Such "boardinghouse reaches" inevitably concluded with a fruit cobbler or pie, hot tea or coffee. The tavern beckoned the men to continue conversation and drinking as soon as the meal concluded.

A strong "we take care of our own" mentality predominated in Kansas City for those people arriving with few means or resources. The Swedish immigrant experience is representative. August Johnson, an employment contractor, helped fellow Swedes acclimate. He stood on the train platform with a box of cigars calling out, *Talar någon svenska*? ["Does anyone speak Swedish?"] If men cried out "Ja!" Johnson offered them cigars and escorted them to a Swedish boardinghouse for a welcome meal of brown beans and rye bread, boiled potatoes, and *lutfisk*.[21] The Swedish Brewery was another popular boardinghouse, located at Fifth and Holmes in what had once been a brewery. A Mr. Bergendahl leased the building and converted it into a twenty-family rooming house. Boarding Boss Johnson's House was particularly popular with Swedish women who worked nearby as housemaids.[22]

With so many boardinghouses, some inevitably found a place in Kansas City lore, occasionally for their notoriety. The Gillis House (sometimes called the Troost, Western, or American House) was one such place. Built by Dr. Benoist Troost in 1849, it provided a temporary home to several

Gillis House, 1870, a distant view as seen through the stone supports of the Hannibal Bridge.
Missouri Valley Special Collections, Kansas City Public Library, Kansas City, Missouri

early Kansas City settlers. Perched precariously on a cliff and facing the Missouri River, Gillis House was difficult for boat passengers to miss. Among its more famous occupants were Kersey and Sarah Coates. Prior to becoming the owners of the Coates House Hotel and Coates Opera House, Kersey and his wife had little choice but to board. Sarah recalled that in 1856, Gillis House was "surmounted by a steeple containing a large bell whereby the signal is given for rising in the morning and for attendance at meals." A "long table was set, capable of holding fifty or sixty persons. The emigration at this time was so immense that often three times this number would obtain meals here."[23] The rough food and accommodations were made only more so by crowds of California '49ers. As the Border War intensified, Free-Soilers, including Kersey and Sarah, were taunted and threatened by Confederate sympathizers. No one, regardless of their politics, went to bed at night without revolvers under their pillows.[24] After the Civil War, when the Coates House Hotel opened, its immediate reputation as the very best accommodation and restaurant in Kansas City surely had something to do with the couple's determination to bring comfort, quiet, civility, and refined hospitality to Kansas City: to create the antithesis of the Gillis House.

The Coates's private residence at Tenth and Pennsylvania was likewise a civilized haven, the centerpiece of the Coates's planned exclusive neighborhood dubbed "Quality Hill." The couple made their new home an expanse of flower gardens, terraces, and porches. Even in its unfinished state, the Coateses opened their home up for the French-style dinners and balls that had the vestiges of older French Creole society.[25] Although they were Pennsylvania Quakers, and the Quality Hill neighborhood initially an enclave of "Yankees," the Coateses gained acceptance. During the Civil War, Sarah was a highly admired nurse who refused to consider the color of a man's uniform if he lay injured, thirsty, or hungry.

CITY BEAUTIFUL, HOME BEAUTIFUL

When travelers stepped off steamboats before the Civil War, they were immediately sharing a too-narrow space with hundreds of other people, livestock, wagons, piles of cargo destined downriver, and warehouses. The opening of the Hannibal Railway Bridge after the Civil War and the growth of meatpacking, stockyards, railroads, and milling industries only added to the confusion, as well as to the stench. The mud was often unbearable as scores of men slaved to cut roads through the bluffs and level the smaller ones. "Gulleytown," the city's moniker, fit. When the English gentlewoman Rose Kingsley by "some unlucky chance" ended up rerouted to Kansas City on her way to Denver in 1871, her words were illustrative: "My heart sank, for of all places to wait at, a more unpleasant one on a hot day than Kansas City . . . could not be found."[26]

Pearl Street and Quality Hill were to a degree protected from the worst of the noise and odors, but rapid industrialization and population growth motivated Kansas Citians with financial means to move farther east and south. While many of their fortunes were made from meatpacking and related industries, they were embarrassed by the ugliness of it all, determined to ensure that future planning efforts resulted in aesthetics more so than mere pragmatism. As its contribution to the nationwide City Beautiful Movement, Kansas City set aside an unprecedented 2,050 acres for parks and twenty-six miles for boulevards that artfully connected parks and new residential developments. Union Depot, the city's West Bottoms train station, was demolished shortly after the 1903 flood, and the new Union Station owed its own architectural grandeur and landscaping to the City Beautiful Movement. Instead of travelers pulling into the Bottoms and looking out on cows, saloons, gun-slinging drunks, and prostitutes, they pulled into a Beaux-Arts structure of 850,000 square feet. "Here, in solid marble and limestone, was testimony that their future would be bright," wrote geographer James R. Shortridge, characterizing the public's reaction to Union Station.[27] Much has been written about the City Beautiful Movement's effect on Kansas City's layout, but it also had implications for home life and dining between the two world wars.

The Woman's City Club, formed in December 1916, helps get at those implications. As with Woman's Clubs nationwide, Kansas City's was made up of well-connected women, including First Lady Bess Truman, who engaged in civic initiatives and also socializing. While spearheading successful drives to clean up trash, establish a Children's Cardiac Convalescent Center, and ensure safe milk supplies, these women also met at one another's homes for luncheons, teas, and receptions. Both the 1920 Woman's City Club's *Our Own Cook Book* and its seventieth-anniversary *Our Favorite Recipes* testified to the importance these women placed on gracious home entertaining, in part as antidote to the public ugliness they combated. Their hospitality standards reflected those of earlier eras in Kansas City.

Woman's City Club members were accustomed to a formal style of multiple courses for dinner parties. Hence, *Our Own Cook Book*'s first recipes were for appetizers, including an oyster cocktail and several canapés, some elaborate, such as eggs stuffed with caviar encased in tomato aspic. Removed from their individual molds, the eggs were sliced and served on toast points covered with shredded lettuce and whipped-cream-lightened mayonnaise.[28] Gentility at its best, one might say. Because the City Club conducted much of its business around meals, the cookbook also included several luncheon recipes and menu suggestions. It also devoted a segment to afternoon teas, including recipes for finger sandwiches and various small cakes and pastries.

Many City Club members lived in the exclusive developments created by J. C. Nichols, and both he and his wife, Jessie Miller Nichols (a City Club member), centered their aspirations for gracious living on a fundamental question that J. C. asked city planners: "Don't you believe that the creation of a beautiful setting would do much to bring fresh capital here?"[29] His question was not rhetorical; it motivated planners to shift their traditional focus on cost savings toward a riskier blueprint to make Kansas City residential developments exemplary, both for other Kansas City developers and nationwide. For one, Nichols's developments in the Brush Creek Valley and the Country Club District made distance from downtown an asset, not a liability. Sunset Hills and Mission Hills were by Nichols's calculation thirty-two minutes away from downtown by automobile, and the developments were not designed to make it easy for people to come into or out of the district via trolley bus or streetcar.[30] While the Country Club Plaza would over time become a citywide attraction, in its earliest days it was designed to ensure that women did not have to venture downtown unless they had an express wish to do so; then it would be by automobile. Nichols explained to the Women's Community Council of the Country Club District that it was "planned and built" for them and their children; "women are the home buyers and builders and makers." As a result, home interiors and landscaping were created in ways to make domestic life and entertaining friends and family more enjoyable for women. As Nichols put it, women would be "more in and about the home, more a part of it."[31]

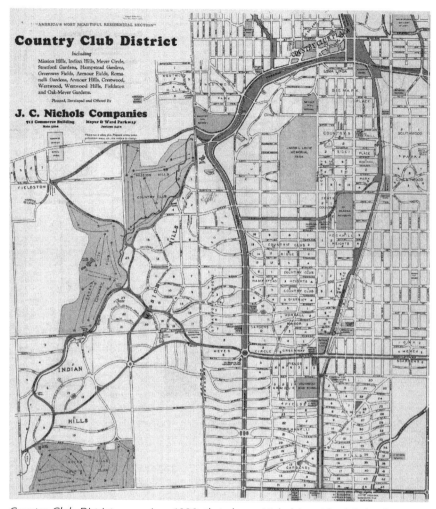

Country Club District map, circa 1920, that shows Nichols's residential developments, parks, and shopping centers.
Missouri Valley Special Collections, Kansas City Public Library, Kansas City, Missouri

The 1921 article in the *Ladies' Home Journal* that quoted Nichols above likewise praised the Country Club District. "A Home District Beautiful," as the article was titled, explained how kitchens were "on the street sides" and the "bedrooms, breakfast room, dining room, living room and sun room . . . on the garden side [backyard] so as to relate the living part of the house more closely to the garden." With this configuration, privacy was ensured, reflecting a nationwide movement away from front-porch congeniality and toward backyard intimacy. Nichols helped usher in an era where an invitation to one's home took on added meaning, that one was sought out and highly regarded. The home design in these exclusive developments facilitated the hostess's ease in entertaining her guests both outside on the back terrace and in the large dining room adjacent to the kitchen.

With self-perpetuating restrictive covenants to control who could and could not move in, as well as steep prices, residents who qualified to buy in these developments typically had the means to budget an additional $272 annually to maintain a live-in servant. Upfront building and furnishing costs for said servant would also necessitate a one-time investment of $1,005 to add on a ten-by-ten-foot bedroom, a bath, and to purchase furniture, bed linens, aprons, and the servant's own dishes and flatware.[32]

Most Kansas Citians obviously could not afford such luxuries and such homes, and hundreds were wrongfully denied access to such privileges based exclusively on their race and ethnicity, no matter how much money they made. While Woman's City Club members, Junior League members, and their families had a strong influence on what gracious hospitality and at-home dining ideally should be, Kansas Citians of all classes and races were already accustomed to treating guests to great food and hospitality, not only because of the predominant culture into which they entered upon arrival, but also because many immigrants came from cultures that championed similar virtues. Doug Worgul's title to his book, *A Table Full of Welcome: A Cookbook Celebrating Kansas City's Culinary Diversity* (2002), suggested as much.

Kansas City Filipino traditions, for example, focus on Fiesta, which is akin to "a state of grace," wrote Worgul. Fiestas, or feast days, began centuries ago in the Spanish-controlled Philippines when time was set aside to honor Catholic saints. Kansas City Filipinos celebrate Fiesta by opening their homes to strangers and offering them dinner on the best china.[33] Conversely, Filipinos are expected to leave their own homes to accept others' hospitality. This breaking down of barriers and treating strangers as family is not merely an opportunity to meet new people; as Kansas City resident Adela Tan explained to Doug Worgul, "Cooking is like a prayer. You do it with your heart. Then you give it to others. And it makes everyone better in their bodies and souls."[34]

A Table Full of Welcome reminded readers of Kansas City's earliest foodways when Worgul profiled Raymond W. Red Corn III, an Osage Native American. "Guilt is a rotten appetizer," Worgul admitted. "Like, perhaps, many European Americans, I experience a certain amount of retroactive guilt in the presence of Native Americans." Nonetheless, Red Corn greeted Worgul by plucking a gorgeous piece of fry bread out of the basket and dropping it into Worgul's hand before he even said hello. Over a meal of fry bread, corn soup, Osage meat pies, Osage squash, and hominy pork stew, Red Corn's family discussed Osage culinary history and identity. What stood out for Worgul was Red Corn's follow-up e-mail: "Thank you," he wrote, "for dining with us last night. In Anglo culture the guest thanks the host for the dinner. But with the Osage, it's the other way around. In Osage culture the host thanks the guest for the honor of their company and for the privilege of serving them. So thank you."[35] While Red Corn did point out a difference between Osage culture and Anglo culture, many Kansas Citians have oftentimes thanked their dinner guests; that custom might be traced as far back as early 1700s, when the Osage and Kansa met the French at Kawsmouth and invited them to a meal.

AL FRESCO DINING AND HOME ENTERTAINING

Kansas Citians have long made al fresco dining into an art. The custom had to do initially with the weather itself, given that Kansas City summers are long and sweltering; hence, indoor cooking and eating could become unbearable. Necessity bred habit, habit bred pleasure. Madame Chouteau's and Mrs. Coates's wide porches were conducive for socializing over meals. The porches of the nineteenth century gave way to the patios or terraces of the twentieth century, and in both cases, they facilitated eating and entertaining outside.

J. C. Nichols's contemporary, architect Mary Rockwell Hook, is critical to the story of how Kansas Citians made al fresco dining into an art. Hook came from a wealthy family. Her mother was a historian for the Episcopal Diocese based in Kansas City, and her father was a banker and grain merchant. They supported their daughter's architectural ambitions after she graduated from the Art Institute of Chicago and studied at L'École des Beaux-Arts in Paris. Hook's Kansas City–designed houses, many in Sunset Hills, speak to a design philosophy that facilitates the seamless back-and-forth movement between outside and inside spaces, as well as floor plans that make the best use of natural light. Kitchen windows are often positioned so that the light comes from the east and north rather than from the glare of the ferocious sun out of the west. Liberal use of skylights and two-story-tall windows throughout Hook homes are also common. Most important was Hook's focus on the interplay between inside and out. Inspired by Italian villas she had visited, Hook created houses that often feature terraces that include outside fireplaces, grills, and/or ranges, and that do not seem to be strictly outside; transitional zones between the two spaces create fluidity.[36] Built skillfully into the steep wooded bluffs south of Brush Creek, Hook houses look out over some of the most beautiful scenery in Kansas City.[37] In an era well before the nationwide trend to utilize outdoor spaces for cooking and entertaining (beyond the 1950s-era backyard grill and picnic table) Hook houses exemplified the priority that Kansas Citians have traditionally placed on at-home entertainment and ensuring that it is intimate, meaningful, and special. Creative use of outdoor spaces continues to define Kansas City home styles.

Suggested menus in twentieth-century Kansas City cookbooks likewise prioritized al fresco entertaining, as well as entertaining in general. The Kansas City Junior League's 1975 *Company's Coming*, its 1984 *Beyond Parsley*, and its 1992 *Above and Beyond Parsley* are illustrative. Even if cooks were only entertaining their families, the preface to *Company's Coming* explained it is "one of the most fun ways of developing . . . style in food presentation."[38] Suggested menus included a patio dinner featuring tomato dill consommé, green pea salad, butterflied leg of lamb accompanied by cheese potatoes, a peach-blueberry custard pie, and a Rhône wine. A garden picnic menu suggested chilled Greek lemon soup, wine-poached salmon, Armenian bread, chocolate-cinnamon torte, and a Wente Brothers Pinot Chardonnay. *Beyond Parsley* and *Above and Beyond Parsley* did not offer suggested menus, but many recipe notes nudged readers to consider food presentation, how to serve guests a dish with sophisticated but casual elegance, and how to exploit natural settings and edible flora. Entertaining was the guiding principle behind all three Kansas City Junior League cookbooks.

How did such meals play out? How did cookbooks move from an idealized world on paper and staged photography to an actual world of cooks, families, and guests—weighed down with a retinue of modern-day challenges, competing commitments, and inevitable time shortages? Traditionally (and one could argue currently), many Kansas Citians made dining at home into an event precisely because it *was* an event, one that took more sacrifice than a meal at a restaurant. However, the meal at home was one *worth* the sacrifice. Company mattered. Meals where guests were invited took place over hours, not minutes. Hosts and hostesses did significant behind-the-scenes work to make sure guests felt not only welcomed, but highly valued. A refrigerator crammed with drink selections to which guests were urged repeatedly to help themselves; a kitchen counter loaded with a selection of appetizers put out on colorful plates; the warmth and generosity of the hosts, who anticipated a guest's need or desire before she herself was even aware of it: these traits of Kansas City entertainment persist today.

Kansas City Junior League cookbooks were sophisticated productions, available in area bookstores, and heavily marketed. As such, they were self-conscious productions, deliberately designed to put forth Kansas City's best self, so to speak. However, numerous Kansas City cookbooks not designed for retail purchase spoke to the same fundamental values. *Memories Good Enough to Eat*, the cookbook of Kansas City's oldest Reform Jewish congregation, testified to the sacredness of home dining and sharing meals with friends. "So much of the tradition and strength of Judaism is found in the home, and so much of the spirit of Jewish home life comes into focus around the supper table," the editors wrote in the cookbook's 1970 publication, the centennial of Temple B'nai Jehudah.[39] While acknowledging that over the course of the century, women's opportunities as well as responsibilities expanded, family size shrank, and technology altered both cooking and eating, *Memories Good Enough to Eat* stressed that a profound "appreciation of home ritual survived the hurried pace, the convenience foods and the beyond-the-family distractions of our times."[40] At-home meals were thus more meaningful as a result of such transformations and challenges.

As with the Junior League's *Company's Coming*, *Memories Good Enough to Eat* championed entertaining, offering suggested menus and reasons to invite guests over. A "Buffet for Eight" menu included crabmeat spread, a cold vegetable medley, beef tenderloin on assorted breads, strawberry–sour cream mold, spaghetti casserole, ice cream cake, and sparkling Burgundy; the menu would work well inside the dining room, but also out on the patio or in the garden. A suggested "Sunday Brunch Buffet" included piña coladas; French toast; chicken livers; baked eggs; bagels, lox, and cream cheese; fruit kabobs; stickies (caramel nut rolls); and coffee. Such a menu could allow guests to sit where they wished, to mingle and relax. An "After the Game" menu was of course a product of 1970s food trends, but many Kansas Citians would find its suggestions perfectly appropriate for today, and for that matter, continue to host or attend parties where these foods are served: tomato Ro-Tel dip, avocado crab dip with chips, chili and tamale pie, crackers, garlic toast, lemonade pie, and beer.[41]

"OUR OWN TRADITIONS": KANSAS CITY ETHNIC HERITAGE AND COOKBOOKS

Judith Fertig, a noted Kansas City cookbook author and food writer, pointed out that when an ethnic group feels in danger of losing its heritage due to assimilation, its members often create a cookbook. These complications typically appear around fifty years after the last wave of settlement. Grandmothers and great-grandmothers are passing away, recipes were handed down but not necessarily written down, and the need to preserve and to reinvigorate food traditions for the next generations become paramount concerns.[42] Indeed, *Memories Good Enough to Eat*, published roughly fifty years after the last significant waves of Jews arrived in Kansas City, testified to this pattern. The B'nai Jehudah Sisterhood stressed that its contributors, "through their culinary efforts," were able to "bring back memories of people and events long gone. They have given us a heritage upon which to build a future."[43] Irrespective of a cookbook's ethnic focus, most of them stressed, sometimes explicitly, sometimes implicitly, the fundamental importance of food and hospitality, food and celebration to maintaining cohesion and community.

In 1962, the Guadalupe Center in Kansas City printed a compilation of Mexican-American favorites. Although brief, mimeographed, and without a title page (the front and back paper covers were simply graced with the Mexican flag), recipe portion sizes and small illustrations championed everyday family meals and also foods that lent themselves to festive gatherings. *Chili con queso* served eighteen and was clearly associated with a party. *Tamales de carne* likewise fed a large number and involved an assembly line of family members and friends to make the tamales for Christmas festivities or an annual fund-raiser. *Capirotada*, a pudding consisting of Italian bread, raisins, pineapple, piñon nuts (or peanuts), almonds, and brown sugar was "a Lenten favorite, and you will find it on many tables, particularly on Good Friday," the accompanying note indicated. Several recipes were modest family staples, illustrative of good taste but little effort, including *pastel de enchilada* (enchilada pie), multiple variations of *frijoles* (pinto beans), *chili con carne* and *chili con frijoles, turquitos* (chili pie), and *nopales con salsa de chile* (greens or cactus paddles with chili sauce).

The beautiful manuscript *Priscilla Art Cook Book* of the First Lutheran Church (1948) was likewise full of family staples and more elaborate foods. Its compilers thanked church members and friends who had graciously shared their recipes so as to preserve "the many special dishes of our own Swedish Heritage."[44] Designed to ensure that the next generations of Swedish Americans kept food traditions alive, a prefatory poem, "Smörgåsbord," included this stanza: "Be not very astounded nor very afraid / By such as *Krop Kakker, Ost Kaka*, they're easily made / It really is simple, just follow the rule / Set down by the experts, ' tis beyond ridicule."[45] Cookbooks such as the *Priscilla Art Cook Book* and the Guadalupe Center's recipe collection included English translations of various recipe titles, as well as other elaborations on technique, equipment, or dining rituals. These efforts indicated that the targeted audience might be unsure of how to proceed or no longer fluent in the native language; however, such cookbooks were also geared toward inclusiveness, an invitation for anyone with a desire for insight to look into a culture's foodways.

In this respect, Inez Yeargan Kaiser's *Soul Food Cookery* was particularly important. Published in 1968 and selling out quickly enough to go into a revised edition the same year, *Soul Food Cookery* has the distinction of being the first book to make commercial use of the term "soul food."[46] *Soul Food Cookery*'s author is a native Kansas Citian who taught home economics before pursuing a career in marketing. *Soul*

Food Cookery did not speak exclusively to a Kansas City audience, nor strictly to an African American audience; rather, it invited outsiders in, with Kaiser's wish that the book help readers "to develop an appreciation for food that has been prepared and enjoyed for years by minority people, especially Negros. These recipes may in some way bridge the gap in our society, and enable [readers] to understand the cultural background of all people as well as develop a channel for better communications through one of the basic needs of life—food."[47]

Many recipes in *Soul Food Cookery* were economically thrifty, including those in its chapter "Party and T.V. Snacks"; furthermore, baked beans and cheese on hamburger buns, deviled sardines, deviled eggs, and hamburger turnovers were easy to make and serve in large or small portions, depending on the size of the party. Other recipes spoke strongly to Kansas City's African American culinary traditions, with recipes for fried pig's feet, brains and eggs, neckbones and corn mush, and possum, which was prepared by slow boiling the meat on the stove with fresh red pepper, and from there baking it skin side up until crisp and brown. Kaiser also did in *Soul Food Cookery* what other ethnic groups did: she connected her readers through "emotional feeling and sentiment" to foods that they might no longer have to eat because they were "so limited," but that they chose to eat for heritage and pride.[48]

FESTIVALS AND CELEBRATIONS

The prefatory "Brief History of the Saint Dionysios Greek Orthodox Church" in *Food Fit for the Gods* (first edition 1969) resembled *Soul Food Cookery* in its invitation to outsiders to take a closer look at Kansas City Greek cuisine and traditions. And, as was often the case with ethnic cookbooks, it was for sale at a large, public festival that featured a lot of food. St. Dionysios was founded in 1926 in Kansas City, Kansas, and its annual June festival is one of the city's most anticipated. Many Kansas Citians make these types of celebrations part of their summer routine because the food is delicious, the live music and dancing create a wonderful vibe, and people enjoy meeting friends and strangers alike. At the Saint Dionysios Greek Festival, both patio and parking lot are set up with food booths, and long lines of eager and admiring guests watch cooks grill and flame cheese *saganaki* and prepare *souvlakia.*

Such ethnic festivals have their roots in the 1800s, when the city helped sponsor the annual Kansas City Irish Picnic. After the Civil War, Irish populations throughout the United States celebrated Celtic heritage with a picnic commemorating *Bael-an-atha-Buidhe*, a 1600s Irish battle where Red Hugh O'Neill ousted an English force of four thousand men. Kansas City's first Irish Picnic was held on September 2, 1887, when hundreds gathered at a local park to feast on barbecued meats, relishes, potato salad, and barrels of beer, all served up by the women of Holy Name Parish. August 13, 1916, drew the largest crowd on record for a Kansas City Irish Picnic; some ten thousand visited Walnut Grove near Watt's Mill to spend the day celebrating and feasting.[49] The current Kansas City Irish Fest, also held in late summer and routinely voted Kansas City's best public festival, can trace its roots back to the Irish Picnics that reached their apex around the time of the Great Depression and then declined in attendance due to hard times.

August, when many Kansas City festivals take place, gives way in September to the anticipated ongoing food event of the year: the Arrowhead Stadium tailgate parties—more popular, many would argue, than the Chiefs football games themselves. On scheduled away games, many neighbors turn their driveways into a tailgate party, with an open trunk or pickup bed full of beer, a large grill or smoker set up, and a sheet covering the garage door to broadcast the game. People inevitably stop by and join the festivities, and the party grows. Home Chiefs games, however, are the main attraction. The Truman Sports Complex parking lot opens at 8:30 on Sunday game days, but hundreds of vehicles line up at 6:00 a.m. for entrance. Ty Rowton, a self-declared "superfan," rightly explained that arriving just before sunup "just kind of gets you in the mood for the game. There's a lot of camaraderie with meeting people at the game," he explained.[50] Another self-declared superfan, David Goings, elaborated on the importance of the food: "Tailgating is all about the food—and we're not talking hot dogs." He elaborated on his family's tradition: "We cook something different every game, and throughout the years, we've never really duplicated anything. We've cooked everything from ribs to lobster to salmon to brisket." Bacon is also popular, in keeping with nationwide culinary trends. "Bacon is like currency," the *Visit Kansas City* website explained in its information to potential visitors about tailgating. "Beautiful, edible currency. Not sure what to talk about while at a Chiefs tailgate party? Talk about bacon. Want to gain access into someone else's party? Tote around a packet of bacon and a sixer of Bud." Nonetheless, most would also agree with the Kansas City Convention and Visitors Association that the most important part of tailgating culture is barbecue; that is "what holds court."[51] More specifically, many tailgaters hold impromptu competitions and tastings that center on the rub and the sauce, the things that make Kansas City barbecue distinct when virtually everyone already knows how to smoke chicken and ribs or grill hamburgers.

It is fitting, then, to conclude this chapter on home cooking with barbecue, as it continues after almost two centuries to reign supreme at virtually any family outdoor gathering in Kansas City. Houses inevitably have outdoor grills, including earth-dug pits with a grate over the top, tandoori ovens, charcoal or gas grills, impromptu smokers fashioned out of a steel drum, or in some cases, $10,000 competition smokers. A slow drive through Swope Park (the largest city park) on a weekend morning on any mild day will speak the truth of Kansas City's obsession. Shelter after shelter will have a truck, SUV, or a car beside it, and a family or group will be setting up the smoker for later afternoon revelry. All races, ethnicities, classes, as well as family sizes, are represented. The same ritual happens on a smaller scale at all city and county parks that have shelters. This passion for barbecuing led to the creation of the Kansas City Barbeque Society (KCBS), one of the nation's most important organizations for sanctioning contests and certifying barbecue judges. It began in 1985 after Carolyn and Gary Wells and Rick Welch decided that with the large number of Kansas City barbecue competitors, a club would serve everyone for reasons of coordination. The Kansas City Barbeque Society began with a $12 yearly membership, a newsletter, and a "Spring Training Practice Competition" held at a member's farm. Ten years later, there was no longer a need for a spring training, and indeed, hundreds of Kansas Citians are members of the KCBS and compete. They join upwards of nineteen thousand other KCBS members worldwide and face off in one (or several) of the 450 barbecue contests held nationwide, and/or they judge KCBS events.[52]

The most auspicious competition is the American Royal World Series of Barbecue, which began in 1980 as part of the Kansas City American Royal, a livestock and horse show. Also important to competitors and spectators alike are the Kansas City Kosher BBQ Competition and Festival, the Balloons & BBQ Festival at the Kansas Speedway (in Kansas City, Kansas), and the Great Lenexa BBQ Battle. Joining a barbecue team in Kansas City is roughly equivalent to joining a bowling league elsewhere. While participants take barbecuing very seriously, they nonetheless are oftentimes a part of such a group because it fosters goodwill and team spirit and allows them a way to express pride in the city they call home.

Chapter Nine

We've Grown Accustomed to These Tastes

Kansas City's Signature Dishes

Kansas Citians can easily take for granted certain foods and flavors—until they leave town and realize that they can't find those foods and flavors anywhere else. At the same time, Kansas Citians grow accustomed to thinking that their favorite restaurant will always be there—until it disappears. That the loss is deeply felt is evident in the Kansas City cookbooks, newspaper profiles, and retrospectives devoted to recipes and elegiac stories of lost restaurants. This chapter covers some of those recipes as well as distinctive flavors that Kansas Citians yearn for if they travel or move away.

BARBECUED BURNT ENDS

"You can't get a good cheesesteak out of Philly" and "You can't get a great Cubano outside of Miami." "Cincinnati Chili outside Cincinnati? It's not going to happen." These statements resonate with Kansas Citians when they travel and cannot find barbecued burnt ends (and of course many locals would argue barbecue in general, but I will leave that argument for someone else). Burnt ends, the "beef crackling that has been blackened with smoke," as Kansas City food writer Bonjwing Lee described beef brisket ends, have long been a Kansas City specialty, perhaps because Kansas City barbecued brisket is already more heavily smoked and chewier than its cousin, Texas-style barbecue, noted Judith M. Fertig and Karen Adler.[1]

The problem with burnt ends is that many people crave them, but given that they are technically the charred *bits* at the *ends* of the brisket, demand far outweighs the supply. To compensate, many barbecue restaurants approximate the flavor and texture of burnt ends with varying degrees of success. Bonjwing Lee's "The Burnt Ends of Kansas City: A Guided Tour" (2014) is a must-read for those interested in finding the best Kansas City barbecue restaurants that specialize in this delicacy.

Brisket is a primal cut consisting of two muscles separated by a layer of fat. The top muscle, called the point or deckle, is smaller and more marbled than the lower, larger "flat." To approximate burnt ends, some barbecue restaurants twice-cook the more marbled point, first by regular smoking until it is fork-tender, and then a second time when, if done carefully, it takes on that unparalleled char but interior succulence. This method can produce delicious results, in other words. However, some barbecue restaurants will smoke the flat and instead of slicing it thin for sandwiches, they will chunk it up and serve it as "burnt ends." The natural dryness of the flat, however, demands that the meat be soaked in sauce, often a telltale sign of an inferior product no matter what the cut or the meat. Still other barbecue restaurants will chop up the entire brisket, point and flat both, and smoke it again. Kansas Citians not only have their favorite restaurants that prepare this dish to their tastes, but many also smoke briskets themselves to get the flavor of burnt ends as and how they want it.

THE KANSAS CITY STRIP

According to Heather N. Paxton, Kansas City's most famous steak, the Kansas City strip, was created in 1933 by Lou Williams of the Williams Meat Company and Frank H. Servatius, general manager for the American Royal, Kansas City's historic livestock auction and horse show. The Kansas City strip was expertly described by James W. Leathers and Jay B. Dillingham thusly: a steak approximately one inch thick, cut from an oblong muscle of the loin only eight to nine inches wide. It is a boneless cut of meat with a thin layer of fat on one side. A 1,000-pound choice-grade steer producing a 600-pound carcass of meat will yield only 24 one-pound KC strip steaks. The meat comes from behind the thirteenth rib, where it is surrounded by some "mighty fine company"—the sirloin, T-bone, porterhouse, and club steaks.[2]

Although it is easier to refer to the Kansas City strip as a strip loin steak, technicalities matter to Kansas Citians, because the same or similar cut is often referred to as the New York Strip, not because of the New York beef industry, but because of New York City's historic restaurant, Delmonico's. One of its specialties was a "Delmonico steak," and ultimately people changed its name to the "New York strip."[3]

Irrespective of what cut Delmonico's used (some experts claim that Delmonico's used different cuts at different times, and that the meaning of the sirloin itself changed, too), "Delmonico" then as now signifies the best. Given that Armour and Company built one of the nation's first state-of-the-art cold-storage facilities in Kansas City in the early 1880s, and that refrigerated rail cars could move the meat quickly to New York, it is possible that irrespective of the Delmonico cut, the beef was indeed from Kansas City.[4] Paxton gave the "official opinion of the American Royal," and by extension Kansas City's, when she wrote that "the New York Strip Steak has a feather bone, and the Kansas City Strip Steak is boneless and far more flavorful."[5] It is unlikely that the matter is settled for good; suffice it to say that Kansas Citians adore the Kansas City strip, a cut that is slightly less marbled than the rib-eye and more beefy in flavor and texture as a result. Kansas City restaurateurs and butchers specialize in dry-aging prime and choice strips for the best restaurants and for loyal customers.

A high-quality Kansas City strip requires minimal preparation prior to cooking so that the flavor and quality of the beef speaks for itself. Bring the strip to room temperature, liberally salt and pepper it, rubbing the seasoning into the meat, and grill it over medium-hot charcoal for roughly eight minutes on each side (less for rarer), allowing the steak to rest ten minutes before serving it with the traditional Kansas City accompaniments: a baked potato (preferably twice-baked), a tossed salad, and fresh-baked French bread. Quality blue cheese crumbles, either on the steak or on the salad, are also popular. The Kansas City strip also responds well to searing in a hot cast-iron skillet that has been lightly coated with olive oil. The less temptation to overseason the steak and douse it in condiments, the better chance the Kansas City strip has to speak for itself.

KANSAS CITY–STYLE CHEESE ENCHILADAS

Many Kansas Citians miss Mexican food when they travel. Mexicans have been integral to Kansas City history from as far back as the 1700s; as a result, their cuisine has had over two centuries to mature and influence local flavors and traditions. Kansas Citians have thus come to expect excellent Mexican food on just about every corner in the Metro, and they often take this cuisine for granted the way they do barbecue. As of now, over four hundred Kansas City Mexican eateries, from *paleterías* to full-service restaurants, are listed on Internet sites such as Yelp and TripAdvisor. Southwest Boulevard and Kansas Avenue are Kansas City's Mexican food and manufacturing arteries.

While it has many competitors, Art's Mexican Food Company at 615 Kansas Avenue, Kansas City, Kansas, is one of the most successful local manufacturers of tortillas, tortilla chips, taco and tostada shells, and enchilada sauce. In business since 1961, the company has had many decades to establish its reputation for excellence. As a wholesaler, Art's supplies over fifty area grocery stores and sells to around seventy-five area Mexican restaurants.[6] While many produce their own signature enchilada sauces, the flavor of Art's cries out "Kansas City." Because the company will mail-order ingredients, it makes Kansas City–style enchiladas easy to prepare at home.

Cheese Enchiladas (serves four)

10 corn tortillas, small
½ cup vegetable oil
Art's Enchilada Sauce (1½ cups)
12 ounces queso fresco, longhorn Cheddar, or a blend
2 scallions, minced

Right before you are ready to serve the meal, heat vegetable oil in a sauté pan to medium-high heat. Create an assembly line: stack of tortillas, a shallow dish of enchilada sauce, a plate of cheese mixed with minced scallions, a greased 8- by 11½- by 2-inch casserole or four ovenproof plates. Coat bottom of the casserole or each plate with a thin layer of enchilada sauce. Heat oven to 425 degrees Fahrenheit. Briefly submerge a tortilla in hot oil until soft and pliable. Lift it out with tongs and allow excess oil to drip back in pan. Dip the tortilla in enchilada sauce and drain. Put 3 to 4 tablespoons of cheese and onions down the middle, roll tightly, and put in the casserole or on a plate. Repeat the process until all tortillas are filled and rolled. Pour some sauce over the top, but be careful not to submerge the enchiladas. Sprinkle on leftover cheese. Place uncovered in a hot oven just until cheese is melted, around fifteen minutes for a casserole, or seven to ten minutes for individual plates. Watch carefully. Cool briefly and serve with refried beans, guacamole, and beverage of choice.

MISSOURI'S GREEN RICE CASSEROLE

In 2014, the *New York Times* published a map listing the recipes that each state Googled the most at Thanksgiving. Unsurprisingly for Kansas Citians, green rice casserole was Missouri's number one Googled Thanksgiving recipe. For many, that dish calls to mind Stephenson's Old Apple Farm Restaurant and its version of this classic. The original Stephenson's was located at 40 Highway and Lee's Summit Road in Independence, Missouri, and it was a product of the same "blue highways" era that gave rise to teahouses and roadside restaurants. However, instead of a woman at the helm, Stephenson's was run by two brothers, Lloyd and Leslie, who returned home to their family's farm after World War II. The Stephenson family had operated a produce stand since the 1870s, but it made sense for the brothers to capitalize on increased automobile traffic by expanding the business. They built a luncheonette and sold smoked meat sandwiches, apple cider, and the usual offerings of seasonal fruits and vegetables.

From a ten-booth operation, Stephenson's grew into a large restaurant, and from there, the brothers opened Stephenson's Apple Tree Inn in the Northland, as well as the Cider Mill Restaurant near Bella Vista, Arkansas, in Jane, Missouri. By the time the last remaining, original, Stephenson's closed in 2007, dishes such as chicken baked in butter and cream, marshmallow salad, green rice casserole, and apple fritters had little presence on any other Kansas City restaurant menus. Rather, they had become "heritage foods," made for a special Sunday dinner or more likely, a holiday gathering when people honored their Midwestern roots along with their family. Perhaps this is the reason that memories of Stephenson's persist. Chef Jasper Mirabile Jr. offered his memory, one that resonates with many Kansas Citians:

> I still remember sitting in the back seat of my father's Cadillac with my three brothers taking a Sunday drive and ending up at Stephenson's. We would feast on the apple harvest and of course, a multi-course country dinner with ham steak, creamy butter chicken, green rice and fresh apple butter. If I had written the book "1000 Places to See Before You Die" before Stephenson's closed, a visit to this iconic KC restaurant would be on my list.[7]

Every family has its own favorite version of green rice casserole, with the green color coming from either parsley or broccoli. The recipe below was the one I grew up with.

Green Rice Casserole (serves six to eight as a side dish, depending on one's appetite)

1 cup long-grain white rice, prepared by cooking in 2 cups lightly salted water

2 large eggs

1½ cups half-and-half

⅔ cup finely minced curly parsley, packed tightly

⅓ cup finely minced scallions, green part only

½ cup extra-sharp grated Cheddar cheese, packed tightly

2 tablespoons fresh lemon juice and 1 lemon's worth grated peel (yellow part only)

1 garlic clove, smashed and minced

¼ cup vegetable oil

1 teaspoon celery salt

1–2 teaspoons salt, to taste

1 teaspoon fresh-ground black pepper

A liberal dusting of Hungarian paprika on the top of the casserole

Allow the cooked rice to cool before proceeding. It should be thoroughly dry and fluffy.

Preheat oven to 350 degrees Fahrenheit. Grease a 1½- to 2-quart casserole. Beat eggs and add to them the half-and-half. Add all other ingredients, except for the paprika. Pour into the casserole, dust with paprika, and bake covered for 30 minutes. Uncover the casserole and bake an additional 15 minutes, until the top is golden.

SPINACH SALAD WITH CREAMY HORSERADISH DRESSING

Cafeterias and fancy Continental restaurants typically have little in common, unless one happened to grow up in Kansas City when Justus Putsch owned the classy Putsch's 210 and Putsch's Cafeteria; both offered his signature spinach salad. Many Kansas Citians made Putsch's 210 restaurant a special occasion but ate routinely at Putsch's Cafeteria, given that its excellent food was moderately priced. By the 1970s, a branch of Putsch's Cafeteria could also be found at shopping centers and malls throughout the Metro. As with green rice casserole, recipes for variations on Putsch's spinach salad and dressing are widely available, in print and on the Internet. They show a distinctly Midwestern and Southern preference for topping salads with a creamy mayonnaise dressing and other indulgent ingredients that coat the greens. The bite of horseradish in this version really makes the salad stand out. Adjust the amounts accordingly, but if you do not make your own prepared horseradish, look for a version free of additives and corn syrup.

Spinach Salad with Creamy Horseradish Dressing (serves six as a side salad or starter, two to three as a main course)

Dressing:
¾ cup mayonnaise
1½ teaspoons sherry vinegar
A couple dashes of hot sauce, or more to taste
¼ teaspoon salt
½ teaspoon fresh-ground black pepper
3 teaspoons prepared horseradish, or to taste

Blend all ingredients thoroughly and chill.

Salad:
¼ cup finely diced celery
¼ cup finely minced Vidalia, Walla Walla, or other sweet onion
3–4 cups chopped fresh spinach
⅓ cup diced extra-sharp Cheddar cheese
3 eggs, hard-boiled, 2 diced, one sliced neatly for garnish

Toss ingredients except for the hard-boiled egg garnish. Mix with the dressing right before serving.

MYRON GREEN CAFETERIA AND YARBOROUGH'S
FAMILY RESTAURANT: CINNAMON ROLLS

Myron Green was a popular Kansas City cafeteria. Along with its addictive macaroni and cheese, roast beef and mashed potatoes, fried fish, and cherry pie, Myron Green specialized in huge cinnamon rolls. Given their sugary decadence, it is ironic that Myron Green started out as a Michigan-based dentist who left behind that career to become a toothpaste salesman. Green's contention that food for travelers was subpar resembled that of his near contemporary, Fred Harvey, and like Harvey, Green's contention led to his final career: restaurateur. Although Green first opened a cafeteria in Denton, Texas, in 1907, he soon relocated to Kansas City and opened his first Myron Green Cafeteria in 1916. An advocate of women's employment and also convinced that customers would trust women as better cooks than men, Green employed primarily women to run his cafeteria kitchens.[8]

While Myron Green set the standard for restaurant cinnamon rolls, his up-and-coming competitors were Anne Peterson and Leona Yarbrough. Peterson was a Swedish immigrant who ran a small family restaurant in Fairway, Kansas (close to the Country Club Plaza), and Leona Yarbrough was Peterson's head baker. While the restaurant's cinnamon rolls were tiny compared to Green's, they attracted devoted patrons. Eventually, Yarborough bought Anne Peterson's restaurant in the late 1960s, and the cinnamon rolls remained popular until Yarborough's Restaurant also closed for good in 2009.

Traditionally, Kansas Citians enjoy cinnamon rolls as an accompaniment to meals, not merely as a breakfast treat. Many anticipate the basket of cinnamon rolls even more than the fried chicken when they sit down to dinner at Stroud's, for example. For many decades, Missouri, Kansas, and Nebraska schoolchildren anticipated Fridays, when cafeteria cooks served up homemade chili and cinnamon rolls to welcome the coming weekend—a combination that many people from elsewhere find odd. The chili–cinnamon roll combination nonetheless remains popular at home-style area restaurants, particularly the Corner Café in Kansas City's Northland, and at Runza, a Nebraska-based chain with locations in Lawrence and Shawnee Mission, Kansas.

Below is a revised recipe for Myron Green Cafeteria's cinnamon rolls, reprinted with permission from the *Kansas City Star*. It appeared on May

5, 1999, as "Second Time around for Cinnamon Rolls" in the food section some months after an earlier version of the recipe appeared, one that *Star* readers found problematic because it created too many rolls for a family to consume comfortably. As it is, this recipe will produce ten very large rolls. Although a 9- by 13-inch pan is recommended in the *Star* recipe, I found it easier to bake six rolls in a 9- by 13-inch pan, and fit the remaining four in an 8- by 8-inch pan. It will also be easier for home cooks if they prepare and roll the dough before making the margarine–brown sugar mixture, as the mixture will harden quickly. Just warm the mixture; avoid boiling it. Dot, then spread, the mixture on the dough for optimum results. Finally, unsalted butter can easily replace the margarine and shortening in the original recipe.

Myron Green Cinnamon Rolls

For filling:
2½ tablespoons margarine
½ cup plus 2 tablespoons brown sugar
3½ teaspoons light corn syrup
2 teaspoons water
1½ teaspoons cinnamon
6 tablespoons sugar

For dough:
2 packages active dry yeast
1¼ cups warm water
5 cups bread flour, divided
1¼ teaspoons salt
6 tablespoons sugar
6½ tablespoons nonfat dry milk powder (not reconstituted)
2½ teaspoons shortening
2 eggs

For filling: Melt margarine in small saucepan over low heat. Add brown sugar, corn syrup, and water. Heat, stirring constantly, until well mixed and heated through. Cover and set aside to cool. Mix together cinnamon and sugar; set aside. **For dough:** In a large mixing bowl, dissolve yeast in warm water. Add 4½ cups flour, salt, sugar, and dry milk powder (do not reconstitute milk). Blend at low speed with heavy-duty mixer, equipped with dough hook if available, about 5 minutes, or until a dough forms. Add shortening and eggs and blend 3 to 5 minutes or until well blended. Blend in remaining ½ cup flour and blend until dough begins to form a ball. Dough will be quite soft. Cover and allow dough to stand in warm place, free from drafts, until doubled in bulk, about 1 hour. Punch dough down and turn onto lightly floured board. Roll dough into a rectangle about 15 by 12 inches and ¼ inch thick. Spread margarine-syrup mixture evenly over dough. Sprinkle with cinnamon-sugar mixture. Roll dough, jelly-roll fashion, beginning at long end. Slice into 10 rolls, each about 1½ inches thick. Arrange in lightly greased 9- by 13-inch baking pan. Cover and allow to rise until doubled in bulk, about 30 minutes. Preheat oven to 400 degrees Fahrenheit. Bake 20 minutes or until golden brown. Remove from oven and allow to cool 10 minutes. Invert pan, then serve rolls warm, bottom side up.

MRS. DOWD, "MAMA" RUBY, AND "CHICKEN BETTY" LUCAS: PAN-FRIED CHICKEN

By the early twentieth century, Kansas City was home to so many restaurants offering fried chicken dinners that locals were disinclined to go to the trouble of making the meal themselves. Helen Stroud was a relative newcomer to the fried chicken competition when she changed from barbecue to chicken in the mid-1940s, and the Wishbone likewise did not open until 1946. Many would argue that Kansas City's fanciest fried chicken restaurant in the early part of the twentieth century was Mrs. Tena Mae Dowd's Green Parrot Inn. Dowd had operated a small restaurant in Wichita, Kansas, but when her husband's work brought him to Kansas City in 1929, she decided to keep cooking and expand her repertoire. Dowd and her husband purchased an inauspicious house on a hill at Fifty-Second and State Line Road and transformed it into an elegant restaurant that eventually seated three hundred.

Along with Myron Green, the Green Parrot Inn was the only Kansas City restaurant that Duncan Hines recommended in his popular *Adventures in Good Eating: Good Eating Places along the Highways of America* (1943 edition), and with excellent reason. The Green Parrot's surroundings were pastoral; its outdoor accommodation exemplified Kansas City's love of al fresco dining. The menu selections were expansive, offering Parker House rolls and cinnamon rolls, fruit salads, hominy grits au gratin, green bean casserole, strawberry pie, and peach batter cake, but it was her fried chicken that garnered the most rave reviews.[9]

By 1936, Dowd and her brother, Mr. J. H. Toothman, were also operating a Green Parrot Inn in Kirkwood, a St. Louis suburb, and not tiring of the business, Dowd and her sister, Vira B. Fredericks, also started a Green Parrot Inn in Houston, Texas. By this time Dowd's husband and her two sons were also working to help her run the three Green Parrot Inns. Prior to closing in 1955, hundreds of wedding receptions, rehearsal dinners, anniversaries, fraternal and charitable club luncheons, and surprise birthday parties had taken place at the Kansas City Green Parrot Inn, not to mention thousands of family dinners.[10]

Ruby's Soul Food Café at Fifteenth and Brooklyn might have been the antithesis of the Green Parrot Inn when it came to décor and elegance, but not when it came to hospitality and fried chicken. Ruby Lee Watson McIntyre was born on the Howe Plantation in 1920 in Lexington, Tennessee, and she began learning to cook for Miss Effie Howe around age five. While everybody "else went into the field and picked cotton," McIntyre recalled, "I stayed in the house and did all the cooking." In the early 1940s, McIntyre came to Kansas City with her family. In 1951, she opened her soul food restaurant.[11]

She was "a tall, skinny, feisty woman" who "served southern food masterpieces along with a calming charm," as Fred Philips characterized her.[12] "She has made it hard for all other southern cooks in my life—that have hosted dinners and brought out their cobblers, fried chicken and cabbage—because once you had food at Ruby's the other cooks didn't fare very well," wrote Teresa Urban in a commemoration after Ruby passed away in May 2015. All the soul food classics were on the menu, but her pan-fried chicken commanded respect, not just admiration. With only a heavy cast-iron skillet, she fried her chicken "in good old Lard. She kept an eye on anything that was frying with a single dinner fork," marveled longtime fan and "adopted son" Donnie Bowerman.

Bowerman, along with other Kansas City police officers, firefighters, and *Kansas City Star* reporters, made Ruby's their "home away from home," and "Mama Ruby," as she was known by all her patrons, treated them like sons and daughters. As with Bryant's, Gates & Son, and later, BB's Lawnside Barbecue, Ruby's attracted customers of all classes and races. In infrequent moments when matters of race came up, Bowerman noted that McIntyre "would not unquietly say, 'There's only one color here in my place, and it's the golden brown of my fried chicken. Y'all remember that.'" She would then go back to her small kitchen where more chicken was frying.[13] Patrons loved her for that, and many gained "spare tires" eating her food.

And then there was "Chicken Betty" Lucas, who also cemented Kansas City's reputation for delectable pan-fried chicken. A onetime head cook for Helen Stroud, Lucas moved around the Metro, taking legions of fans with her. Correctly dubbing Lucas the "Pied Piper of Chickendom," *New York Times* food critic Mimi Sheraton brought Lucas to national attention in 1980. She had such "a faithful following of customers," Sheraton noted, that restaurateurs were desperate to entice Lucas into their kitchens.[14] Lucas proudly stood behind a cast-iron skillet and fried chicken for many restaurants over her long career, including Boots & Coates, Gomer's Fried Chicken and Liquors, Westport Diner, and Granny's. Her "pan fried chicken is moist inside and crispy outside as it should be," wrote restaurant reviewers Colin and Sylvia Clarendon when they ate at Granny's in the early 1980s. "Chicken livers and gizzards are also fried, and come with a delicious bowl of thick, fattening gravy."[15]

Most Kansas City fried-chicken cooks gave their chicken an egg-wash coating before dredging it in flour, while some, most notably Helen Stroud, relied solely on flour. What they all relied on, at least in the early days of their fame, was lard. They also agreed that the best fried chicken had to have a shattering thin-crusted batter, not the fast-food kind where, as Lucas bluntly put it, "the breading cracks off like a plaster cast."[16]

The recipe below is simple in theory, but technique and correct temperatures can be challenging. Dowd advised cooks to use a heavy cast-aluminum skillet, although many would argue that cast iron is better, and in this era, a heavy stainless-steel skillet will also do a fine job. Importantly, most chickens today are factory farmed and bred to be much larger than the chickens of old; hence, it is better to use a free-range bird and a heritage breed if possible. Their smaller size will facilitate frying, and the taste of the meat will be superior as well. If using a factory-farmed bird, it is best to plan on finishing the cooking in the oven to ensure that it is cooked through. While brining chicken was not traditional with the old-fashioned fried chicken cooks, many today do brine their birds to ensure tenderness and flavor.

Kansas City Pan-Fried Chicken (serves four)

Enough lard to fill a large skillet one-third full (peanut oil is an excellent option for those opposed to lard)
Salt and pepper (liberal amounts)
1 three- to four-pound chicken, cut into 9 pieces (8 if you do not wish to fry the backbone, or 11 if cutting the breasts into 4 pieces)
An egg wash made of 1 egg beaten with ¾ cup milk
Flour

Ensure the chicken is dried off and at room temperature before starting. Create an assembly line: egg wash in a shallow bowl, flour mixed with salt and pepper in a pie pan. Heat lard or oil to 350 degrees Fahrenheit (if you add a pinch of flour to the oil, it should immediately sizzle). Liberally salt and pepper chicken pieces. Dip them in the egg wash and allow the excess to drip off. Dredge the chicken thoroughly in flour, ensuring that no skin is visible.

Gently add the chicken to the hot lard, being careful never to crowd the pieces. Mrs. Dowd recommended at this point to cover the pan tightly and fry it for roughly 10 minutes to accelerate the cooking—a smart idea. Remove the pan lid and continue to cook until the pieces' undersides are coppery brown. This should take about 12 minutes, but if the pieces are browning too quickly, reduce the heat. Turn the chicken with tongs and fry on the other side at a slightly lower temperature for another 12 or so minutes. When the chicken reaches an internal temperature of 165 degrees Fahrenheit and the juices run clear when pierced in the thickest part, it is ready. Transfer the pieces to a wire rack and allow them to rest 5 or 10 minutes before serving.

HARVEY'S WESTPORT ROOM: CHICKEN MACIEL

Kansas City does not only eat fried chicken. It is a favored meat in all its guises: baked, broiled, smoked, grilled, and *en casserole*. In this last respect, "Chicken Maciel" became one of Kansas City's signature dishes. When a patron ordered it at the Westport Room in the 1950s, Joe Maciel, the maître d'hôtel, prepared it table side and served it with the accompaniment of a gong. The menu credited Maciel himself with the dish's creation and described it as such: "Large pieces of Chicken in Rich Sherry Wine Sauce flavored with Curry, served in Chafing Dish with Buttered Rice. . . . $2.85." As the rail dining cars and Harvey Houses began serving Chicken Maciel, it gained increasing popularity, and countless versions began appearing in cookbooks, newspaper articles, and family recipe files. The creation of the Internet gave rise to even more versions.

Chicken Maciel remained popular after the Westport Room closed in 1968, in part because the Maciel family opened Maciel's III, a Mexican-Continental restaurant at 4744 Rainbow Boulevard that continued to feature the dish, again accompanied by a gong when it was served. Reviewers Colin and Sylvia Clarendon noted that during that era, Chicken Maciel was "made with curry, wine, other spices, Swiss and parmesan cheese, and surrounded by mounds of tender, delicious yellow rice with an overall Mediterranean quality." They cautioned that diners "must be prepared for a hot dish, as the curry does make it spicy! It is served with a green salad and Lyolene toast that is buttered and squashed flat in a toasting machine."[17] Likely, a broiled Swiss-Parmesan cheese topping came later than Joe Maciel's original concoction, given that he prepared the dish table side. Furthermore, some recipe versions call for the rice to be blended into the chicken-cream-curry mixture as a casserole. What follows is the historic Chicken Maciel recipe, reprinted by permission from the Kansas City Museum and Union Station Kansas City. It was given to curators of these collections by Mr. Maciel's widow in 2001. In my recipe, I use two teaspoons of Madras-style curry powder, not two tablespoons, and a velouté sauce (part milk and part chicken stock) rather than a béchamel. A healthy pinch of saffron adds flavor and color to the rice, although the original recipe notes that one can substitute yellow food coloring.

Chicken Maciel (serves six liberally if accompanied by a green salad and bread)

4 medium-size chicken breasts
½ cup butter
2 tablespoons curry powder
¼ cup cream sherry wine
3 cups medium cream sauce
3 cups saffron-colored cooked rice (recipe follows)
1 cup grated Swiss cheese

Steam or simmer the chicken breasts until tender; skin and debone the meat and dice into 1-inch squares. Melt the butter. Add the curry powder, cream sherry, and chicken; sauté for 5 minutes. Add the cream sauce and bring to a full simmer to thoroughly combine the ingredients.

Ring a casserole or chafing dish with the hot rice. Pour the creamed mixture in the center and top with grated Swiss cheese. Place under broiler until lightly browned. This dish serves six.

Saffron-Colored Rice

1 cup long-grain rice
2 cups water
1 teaspoon salt
1 pinch saffron or yellow food coloring

Combine ingredients in a 1½-quart saucepan. Cook on high until steam escapes around the lid. Reduce heat to low and simmer for 30 minutes without removing the lid. Makes 3 cups steamed rice.

Notes

CHAPTER 1. "HERE STANDS A CITY BUILT O' BREAD AND BEEF": KANSAS CITY'S NATURAL AND MATERIAL RESOURCES

1. William E. Foley, *The Genesis of Missouri: From Wilderness Outpost to Statehood* (Columbia: University of Missouri Press, 1989), 7–8.

2. James Shortridge, *Kansas City and How It Grew, 1822–2011* (Lawrence: University of Kansas Press, 2012), 10–11.

3. Ibid., 2, 4.

4. Ibid., 14. Much of the following information comes from information in Shortridge's study. See also pages 14–15.

5. Jacob Ferris, *The States and Territories of the Great West* (New York: Miller, Orton, and Mulligan, 1856), 305–6.

6. Quoted in Federal Writers' Project, *Missouri: Guide to the 'Show-Me' State* (New York: Duell, Sloan and Pearce, 1941), 247.

7. Charles Nelson Glaab, *Kansas City and the Railroads: Community Policy in the Growth of a Regional Metropolis* (Lawrence: University of Kansas Press, 1993), 18.

8. Ibid., 43. This information and some of what follows relies on Glaab's research. See in particular pages 18, 40–41.

9. James Shortridge, *Kansas City and How It Grew, 1822–2011*, 34.

10. Classified advertisement, *The Christian Nation*, November 11, 1908.

11. Henry Washington Chick, "As I Remember," 1965. Missouri Valley Special Collections. Kansas City Public Library, Kansas City, Missouri.

12. James Shortridge, *Kansas City and How It Grew, 1822–2011*, 35. Information on the development of the early meatpacking industry that follows is also from Shortridge. See pages 35–36.

13. "Hereford History," *American Hereford Association*, 2015. Available at http://hereford.org/node/47.

14. Alice Lanterman, "Development of Kansas City as a Grain and Milling Center," *Missouri Historical Review* 42, no. 1 (1947): 20–21.

15. "Moving a Great Crop," *The Roller Mill* 16 (September 1897): 146.

16. Alice Lanterman, "Development of Kansas City as a Grain and Milling Center," 23–24.

17. Ibid., 32–33.

18. *Kansas City: An Intimate Portrait of the Surprising City on the Missouri* (Kansas City: Hallmark Cards, 1973), 42.

19. Francis Parkman Jr., *The Oregon Trail*, Penguin Classics Edition (New York: Penguin Books, 1982), 44.

20. When Singer bought the distillery from the Holladays, it was called Old Weston Distilling Company. The name was changed to McCormick after Singer purchased the right to the name of a neighboring distillery in Waldron, Missouri.

21. Leigh Ann Little and John M. Olinskey, *Early Kansas City, Missouri* (Charleston, SC: Arcadia Press, 2013), 69.

22. United States Geological Survey, Kansas-Missouri Floods of July 1951: Water Supply Paper 1139. 1952. http://pubs.usgs.gov/wsp/1139/report.pdf; "Flood Crest Nears Missouri Capital," *New York Times*, July 18, 1951.

23. Jimmy M. Skaggs, *Prime Cut: Livestock Raising and Meatpacking in the United States, 1607–1983* (College Station: Texas A&M University Press, 1986), 179.

24. Michael J. Broadway, "Meatpacking," in *Encyclopedia of the Great Plains*, ed. David J. Wishart (Lincoln: University of Nebraska Press, 2004), 426.

25. "The Farmer's Wheat, the Baker's Flour," *Heartland Mill*, 2010.

CHAPTER 2. PREHISTORIC AND NATIVE AMERICAN FOODWAYS OF THE KAWSMOUTH REGION

1. Elias Yanovsky, *Food Plants of the North American Indians*. U.S. Department of Agriculture, Misc. Pub. no. 237 (Washington, DC, July 1936), 10.

2. Jeannette M. Blackmar and Jack L. Hofman, "The Paleoarchaic of Kansas," in *Kansas Archaeology*, eds. Robert J. Hoard and William E. Banks (Lawrence: University of Kansas Press 2006), 58–59, 62. Information on Kawsmouth hunter-gatherer food and cooking technology comes from Blackmar and Hofman. See as well pages 47, 67, 69–70.

3. Matthew Alfs, *Edible and Medicinal Wild Plants of the Midwest* (New Brighton, MN: Old Theology Book House, 2013), 244–46.

4. Ancient horses did inhabit the Central Plains region eleven thousand years ago, but these mammals, along with mammoths, mastodons, and camels, went extinct.

5. Rudolph Waldo Wedel, *Prehistoric Man on the Great Plains* (Norman: University of Oklahoma Press, 1961), 38.

6. Brad Logan, "Woodland Adaptations in Eastern Kansas," in *Kansas Archaeology*, eds. Robert J. Hoard and William E. Banks (Lawrence: University Press of Kansas, 2006), 78.

7. It is possible that the culture lasted as late as 750 CE, but the most recent radiocarbon dating puts the likely decline of Kansas City Hopewell at around 600 CE. See Brad Logan, "Woodland Adaptations in Eastern Kansas," in *Kansas Archaeology*, 80.

8. "Ancient Times," *City of Riverside, Missouri.* http://www.riversidemo .com/community/page/ancient-times. Accessed February 12, 2015.

9. Brad Logan, "Woodland Adaptations in Eastern Kansas," 80, 85.

10. Thank you to William McFarlane, professor of archaeology at Johnson County Community College, for this helpful analogy.

11. Patricia J. O'Brien and Frances B. King, "The Yeo Site (23CL199): A Kansas City Hopewell Limited Activity Site in Northwestern Missouri and Some Theories," *Plains Anthropologist* 27 (1982): 39.

12. Sissel Johannessen, "Farmers of the Late Woodland," in *Foraging and Farming in the Eastern Woodlands*, ed. C. Margaret Scarry (Gainesville: University of Florida Press, 1993), 60.

13. Michael J. O'Brien and W. Raymond Wood, *Prehistory of Missouri* (Columbia: University of Missouri Press, 1998), 275–76.

14. Donna C. Roper, "The Central Plains Tradition," in *Kansas Archaeology*, eds. Robert J. Hoard and William E. Banks, 128.

15. Terrell L. Martin, "Prehistoric Settlement of Western Missouri during the Mississippian Period," *Missouri Archaeologist* 68 (2007): 10.

16. Matthew Alfs, *Edible and Medicinal Wild Plants of the Midwest*, 261.

17. Terrell L. Martin, "Prehistoric Settlement of Western Missouri during the Mississippian Period," 10.

18. Donna C. Roper, "The Central Plains Tradition," 118–19, 120, 128.

19. Terrell L. Martin, "Prehistoric Settlement of Western Missouri during the Mississippian Period," 3, 11.

20. As is the case with Hopewell, Steed-Kisker, and other prehistoric people, the term "Oneota" does not designate a particular tribe, but rather, a type of pottery and related artifacts.

21. Michael J. O'Brien and W. Raymond Wood, *Prehistory of Missouri*, 295; James Marshall, "The Kansa," in *Kansas Archaeology*, eds. Robert J. Hoard and

William E. Banks, 219–32, 230–31. Portions of the following pages on the Kansa are taken from Marshall's research. See also pages 220–21.

22. This Kansa oral history is verified by Henri de Tonti, Robert de La Salle's lieutenant. In 1700, he explained in a letter to his brother that the Oyo (Ohio) River was called by the natives *Akanceasipi*, the Algonquin word for "River of the Kansa." Because French explorers were familiar with Algonquin languages, they used Algonquin references.

23. David Ives Bushnell Jr., *Villages of the Algonquin, Siouan, and Caddoan Tribes West of the Mississippi* (Smithsonian Institution. Bureau of American Ethnology. Bulletin 77. Washington, DC: Government Printing Office, 1922), 82, 92–93.

24. Robert H. Lowie, *Indians of the Plains* (Lincoln: University of Nebraska Press, 1982), 40.

25. Louis F. Burns, *Osage Indian Customs and Myths* (Tuscaloosa: University of Alabama Press, 2005), 108; Melvin Gilmore, *Uses of Plants by the Indians of the Missouri River Region* (Washington, DC: U.S. Government Printing Office, 1919), 59.

26. Louis F. Burns, *Osage Indian Customs and Myths*, 109. Much of the following information on Osage foodways is taken from Burns. See also pages 110–11.

27. Robert H. Lowie, *Indians of the Plains*, 22; William E. Unrau, *The Kansa Indians: A History of the Wind People, 1673–1873* (Norman: University of Oklahoma Press, 1986), 38.

28. Edwin James, *Account of an Expedition from Pittsburgh to the Rocky Mountains* (London: Longman, Hurst, Rees, Orme and Brown, 1828), 2:136.

29. Quoted in David Ives Bushnell Jr., *Villages of the Algonquin, Siouan, and Caddoan Tribes West of the Mississippi*, 119.

30. Louis F. Burns, *Osage Indian Customs and Myths*, 121.

31. William E. Unrau, *The Kansa Indians: A History of the Wind People, 1673–1873*, 38.

32. Rudolph Waldo Wedel, *Prehistoric Man on the Great Plains*, 38.

33. Louis F. Burns, *A History of the Osage People*, 81; Kay Young, *Wild Seasons: Gathering and Cooking Wild Plants of the Great Plains* (Lincoln: University of Nebraska Press, 1993). Young's work on native edible plants and her details about Native American use of them constitute much of the information in this section of the chapter. See the following pages: 62, 69, 138–39; 150–51, 176–88, 270.

34. John Bradbury, *Travels in the Interior of America in the Years 1809, 1810, and 1811* (Liverpool: Smith and Galway, 1817), 37; Louis F. Burns, *A History of the Osage People* (Tuscaloosa: University of Alabama Press, 2004), 81.

35. Louis F. Burns, *A History of the Osage People*, 120.

36. Melvin Gilmore, *Uses of Plants by the Indians of the Missouri River Region*, 84.

37. Ibid., 85; Elias Yanovsky, *Food Plants of the North American Indians*, 49.

38. Louis F. Burns, *Osage Indian Customs and Myths*, 97.

39. William E. Unrau, *The Kansa Indians: A History of the Wind People, 1673–1873*, 30–31.

40. Louis F. Burns, *Osage Indian Customs and Myths*, 97–98.

41. Ibid., 101–2.

42. Quoted in William E. Unrau, *The Kansa Indians: A History of the Wind People, 1673–1873*, 40, 44.

CHAPTER 3. THE OLD WORLD MEETS THE NEW

1. Father Bernard Donnelly, *Scattered Sheets: Reminiscences of Father Bernard Donnelly, as Transcribed by Miss Mary Hunter, 1877* (St. Joseph: Two Trails Press, 2001), 42.

2. William E. Unrau, *The Kansa Indians: A History of the Wind People, 1673–1873*, 12–13.

3. Charles E. Hoffhaus, *Chez les Canses: Three Centuries at Kawsmouth, the French Foundations of Metropolitan Kansas City* (Kansas City: Lowell Press, 1984), 6, 11.

4. Quoted in Charles E. Hoffhaus, *Chez les Canses: Three Centuries at Kawsmouth, the French Foundations of Metropolitan Kansas City*, 10.

5. Kristie C. Wolferman, *The Osage in Missouri* (Columbia: University of Missouri Press, 1997), 20. Incidentally, many Kansas Citians affectionately call the Missouri River the "Muddy Mo" or "Big Muddy," an allusion to its original name, the *Pekittanoui*, or Muddy Water.

6. Louis F. Burns, *A History of the Osage People*, 71.

7. Quoted in Charles E. Hoffhaus, *Chez les Canses: Three Centuries at Kawsmouth, the French Foundations of Metropolitan Kansas City*, 7–8.

8. Kristie C. Wolferman, *The Osage in Missouri*, 21, 24.

9. Louis F. Burns, *A History of the Osage People*, 87, 92.

10. Pierre-Jean DeSmet, *Life, Letters and Travels of Father Pierre-Jean DeSmet, S.J. 1801–1873* (New York: Francis P. Harper, 1905), 4: 1394.

11. Ibid., 1397.

12. Louis F. Burns, *Osage Indian Customs and Myths*, 110.

13. Charles E. Hoffhaus, *Chez les Canses: Three Centuries at Kawsmouth, the French Foundations of Metropolitan Kansas City*, 34.

14. Ibid., 42, 43. The map of Fort Orleans in Hoffhaus's book gives the minutiae of the fort layout and the location of its various gardens and crops. The original *Plan du Fort d'Orleans* is housed in the Missouri Valley Special Collections, Kansas City Public Library.

15. *Cher Oncle, Cher Papa: The Letters of Francois and Berenice Chouteau*, eds. Dorothy Brandt Marra, Marie-Laure Dionne Pal, and David Boutros (Kansas City: Western Historical Manuscript Collection, 2001), 18.

16. Such was the way that the Jesuit fathers at Kaskaskia characterized these relationships with their superiors in 1713. Charles E. Hoffhaus, *Chez les Canses: Three Centuries at Kawsmouth, the French Foundations of Metropolitan Kansas City*, 31.

17. Sylvia Van Kirk, *Many Tender Ties*: *Women in Fur-Trade Society, 1670–1870* (Norman: Oklahoma University Press, 1983), 53. *Sagamité* was a stew of parched corn, cornmeal, beans, vegetables, and game flesh or brains. French settlers in Louisiana called a similar Native-inspired dish *Maquechou*.

18. Jay Gitlin, *The Bourgeois Frontier: French Towns, French Traders, and American Expansionism* (New Haven: Yale University Press, 2010), 92.

19. Tai S. Edwards, "The Osage Struggle to Survive in the Nineteenth-Century Trans-Missouri West," *Kansas History* 36 (Winter 2013–2014): 220–21.

20. Ibid., 221.

21. Louis F. Burns, *Osage Indian Customs and Myths*, 118.

22. Jay Gitlin, *The Bourgeois Frontier: French Towns, French Traders, and American Expansionism*, 106.

23. *Cher Oncle, Cher Papa: The Letters of Francois and Berenice Chouteau*, eds. Dorothy Brandt Marra, Marie-Laure Dionne Pal, and David Boutros, 48; Tanis C. Thorne, *The Many Hands of My Relations: French and Indians on the Lower Missouri* (Columbia: University of Missouri Press, 1996), 150.

24. Patricia Cleary Miller, *Westport: Missouri's Port of Many Returns* (Kansas City: Lowell Press, 1983), 38.

25. Tai S. Edwards, "The Osage Struggle to Survive in the Nineteenth-Century Trans-Missouri West," 222.

26. Louis F. Burns, *Osage Indian Customs and Myths*, 118.

27. Quoted in William E. Unrau, *The Kansa Indians: A History of the Wind People, 1673–1873*, 154.

28. Charles E. Hoffhaus, *Chez les Canses: Three Centuries at Kawsmouth, the French Foundations of Metropolitan Kansas City*, 140–41.

29. Tanis C. Thorne, *The Many Hands of My Relations: French and Indians on the Lower Missouri*, 149.

30. Gilbert J. Garraghan, *Catholic Beginnings in Kansas City: An Historical Sketch* (Chicago: Loyola University Press, 1920), 40. Many of Roux's comments on the next pages come from Garraghan's history, one of the few sources of this published correspondence. See also pages 48–49, 60–61.

31. Quoted in Tanis C. Thorne, *The Many Hands of My Relations: French and Indians on the Lower Missouri,* 152.

32. In an August 10, 1829, letter to his brother Cadet Chouteau, Francois asked him to bring Berenice two bottles of olive oil. Cadet kept his brother's tab on groceries he purchased. See Charles Van Ravensway, *Cher Oncle, Cher Papa: The Letters of Francois and Berenice Chouteau,* 60.

33. *Cher Oncle, Cher Papa: The Letters of Francois and Berenice Chouteau,* 260. Without mentioning Father Roux, Charles Van Ravensway went into detail about the popular Missouri French balls of the sort that Father Roux criticized. See Charles van Ravensway, "Missouri Cookery," *Bulletin of the Missouri Historical Society* 3 (1946–1947): 53.

34. Quoted in Tanis C. Thorne, *The Many Hands of My Relations: French and Indians on the Lower Missouri,* 153.

35. Ibid.

36. Bernard Donnelly, *Notes from Scattered Sheets: Reminiscences of Father Bernard Donnelly, as Transcribed by Miss Mary Hunter, 1877,* 101–2.

37. Charles Van Ravensway, "Missouri Cookery," 53–54.

38. The history of Westport and early Kansas City settlement that informs my history comes from Patricia Cleary Miller's *Westport: Missouri's Port of Many Returns.* See the chapter "Boom Town (1833–1860)."

39. Edward R. Schauffler, "Westport's No. 1 Romance," *Swing* (November 1945): 37.

40. Carrie Westlake Whitney, *Kansas City, Missouri: Its History and Its People 1808–1908* (Chicago: S. J. Clarke Publishing Co., 1908), 1: 651.

41. William D. Grant, *Romantic Past of the Kansas City Region, 1540–1880* (Kansas City: Business Men's Assurance Company of America, 1987), 34.

42. Nellie McCoy Harris, "Memories of Old Westport," *Annals of Kansas City* 1, no. 4 (1947): 470–71.

43. Carrie Westlake Whitney, *Kansas City, Missouri: Its History and Its People 1808–1908,* 1: 645–46. Information on bees and dining days come from Whitney's history. See also volume 1, page 652.

44. Nellie McCoy Harris, "Memories of Old Westport," 471–72, 474; Carrie Westlake Whitney, *Kansas City, Missouri: Its History and Its People 1808–1908,* I: 652.

45. Charles Carroll Spalding, *Annals of the Kansas of Kansas* (Kansas City: Van Horn & Abeel's Printing House, 1858), 19–21.

CHAPTER 4. CONTRIBUTING TO
KANSAS CITY'S GREATER GOOD:
IMMIGRANTS AND THEIR FOOD TRADITIONS

1. Keith J. Guenther Jr., "The Development of Mexican-American Cuisine," *National and Regional Styles of Cookery: Proceedings. Oxford Symposium*, ed. Alan Davidson (Oxford: Oxford University Press, 1981), 268.

2. Ibid., 268, 270.

3. Thomas Pinney, *A History of Wine in America: From Prohibition to the Present* (Berkeley: University of California Press, 1989), 236.

4. Keith J. Guenther Jr., "The Development of Mexican-American Cuisine," 268–69. Guenther does not discuss Kansas City or Kawsmouth, but I speculate that when mission fathers made their trips to Mexico City to stock up on such foods, their value made them lucrative trade items for a continued journey north along the Santa Fe Trail, and hence, through Westport.

5. Daniel Serda, "Finding Latin Roots: Hispanic Heritage in Kansas City," *Kansas Preservation* 33, no. 3 (2011): 9–10.

6. Chef Jesse Vega, interview with the author regarding Kansas City Hispanic foodways, September 20, 2014.

7. Charles Ferruzza, "King of Tamale, " *KC Pitch* (July 5, 2001), http://www .pitch.com/kansascity/king-of-tamale/Content?oid=2163635.

8. Gina Marie Zarrin-Kia, June 7, 2013, comment regarding Jim's Tamales on Facebook group *Things and Places We Loved in Greater KC When We Were Much Younger*. Accessed May 5, 2015.

9. Jim's Tamales closed for good in August 2013, although up until 2015, John David DiCapo sold Jim's Famous Hot Tamales wholesale to grocery stores and some restaurants after he purchased a licensing agreement with Jim Van Zant III, Jim Shepard's grandson. As of this writing, John David DiCapo's business is for sale, and the future of Jim's Famous Hot Tamales uncertain.

10. Keith J. Guenther Jr., "The Development of Mexican-American Cuisine," 273.

11. Chef Jesse Vega, interview with the author on Hispanic foodways, September 20, 2014; Chef Jess Barbosa, telephone interview with the author, March 27, 2015.

12. *Manny's Mexican Restaurant of Kansas City* (2013), http://www.mannyskc .com.

13. Patrick O'Neill, *From the Bottom Up: The Story of the Irish in Kansas City* (Kansas City: Seat O' the Pants Publishing, 2000), 17.

14. William V. Shannon, *The American Irish: A Political and Social Portrait* (Amherst: University of Massachusetts Press, 1989), 8.

15. John Livingston Wright, "Kitchen Racket," *Down the Road with a Tramp Writer, Poems* (Boston: Black Lion Press, 1909), 56.

16. Pat O'Neill, *From the Bottom Up: The Story of the Irish in Kansas City*, 51.

17. Ibid., 123. O'Neill's book is the most comprehensive study of Irish roots of Kansas City, and much of the information on the next pages comes from O'Neill's book. See 59–60, 85, 93, 110, 141, and 190–91.

18. "Thomas Joseph Pendergast (1872–1945)," Historical Society of Missouri, Historic Missourians. University of Missouri, http://shs.umsystem.edu/historicmissourians/name/p/pendergast/.

19. Dorothy J. Caldwell, "Christmas in Early Missouri," *Missouri Historical Review* 65, no. 2 (1971): 128.

20. James Shortridge, *Kansas City and How it Grew, 1822–2011*, 26.

21. Quoted in Rick Montgomery and Shirl Kasper, *Kansas City: An American Story* (Kansas City: Kansas City Star Books, 1999), 44–45.

22. *One Hundred Years of Brewing: A Complete History of the Progress Made in the Art, Science and Industry of Brewing* (Chicago: H. S. Rich & Company, 1901), 218; H. James Maxwell and Bob Sullivan Jr., *Hometown Beer: A History of Kansas City Breweries* (Kansas City: Omega Innovative Marketing, 1999), 124.

23. Brian Burnes, Dan Viets, Robert W. Butler, *Walt Disney's Missouri: The Roots of a Creative Genius* (Kansas City: Kansas City Star Books, 2002), 51.

24. James Maxwell and Bob Sullivan Jr., *Hometown Beer: A History of Kansas City Breweries*, 272–74.

25. *Boulevard Brewery* (2015), http://www.boulevard.com/.

26. Dennis Boone, "All in the Family," *Ingram's Magazine* (2000–2015), www.ingrams.com/article/all-in-the-family/.

27. *Andre's Confiserie Suisse* (2013), http://andreschocolates.com.

28. "About KC Chefs," *American Culinary Federation Greater Kansas City Chefs Association* (2014–2015), http://acf.kcchefs.org/about-kc-chefs/; Obituary: Klaus H. Sack, January 18, 1936–July 7, 2014, Chapel Hill Memorial Funeral Home, Kansas City, July 7, 2014.

29. James Shortridge, *Kansas City and How It Grew, 1822–2011*, 90; "Virtual Jewish World: Kansas City, Kansas/Missouri," *Jewish Virtual Library* (2015). This website noted that the first Jewish board of trade member joined in 1869: http://www.jewishvirtuallibrary.org/jsource/vjw/kansascity.html.

30. *Social Prospectus of Greater Kansas City, Missouri* (Kansas City: Research Bureau of the Board of Public Welfare, 1913), 11.

31. James Shortridge, *Kansas City and How It Grew, 1822–2011*, 90; *Social Prospectus of Kansas City, Missouri*, 54.

32. Calvin Trillin, *Messages from My Father* (New York: Farrar, Straus and Giroux, 1996), 48, 101–2.

33. "Open Today!" Advertisement for Bretton's. *Kansas City Times* (October 27, 1949), 29; Charles Ferruzza, "Kansas City Loved Polynesian Cuisine—It Still Does," *KC Pitch* (November 4, 2014), http://www.pitch.com/FastPitch/archives/2014/11/04/kansas-city-loved-polynesian-cuisine-it-still-does.

34. David Sax, *Save the Deli: In Search of Perfect Pastrami, Crusty Rye, and the Heart of Jewish Delicatessen* (Toronto: McClelland and Stewart, 2009), 111–12.

35. James Shortridge, *Kansas City and How It Grew, 1822–2011*, 90–91.

36. Ibid., 90–91; Terence O'Malley, "Black Hand Strawman: The History of Organized Crime in Kansas City" (lecture, Kansas City Public Library, Kansas City, Missouri, January 15, 2012).

37. Ronald Miriani, *Kansas City's City Market* (Kansas City: Kansas City Public Library, 2007), 10.

38. James Shortridge, *Kansas City and How It Grew, 1822–2011*, 91.

39. Hasia R. Diner, *Hungering for America: Italian, Irish, and Jewish Foodways in the Age of Migration* (Cambridge: Harvard University Press, 2001), 34, 43.

40. John Mariani, *How Italian Food Conquered the World* (New York: Palgrave Macmillan, 2011), 37.

41. *Cascone's Italian Restaurants*, 2014, http://www.cascones.com/; Joyce Smith, "Cascone's Remains a North Oak Landmark," *Kansas City Star*, 816 Business section (December 23, 2014).

42. The heritage and importance of Jasper's Restaurant to Kansas City is detailed in Jasper Mirabile Jr., *Jasper's Kitchen Cookbook: Italian Recipes and Memories from Kansas City's Legendary Restaurant* (Kansas City: Andrews McMeel Publishing, 2009). See in particular the preface, "A Love Affair with Jasper's" by Josephine Mirabile, and chapter 1, "In the Beginning," by Jasper Mirabile Jr.

43. Charles Ferruzza and Jonathan Bender, "KC's Bakeries Turn Up the Flour Power," *KC Pitch* (May 15, 2012), http://www.pitch.com/kansascity/kansas-city-bakeries-artisan-bread/Content?oid=2881235&showFullText=true; *Roma Bakery* (2004), http://www.romabakerykc.com.

44. Joyce Smith, "Scimeca's Market Has a New Name," *Kansas City Star* (November 30, 2001).

45. James Shortridge, *Kansas City and How It Grew, 1822–2011*, 95–96.

46. Doug Worgul, *A Table Full of Welcome: A Cookbook Celebrating Kansas City's Culinary Diversity* (Kansas City: Kansas City Star Books, 2002), 53. The story of Joe Krizman Sr. is told in Worgul's book. See also *Krizman's House of Sausage* at http://www.krizmansausage.com.

47. Shirl Kasper, "All in the Family: A Third Generation of Krizmans Is Making Sausage in KCK," *Kansas City Star*, *Star Magazine* (June 2, 1996); Jill Wendholt Silva, "Peter May's House of Kielbasa Is a Family Affair," *Kansas City Star* (May 5, 2014).

48. Tammy Ljungblad,"Strawberry Hill Povitica Breads," *KansasCityStar-Video*. YouTube. May 4, 2014.

49. "Asian Community in Kansas City," *Visit KC* (*Kansas City Convention & Visitors Association*), 2015, https://www.visitkc.com/visitors/discover/diversity/asian-community-kansas-city.

50. Huping Ling, *Chinese St. Louis: From Enclave to Cultural Community* (Philadelphia: Temple University Press, 2004), 233. Charles Ferruzza examined the 1900 *City Directory* and the 1909 *City Directory*. It would appear that in that decade, the number of Chinese restaurants went from zero to seven, including King Joy Lo. See "Global Grub," *KC Pitch* (May 24, 2006), http://www.pitch.com/kansascity/global-grub/Content?oid=2185403.

51. Sherrie A. Inness, *Dinner Roles: American Women and Culinary Culture* (Ames: University of Iowa Press, 2001), 103–4.

52. The earliest mention of King Joy Lo that I could find came from a September 20, 1907, *Kansas City Times* advertisement that gave the restaurant's address at 1217 Grand and touted the health-giving qualities of King Joy Lo's food. A reprinted article from the *Kansas City Journal*, dated January 11, 1908, reported a robbery at the restaurant when it was managed by F. G. Lee. Available at Vintage Kansas City, http://www.vintagekansascity.com/100yearsago/2009/01/stick-up-man-robs-restaurant-at-2-m.html; "King Joy Lo." *Things and Places We Loved in Greater KC When We Were Much Younger*.

53. Pat Price, "Old Restaurants Never Die: Famous Flavors Capture Dining Pleasures of Bygone Restaurants," *Kansas City Star*, metropolitan edition, February 3, 1999.

54. Obituary, Billy Chill Von Choi. McGilley & Hoge Johnson County Memorial Chapel, Overland Park, Kansas, March 8, 2011.

55. Colin Clarendon and Sylvia Clarendon, *Clarendon Guide to Kansas City Restaurants* (Memphis: C & S Enterprises, 1982), 99.

56. Carl J. DiCapo, in discussion with the author on Italian foodways and the North End, July 22, 2014.

CHAPTER 5. AFRICAN AMERICAN CONTRIBUTIONS AND KANSAS CITY'S SOUTHERN TRADITIONS

1. Meriwether Lewis and William Clark, *The Journals of Lewis and Clark*, ed. Bernard DeVoto (New York: Houghton Mifflin, 1997), 7.

2. John Mason Peck, *Forty Years a Pioneer: Memoir of John Mason Peck, D.D.*, ed. Rufus Babcock (Philadelphia: American Baptist Publication Society, 1864), 146.

3. Rose M. Nolen, *Hoecakes, Hambone, and All that Jazz: African American Traditions in Missouri* (Columbia: University of Missouri Press, 2003), 22.

4. Dorothy J. Caldwell, "Christmas in Early Missouri," *Missouri Historical Review* 65, no. 2 (1971): 131, 134–35.

5. Nellie McCoy Harris, "Memories of Old Westport," *Annals of Kansas City* 1, no. 4 (1947): 467–68.

6. Charles Coulter, *"Take up the Black Man's Burden": Kansas City's African American Communities, 1865–1939* (Columbia: University of Missouri Press, 2006), 20; Rick Montgomery and Shirl Kasper, *Kansas City: An American Story*, 37.

7. Nellie McCoy Harris, "Memories of Old Westport," 465; Louis O. Honig, *Westport: Gateway to the Early West* (North Kansas City, MO: Industrial Press, 1950), 31.

8. Carrie Westlake Whitney, *Kansas City, Missouri: Its History and Its People 1808–1908* (Chicago: S. J. Clarke Publishers, 1908), I: 651–52.

9. Tricia Martineau Wagner, *It Happened on the Oregon Trail: Remarkable Events That Shape History*, 2nd ed. (Guilford, CT: Globe Pequot Press, 2014), 143–44; "African-American Historic Sites of Independence, Walking/Driving Tour," Independence, Missouri. *City of Independence, Missouri* (2015), http://www.ci.independence.mo.us/UserDocs/ComDev/afam_historic_sites%20 web%20version_6_14.pdf; William H. and Nathan B. Young Jr., *Your Kansas City and Mine*, 1950, repr. ed. with added index (Kansas City: Midwest Afro-American Genealogy Interest Coalition, 1997), 8, 118.

10. Poppy Cannon and Patricia Brooks, *The President's Cookbook: Practical Recipes from George Washington to the Present* (New York: Funk and Wagnalls, 1968), 449.

11. Quoted in Charles E. Coulter, *"Take Up the Black Man's Burden": Kansas City's African American Communities, 1865–1939*, 18.

12. Ibid., 70–71; Sonny Gibson, ed., *Kansas City Early Negro History* (Kansas City: Mecca Enterprises, 2014), 82.

13. Servants, laundresses, and laundry operatives were the top three occupations for African American women during this era. See Charles E. Coulter, *"Take Up the Black Man's Burden": Kansas City's African American Communities, 1865–1939*, 81.

14. Evan S. Connell, *Mr. Bridge* (New York: Alfred A. Knopf, 1969), 13.

15. Melvin B. Tolson, *Caviar and Cabbage: Selected Columns by Melvin B. Tolson from the* Washington Tribune, *1937–1944*, ed. Robert M. Farnsworth (Columbia: University of Missouri Press, 1982), 264–65.

16. Ibid., 264.

17. Charles E. Coulter, *"Take Up the Black Man's Burden": Kansas City's African American Communities, 1865–1939*, 62, 64.

18. Doug Worgul, *The Grand Barbecue: A Celebration of the History, Places, Personalities and Techniques of Kansas City Barbecue* (Kansas City: Kansas City Star Books, 2001), 60.

19. Carrie Westlake Whitney, *Kansas City, Missouri: Its History and Its People 1808–1908,* I: 657.

20. Doug Worgul, *The Grand Barbecue: A Celebration of the History, Places, Personalities and Techniques of Kansas City Barbecue*, 12; Patrick O'Neill, *From the Bottom Up: The Story of the Irish in Kansas City*, 37.

21. Quoted in Doug Worgul, *The Grand Barbecue: A Celebration of the History, Places, Personalities and Techniques of Kansas City Barbecue*, 47.

22. "Henry Perry Has Cooked Good Barbecue for 50 Years," *Kansas City Call*, February 26, 1932; "Henry Perry, The Barbecue King Is Dead," *Kansas City Call*, March 29, 1940.

23. "Henry Perry Has Cooked Good Barbecue for 50 Years," *Kansas City Call*, February 26, 1932.

24. "Henry Perry, The Barbecue King Is Dead," *Kansas City Call*, March 29, 1940.

25. Sonny Gibson, ed., *Kansas City Early Negro History*. Gibson's book is a compendium of primary source documents (articles, advertisements, and photographs) from Kansas City African American history during the Jim Crow era. Numerous Perry barbecue advertisements are found in this collection. See for example page 282.

26. Michael Sweeney, former collection librarian for the Black Archives of Mid-America, in discussion with the author, January 13, 2015.

27. Advertisements, *Kansas City Sun*, September 9, 1916; Sonny Gibson, ed. *Kansas City Early Negro History* 172, 292, 308, 393, 408.

28. Rick Montgomery and Shirl Kasper, *Kansas City: An American Story*, 184.

29. "Death to Popular Barbecue Man, 60: Illness Fatal to Charles L. Bryant," *Kansas City Call*, October 17, 1952.

30. Arthur Bryant interview, ca. 1980, Black Archives of Mid-America, Kansas City, Missouri.

31. "Death to Popular Barbecue Man, 60: Illness Fatal to Charles L. Bryant," *Kansas City Call*, October 17, 1952; quoted in Doug Worgul, *The Grand Barbecue: A Celebration of the History, Places, Personalities and Techniques of Kansas City Barbecue*, 25.

32. Vince Staten and Greg Johnson, *Real Barbecue: The Classic Barbecue Guide to the Best Joints Across the USA* (Lanham, MD: Rowman & Littlefield, 2007), 181.

33. Doug Worgal, *The Grand Barbecue: A Celebration of the History, Places, Personalities and Techniques of Kansas City Barbecue*, 21.

34. Michael Sweeney, Former Collection Librarian for the Black Archives of Mid-America, interview with the author, January 13, 2015.

35. *National Register of Historic Places*, U.S. Department of the Interior Multiple Property Documentation Form. "Historic Resources of the 18th and Vine Area of Kansas City, Missouri," July 22, 1991, http://dnr.mo.gov/shpo/nps-nr/84004142.pdf.

36. Stanley Crouch, *Kansas City Lightning: The Rise and Times of Charlie Parker* (New York: HarperCollins, 2013), 188.

37. Ross Russell, *Jazz Style in Kansas City and the Southwest* (Berkeley: University of California Press, 1971), 21–22.

38. Quoted in Nathan W. Pearson Jr., *Goin' to Kansas City* (Urbana: University of Illinois Press, 1987), 207.

39. Ibid., 95.

40. Stanley Crouch, *Kansas City Lightning: The Rise and Times of Charlie Parker*, 219–20.

41. "Club Reno, aka the Reno Club," *Club Kaycee. Kansas City Jazz History*. 1996. University of Missouri-Kansas City Library Special Collections, http://library.umkc.edu/spec-col/club-kaycee/JAZZSPOT/clubreno.htm; Ross Russell, *Bird Lives: The High Life and Hard Times of Charlie (Yardbird) Parker*, reprinted ed. (Jackson, TN: DaCapo Press, 1996), 51. References are from the DeCapo Press edition.

42. Ross Russell, *Bird Lives: The High Life and Hard Times of Charlie (Yardbird) Parker*, 52–53.

43. Quoted in Nathan W. Pearson Jr., *Goin' to Kansas City*, 2–3.

44. Ross Russell, *Jazz Style in Kansas City and the Southwest*, 25.

45. Stanley Crouch, *Kansas City Lightning: The Rise and Times of Charlie Parker*, 217–18.

46. John Dawson, post in *Kansas City Memories . . . Vintage Photos, Places, and Things Remembered.* Facebook group. December 18, 2014.

47. Charles Broomfield, personal reminiscence, interview with the author, August 13, 2014.

48. "Spook" in this context referred to people who never went to bed, who preferred to be out with the "spooks" after dark. Stanley Crouch, *Kansas City Lightning: The Rise and Times of Charlie Parker*, 218.

49. Quoted in Frank Driggs and Chuck Haddix, *Kansas City Jazz: From Ragtime to Bebop* (Oxford: Oxford University Press, 2005), 25.

50. "New Street's [sic] Hotel Attracts Keen Interest," *Kansas City Call*, December 9, 1949. Ramos Vertical File—Kansas City. Missouri Valley Special Collections. Kansas City Public Library.

51. "Reuben S. Street. In Memoriam." Monday, August 20, 1956. Funeral brochure, Watkins Brothers Chapel, Black Archives of Mid-America; Charles E. Coulter, *"Take Up the Black Man's Burden": Kansas City's African American Communities, 1865–1939*, 121.

52. Buck O'Neil with Steve Wulf and David Conrads, *I Was Right on Time: My Journey from the Negro Leagues to the Majors* (New York: Simon & Schuster, 1996), 75.

53. "New Street's [sic.] Hotel Attracts Keen Interest," *Kansas City Call*, December 9, 1949. Ramos Vertical File—Kansas City. Missouri Valley Special Collections. Kansas City Public Library.

54. *Directory of Colored Residents: Kansas City Missouri, 1937–38.* Black Archives of Mid-America, Kansas City Public Library, Kansas City, Missouri.

55. Radio interview with Sonny Gibson, hosted by Gina Kaufmann, "Unearthed Documents and Memorabilia Tell a Story of Race in Kansas City," *Central Standard.* KCUR. December 2, 2014; "Henry Perry Has Cooked Good Barbecue for 50 Years," *Kansas City Call*, February 26, 1932.

56. Lolis Eric Elie, *Smokestack Lightning: Adventures in the Heart of Barbecue Country* (New York: Farrar, Straus, and Giroux, 1996), 145.

57. Buck O'Neil with Steve Wulf and David Conrads, *I Was Right on Time: My Journey from the Negro Leagues to the Majors*, 197.

58. Thomas Frank, "A Machine for Forgetting: Kansas City and the Declining Significance of Place," *Baffler* no. 7, 1995, http://www.thebaffler.com/salvos/a-machine-for-forgetting; Richard Rhodes, "Cupcake Land. Requiem for the Midwest in the Key of Vanilla," *Harpers*, November 1986, *Harper's Archive*, http://harpers.org/archive/1987/11/cupcake-land-requiem-for-the-midwest-in-the-key-of-vanilla/.

59. Sherry Lamb Schirmer, *A City Divided: The Racial Landscape of Kansas City, 1900–1960* (Columbia: University of Missouri Press, 2002), 191–95; 218.

Lamb's monograph, particularly Chapter 7, does a masterful job of detailing this era in Kansas City history. My account of COPOD activity and strategy is taken from her.

60. Quoted in Rick Montgomery and Shirl Kasper, *Kansas City: An American Story*, 291; "Surprise Sit-In at Restaurant. Owner Closes for Day after Quiet Demonstration," *Kansas City Times*, June 21, 1963; Donald Jason, "Kansas City Vote Widens Bias Law," *New York Times*, April 8, 1964.

61. Sherry Lamb Schirmer, *A City Divided: The Racial Landscape of Kansas City, 1900–1960*, 220.

62. Quoted in Cindy Hoedel, "Remembering the Day 'Everything Changed,'" *Kansas City Star*, June 28, 2014, http://www.kansascity.com/news/special-reports/civil-rights-act-turns-50/article614480.html.

63. Calvin Trillin, "No! One of the World's Foremost Authorities on Ribs, Cheeseburger, French Fries and Frosty Malts Takes a Gourmet Tour of Kansas City," *Playboy Magazine*, April 1972, 108.

64. John Mariani, *America Eats Out: An Illustrated History of Restaurants, Taverns, Coffee Shops, Speakeasies, and Other Establishments That Have Fed Us for 350 Years* (New York: William Morrow, 1991), 239. Mariani's study speaks to the wider culinary context that helped explain recent food trends in Kansas City. See Chapter 15, "America Hurrah!"

65. Phil Mullin, Post in *Things and Places We Loved in Greater Kansas City When We Were Younger*. Facebook group. July 22, 2011.

CHAPTER 6. KANSAS CITY MARKETS AND GROCERIES

1. Louis O. Honig, *Westport: Gateway to the Early West* (North Kansas City: Industrial Press, 1950), 31.

2. The bulk of information on the Ewing-Boone Building comes from archives in Kansas City Public Library's Missouri Valley Special Collections. See Vertical File: Boone Trading Post. See in particular Katherine B. Moore's "Boone's Trading Post," *Kansas City Star*, October 10, 1959, Jim Lapham's "Our Most Historic Building—and Oldest Saloon," and William A. Goff's "The Ewing-Boone Building in Old Westport." Also helpful is "Tours of Historic Westport," Westport Historical Society web page, available at http://westporthistorical.com/. Accessed May 15, 2015.

3. William A. Goff, "The Ewing-Boone Building in Old Westport," Vertical File: Boone Trading Post.

4. Daniel Coleman, "Biography of Charles E. Kearney (1820–1898), Outfitter," Missouri Valley Special Collections, 2008, Kansas City Public Library,

http://www.kchistory.org/cdm4/item_viewer.php?CISOROOT=/Biographies&
CISOPTR=244&CISOBOX=1&REC=1. Dorothy Caldwell, "Christmas in Early
Missouri," *Missouri Historical Review* 65, no. 2 (1971): 131–32.

5. Quoted in Dorothy Caldwell, "Christmas in Early Missouri," 131–32.

6. Walter Wohleking, "From Research to Model: The Stilwell Oyster Car,"
The Cannonball 44, no. 3 (2014): 1, 4–5; "Arthur E. Stilwell," Pullman State
Historic Site, October 2009, *Pullman Museum*, http://www.pullman-museum
.org/theCompany/stillwell.html; Daniel Coleman, "Arthur E. Stilwell, Railroad
President, 1859–1928," Missouri Valley Special Collections, 2008, Kansas City
Public Library, http://www.kchistory.org/cdm4/item_viewer.php?CISOROOT=/
Biographies&CISOPTR=198&CISOBOX=1&REC=13.

7. James R. Shortridge, *Kansas City and How It Grew, 1822–2011*, 18.

8. Charles C. Spalding, *Annals of the City of Kansas* (Kansas City: Van Horn
& Abel's Printing House, 1858), 37.

9. Ronald Miriani, *Kansas City's City Market* (Kansas City: Kansas City
Public Library, 2007), 10.

10. Ibid.,11.

11. "Whyte Brothers Grocery," *Kansas City Times*, December 19, 1971, clipping in the Mrs. Sam Ray Postcard Collection, Missouri Valley Special Collections, Kansas City Public Library; "Extra Special! Notice" [Whyco Store adver-
tisement], *Kansas City Times*, March 14, 1921.

12. Daniel Coleman, "Fred Wolferman, Owner, Wolferman's Gourmet Grocery, 1870–1955," Missouri Valley Special Collections, 2008, Kansas City Public Library, http://www.kchistory.org/cdm4/item_viewer.php?CISOROOT=/Bio
graphies&CISOPTR=273&CISOBOX=1&REC=3; Jason Roe, "Muffin Man,"
This Week in Kansas City History, blog, Kansas City Public Library, http://
www.kclibrary.org/blog/week-kansas-city-history/muffin-man; "Fred Wolferman's Kansas City Coffers Are Filled with Dough Thanks to His Mega-Muffins,"
People Archive, *People*, March 17, 1986, http://www.people.com/people/archive/
article/0,,20093183,00.html.

13. Ardie A. Davis, "McGonigle's: A Chow Town Icon Known for Its Meat,
Barbecue," *Kansas City Star*, June 19, 2014; *McGonigle's*, June 16, 2015, https://
www.mcgonigles.com/; Joyce Smith,"Ball's Grocery Chain Plans Local Expansion," *Kansas City Star*, July 2, 1998.

14. David Ball interview, Johnson County Community College, Overland Park,
Kansas, June 7, 2010. *YouTube*, https://www.youtube.com/watch?v=Fs4u989Rkyc;
Jerry LaMartina, "Balls Food Stores Will Beef Up Hen House Website," *Kansas
City Business Journal*, April 15, 2008; Joyce Smith, "Ball's Grocery Plans Local
Expansion," *Kansas City Star*, July 2, 1998; Barbara A. Washington, "Ball's Tries
New Hen House Concept in Johnson County," *Kansas City Business Journal*, Sep-

tember 24, 1990; Steve Porter, "Hen House to Get on the Ball, Ball's Super Stores, That Is," *Kansas City Business Journal*, August 21, 1989.

15. "Stover, Clara (1893–1975); Stover, Russell (1888–1954)," *Dictionary of Missouri Biography*, eds. Lawrence O. Christensen et. al. (Columbia: University of Missouri, 1999), 728–29; Daniel Coleman, "Clara and Russell Stover, Candy Makers," Missouri Valley Special Collections, 2008, Kansas City Public Library, http://www.kchistory.org/cdm4/item_viewer.php?CISOROOT=/Biographies& CISOPTR=128&CISOBOX=1&REC=1; Rosemary Haward, "Candy from Kansas City," *Swing*, November 1947, 17–19.

16. Rosemary Haward, "Candy from Kansas City," *Swing*, November 1947, 17–19; Charles Ferruzza, "A Sugar Binge," *KC Pitch*, November 9, 2006, http://www.pitch.com/kansascity/a-sugar-binge/Content?oid=2183594.

17. Quoted in Steve Almond, *Candyfreak: A Journey through the Chocolate Underbelly of America* (Chapel Hill, NC: Algonquin Books, 2004), 192.

18. Ronald Miriani, *Kansas City's City Market* (Kansas City: Kansas City Public Library, 2007), 22–23.

CHAPTER 7. "KANSAS CITY, HERE I COME": HISTORIC RESTAURANTS AT AMERICA'S CROSSROADS, 1860s-1970s

1. Felicia Hardison Londré, *The Enchanted Years of the Stage: Kansas City at the Crossroads of American Theater, 1870–1930* (Columbia: University of Missouri Press, 2007), 42–43, 110.

2. "Coates House Hotel," *Kansas City Times*, March 7, 1981, clipping in the Mrs. Sam Ray Postcard Collection, Missouri Valley Special Collections, Kansas City Public Library.

3. While no known Coates à la carte menu exists, many banquet menus do, housed in the Missouri Valley Special Collections at Kansas City Public Library, as well as in numerous contemporary publications, including *The Hotel Monthly*. See also "The Kansas City Banquet," *Michigan Argonaut* 8, no. 26 (May 17, 1890): 220.

4. Felicia Hardison Londré, *The Enchanted Years of the Stage: Kansas City at the Crossroads of American Theater, 1870–1930*, 264–65.

5. "Baltimore Hotel Pompeian Room," *Kansas City Times*, March 4, 1972, clipping in the Mrs. Sam Ray Postcard Collection, Missouri Valley Special Collections, Kansas City Public Library.

6. "Lobster Baltimore in a Chafing Dish," "Assorted Hors D'Oeuvre Baltimore," *International Cooking Library*, 1–5 (1913): 43, 22, 40. *Google Books*,

https://books.google.com/books?id=ljkyAQAAMAAJ&pg=PA10&dq=French+
Chef+Adrian+Delvaux&hl=en&sa=X&ei=PcAWVZzbJ4ecgwTv9oG4AQ&ved
=0CDEQ6AEwAA#v=onepage&q=Adrian%20Delvaux&f=true.

7. Baltimore Hotel, menu, undated. Missouri Valley Special Collections, Kansas City Public Library.

8. Felicia Hardison Londré, *The Enchanted Years of the Stage: Kansas City at the Crossroads of American Theater, 1870–1930*, 244–45.

9. William R. Reddig, *Tom's Town: Kansas City and the Pendergast Legend* (Columbia: University of Missouri Press, 1986), 90.

10. Frank Driggs and Chuck Haddix, *Kansas City Jazz: From Ragtime to Bebop, A History* (Oxford: Oxford University Press, 2005), 22.

11. *Star Magazine Presents: The Best of Remember When: 100 Warm Tales of Life as We Lived It*, ed. Ronda Cornelius (Kansas City: Kansas City Star Books, 2001), 195.

12. Felicia Hardison Londré, *The Enchanted Years of the Stage: Kansas City at the Crossroads of American Theater, 1870–1930,* 245.

13. Quoted in Charles Ferruzza, "The End of a Restaurant Dynasty: Bob Gaines, 1951–2010," *KC Pitch*, August 11, 2010, http://www.pitch.com/FastPitch/archives/2010/08/11/the-end-of-a-restaurant-dynasty-bob-gaines-1951-2010.

14. Karen Gaines, daughter of Ralph Gaines, telephone interview with the author, April 21, 2015.

15. Unless otherwise stated, information on the Italian Gardens comes from Carl J. DiCapo, John David DiCapo, and Frank R. Hayde, *Italian Gardens: A History of Kansas City through Its Favorite Restaurant* (Kansas City, 2010), 8–9, 47, 29, 30, 24.

16. John Mariani, *America Eats Out: An Illustrated History of Restaurants, Taverns, Coffee Shops, Speakeasies, and Other Establishments That Have Fed Us for 350 Years* (New York: William Morrow, 1991), 116.

17. Ibid., 120.

18. Richard B. Fowler, *Leaders in Our Town* (Kansas City: Burd & Fletcher, 1952), 185–88.

19. Rick Greenberg, Valorie Montavy, Judith Cammack, Facebook posts, January 15, March 6, 2015, *Things and Places We Loved in Greater KC When We Were Much Younger.*

20. Stephen Fried, *Appetite for America: How Visionary Businessman, Fred Harvey Built a Railroad Hospitality Empire* (New York, Random House, 2011), 226.

21. Fred Harvey Breakfast Menu, undated; Joe Maciel Menu Collection, Edna Binkley Collection; Kansas City Museum and Union Station; Kansas City Fred

Harvey Lunchroom Menu, Wednesday, January 29, 1958, Harvey House Museum, Belen, New Mexico.

22. Harvey chefs are listed along with signature dishes in George H. Foster and Peter C. Weiglin's *Harvey House Cookbook: Memories of Dining along the Santa Fe Railroad* (Lanham: Taylor Trade Publishing, imprint of Rowman & Littlefield, 1992).

23. Virginia L. Grattan, *Mary Coulter: Builder Upon the Red Earth* (Flagstaff: Grand Canyon Association, 1992), 95; "Cocktail Room at Station, Main Dining Room Will Be Remodeled and Redecorated," *Kansas City Star*, July 16, 1936.

24. "Centenario de Union Station Celebra Famoso Camareo" ["Union Station Centennial Celebrating Famed Waiter"], *Dos Mundos*, October 2014; Colin Clarendon and Sylvia Clarendon, *Clarendon Guide to Kansas City Restaurants* (Memphis, TN: C&S Enterprises, 1982), 122–23; Denise Morrison, director of historical collections, Kansas City Museum, interview with the author, April 3, 2015; Pat Price, "Old Restaurants Never Die," *Kansas City Star*, February 3, 1999.

25. Joseph William (Bill) Gilbert, interview with the author, April 25, 2015.

26. C. R. McAlister, "Flying Mail" column, *Flying Magazine*, May 1992, 15.

27. Jan Whitaker, *Tea at the Blue Lantern Inn: A Social History of the Tea Room Craze in America* (New York: St. Martin's Press, 2002).

28. "Tea House by the Side of the Road—9 East 45th," *Swing* 1 (January 1945).

29. Lina Bureman, "Kansas City Homecoming," *Kansas City Stories, Local History*. Missouri Valley Special Collections, Kansas City Public Library, July 26, 2008, http://www.kclibrary.org/kchistory/kansas-city-homecoming.

30. Quoted in Jacquie Lehatto, "Resolve, Refinement Central to Her: Dora Adelman, Owner of the Wishbone Restaurant," *Kansas City Star*, November 27, 2007.

31. "Best Home-Grown Product: Wishbone Salad Dressing," Best of Kansas City, 2000, *KC Pitch* (2015), http://www.pitch.com/kansascity/best-home-grown -product/BestOf?oid=2209963; "The Wish-Bone Story," Wish-Bone, 2013–2015: http://www.wish-bone.com; Jane Flynn, *A Taste of Kansas City: Then and Now* (Kansas City: Children's Center for the Visually Impaired, 2003).

32. *National Register of Historic Places Nomination Form*, U.S. Department of the Interior Multiple Property Documentation Form, "Compton, Dr. James Residence," January 23, 1979, http://dnr.mo.gov/shpo/nps-nr/79003677.pdf.

33. "Clay County, Oak Ridge Manor and Justice Statue," Mrs. Sam Ray Postcard Collection (SC58). Missouri Valley Special Collections, Kansas City Public Library.

34. Quoted in Charles Ferruzza, "Roadhouse Blues," *KC Pitch*, December 19, 2002, http://www.pitch.com/kansascity/roadhouse-blues/Content?oid=2167742.

35. Ibid.

36. Lisa Chism, "Stroud's: Legendary Chicken and More," *Herlife Magazine*, November 2014, http://herlifemagazine.com/kansascity/cravings/strouds-legendary-chicken-and-more/; John T. Edge, *Fried Chicken: An American Story* (New York: Penguin, 2004), 143–45; "Fans Say There Are Few Rivals to Helen Stroud's Fried Chicken," *Kansas City Times*, June 16, 1972.

37. Michael Braude, "Stroud's Remains a Fried Piece of Heaven," *Kansas City Business Journal* (November 29, 2009), http://www.bizjournals.com/kansascity/stories/2009/11/30/editorial3.html.

38. Quoted in "Fans Say There Are Few Rivals to Helen Stroud's Fried Chicken," *Kansas City Times*, June 16, 1972.

39. James Shortridge, *Kansas City and How It Grew, 1822–2014*, 85.

40. Joseph William (Bill) Gilbert, interview with the author, April 24, 2015.

CHAPTER 8. KANSAS CITY HOME COOKS AND HOMEGROWN FESTIVALS

1. Stephen Fried, *Appetite for America: How Visionary Businessman, Fred Harvey Built a Railroad Hospitality Empire*, 231, 296.

2. Father Bernard Donnelly, *Scattered Sheets: Reminiscences of Father Bernard Donnelly*, 30.

3. Ibid., 69.

4. Jerena East Giffen, "'Add a Pinch and a Lump': Missouri Women in the 1820s," *Missouri Historical Review* 65, no. 4 (1971): 479.

5. Ibid., 482.

6. Charles van Ravenswaay, "Missouri Cookery," *Bulletin of the Missouri Historical Society*, 54.

7. Quoted in Jerena East Giffen, "'Add a Pinch and a Lump': Missouri Women in the 1820s," 479.

8. Charles van Ravenswaay, "Missouri Cookery," 54.

9. Ibid, 54.

10. Jerena East Griffen, "'Add a Pinch and a Lump': Missouri Women in the 1820s," 494–95.

11. Charles van Ravenswaay, "Missouri Cookery," *Bulletin of the Missouri Historical Society*, 54.

12. Nicholas Perkins Hardeman, *Shucks, Shocks, and Hominy Blocks: Corn as a Way of Life in Pioneer America* (Baton Rouge: Louisiana State University Press, 1981), 127–28.

13. Jerena East Giffen, "'Add a Pinch and a Lump': Missouri Women in the 1820s," 501.

14. Carrie Westlake Whitney, *Kansas City, Missouri: Its History and Its People 1808–1908*, I: 648.

15. Dorothy J. Caldwell, "Christmas in Early Missouri," *Missouri Historical Review*, 135; *National Register of Historic Places Nomination Form*, U.S. Department of the Interior Multiple Property Documentation Form, Dr. James Compton Residence, January 23, 1979, http://dnr.mo.gov/shpo/nps-nr/79003677.pdf.

16. Dorothy Brandt Marra, Marie-Laure Dionne Pal, and David Bourtros, eds., *Cher Oncle, Cher Papa: The Letters of Francois and Berenice Chouteau*, 183.

17. *National Register of Historic Places*, U.S. Department of the Interior Multiple Property Documentation Form, "Quality Hill," September 1977, http://dnr.mo.gov/shpo/nps-nr/78001657.pdf.

18. Quoted in Gilbert J. Garraghan, *Catholic Beginnings in Kansas City, Missouri: An Historical Sketch*, 118.

19. Carrie Westlake Whitney, *Kansas City, Missouri: Its History and Its People 1808–1908*, 1: 217–19.

20. John Dawson, "Public Notice of Shannon's Hotel, *The Enterprise*, Oct. 27, 1855," *The Jarboes and Shannons in Early Kansas City*, August 27, 2013, http://pinecountyherald.blogspot.com/2013/08/the-jarboes-and-shannons-in-early.html.

21. Niel M. Johnson, "Swedes in Kansas City: Selected Highlights of Their History," *Swedish-American Historical Quarterly* 43, no. 1 (1992): 34–35.

22. Ibid., 35–37; "To Rent-Rooms," Classified Advertisements, *Kansas City Journal*, November 19, 1899.

23. Quoted in Theodore A. Brown, *Frontier Community: Kansas City to 1870* (Columbia: University of Missouri Press, 1963), 101.

24. Felicia Hardison Londré, *The Enchanted Years of the Stage: Kansas City at the Crossroads of American Theater, 1870–1930*, 32–33.

25. Ibid., 32–33.

26. Rose Georgina Kingsley, *South by West, or Winter in the Rocky Mountains and Spring in Mexico* (London: W. Isbister & Co., 1874), 33.

27. James R. Shortridge, *Kansas City and How It Grew, 1822–2011*, 68–69.

28. *Our Own Cook Book, Woman's City Club of Kansas City Missouri*, compiled and arranged by Mrs. James M. Coburn (Kansas City: Spencer Printing Co., 1920).

29. Quoted in James R. Shortridge, *Kansas City and How It Grew, 1822–2014*, 70.

30. James R. Shortridge, *Kansas City and How It Grew, 1822–2014*, 84–85.

31. Quoted in A. B. MacDonald, "A Home District Beautiful," *Ladies' Home Journal*, February 1921, 23.

32. A. B. MacDonald, "A Home District Beautiful," *Ladies' Home Journal*, 82, 84.

33. Doug Worgul, *A Table Full of Welcome: A Cookbook Celebrating Kansas City's Culinary Diversity* (Kansas City: Kansas City Star Books, 2002), 77.

34. Quoted in Doug Worgul, *A Table Full of Welcome*, 82.

35. Ibid., 125, 131.

36. *National Register of Historic Places*, United States Department of the Interior, Multiple Property Documentation Form, "Residential Structures in Kansas City by Mary Rockwell Hook," August 9, 1983, http://dnr.mo.gov/shpo/nps-nr/64000399.pdf.

37. Ibid.

38. *Company's Coming: Foods for Entertaining Friends and Family* (Kansas City, MO: Junior League of Kansas City, Missouri, 1975), 12.

39. *Memories Good Enough to Eat* (Kansas City, MO: Temple B'nai Jehudah, B'nai Sisterhood [1970]), 3.

40. Ibid., 3, 13.

41. Ibid., 3, 10, 12.

42. Judith Fertig, interview with the author, February 22, 2015.

43. *Memories Good Enough to Eat*, 2.

44. *Priscilla Art Cook Book of the First Lutheran Church* (Kansas City, MO: Spangler, 1948), 3.

45. Ibid., 5.

46. Margaret Siggillino, "1960s," in Sherri Liberman, ed., *American Food by the Decades* (Santa Barbara: Greenwood/ABC-Clio, 2011), 165.

47. Inez Yeargan Kaiser, "Introduction," *Soul Food Cookery* (New York: Pitman Publishing, rev. ed. 1968).

48. Inez Yeargan Kaiser, *Soul Food Cookery*, n.p.

49. Patrick O'Neill, *From the Bottom Up: The Story of the Irish in Kansas City* (Kansas City: Seat O'the Pants Publishing, 2000), 139.

50. "Advice from the Superfans," Tailgating at Arrowhead, *Visit Kansas City*, Kansas City Convention and Visitors Association, 2015, https://www.visitkc.com/.

51. Ibid.

52. "History of the Kansas City Barbecue Society," *Kansas City Barbecue Society*, 2015, http://www.kcbs.us/index.php.

CHAPTER 9. WE'VE GROWN ACCUSTOMED TO THESE TASTES: KANSAS CITY'S SIGNATURE DISHES

1. Bonjwing Lee, "The Burnt Ends of Kansas City: A Guided Tour," *Eater*, July 8, 2014, http://www.eater.com/2014/7/8/6194903/the-burnt-ends-of-kansas

-city-a-guided-tour; Karen Adler and Judith M. Fertig, *The BBQ Queens' Big Book of BBQ* (Boston: Harvard Common Press, 2005), 357.

2. Heather N. Paxton, *The American Royal, 1899–1999* (Kansas City: BkMk Press/University of Missouri-Kansas City, 1999), 32.

3. The most exhaustive discussion I have come across over the history of the Delmonico and New York strip, along with a discussion of the changing meaning of the word "sirloin," is found in Joe O'Connell's "Delmonico Steak: A Mystery Solved," November 30, 2003, updated August 19, 2011, *Steak Perfection*, http://www.steakperfection.com/delmonico/Steak.html.

4. Jimmy M. Skaggs, *Prime Cut: Livestock Raising and Meatpacking in the United States, 1607–1983* (College Station: Texas A&M University, 1986), 94.

5. Heather N. Paxton, *The American Royal, 1899–1999*, 32.

6. *Art's Mexican Food Products*, 2015, http://www.artsmexicanfoodproducts.com.

7. Jasper Mirabile Jr., "On the Apple Trail," *435: Kansas City's Magazine*, October 2012, http://www.435mag.com/October-2012/On-the-Apple-Trail/.

8. David Conrads, "Biography of Myron Green (1876–1953), Restaurateur," Missouri Valley Special Collections, Kansas City Public Library, 1999, http://www.kchistory.org/cdm4/item_viewer.php?CISOROOT=/Biographies&CISOPTR=71&CISOBOX=1&REC=1.

9. Famous Green Parrot Recipes, *Vintage Kansas City*, http://www.vintagekansascity.com/food-and-drink/greenparrotinn/mrsjbdowd.html.

10. John Herbst, "Green Parrot Inn Was 'The Place' to Eat Fried Chicken," *Jackson County Historical Society Journal* 39 (1999): 5; "Green Parrot Inn," clipping from the *Kansas City Times*, February 1, 1975, Mrs. Sam Ray Postcard Collection (SC58), Missouri Valley Special Collections, Kansas City Public Library.

11. Eric Adler, "Ruby McIntyre Remembered for Soul Food Café, Dies at 95," *Kansas City Star*, May 14, 2015; "Ms. Ruby Lee Watson McIntyre, Feb. 18, 1920–May 12, 2015," obituary, Stephenson-Shaw Funeral Home, 2015.

12. Fred Philips, "Back-in-the-Day Feature: Ruby's Soul Food Café," December 23, 2014, *KC Food Guys: Reviewing KC's Best Eats*, http://www.kcfoodguys.com/rubys/.

13. Donnie Bowerman, e-mail to the author, May 15, 2015; Teresa Urban, Facebook post, *Past Patrons of Ruby's Soul Food Café*, May 15–16, 2015.

14. Mimi Sheraton, "Kansas City's Pied Piper of Chickendom," *New York Times*, May 18, 1980.

15. Colin Clarendon and Sylvia Clarendon, *Clarendon Guide to Kansas City Restaurants*, (Memphis: C & S Enterprises, 1982), 93.

16. Quoted in Mimi Sheraton, "Kansas City's Pied Piper of Chickendom," *New York Times*, May 18, 1980.

17. *Clarendon Guide to Kansas City Restaurants*, 122–23.

Bibliography

ARCHIVES CONSULTED

Missouri Valley Special Collections. Kansas City Public Library. Kansas City, Missouri.

Black Archives of Mid-America. Kansas City, Missouri.

Collections Department for the Fred Harvey Archives. Kansas City, Missouri: Union Station, the Kansas City Museum.

PRIMARY SOURCES

Andre's Confiserie Suisse, 2013. http://andreschocolates.com.

Art's Mexican Food Products, 2015. http://www.artsmexicanfoodproducts.com.

Boulevard Brewery, 2015. http://www.boulevard.com/.

Cascone's Italian Restaurants, 2014. http://www.cascones.com/.

Bradbury, John. *Travels in the Interior of America in the Years 1809, 1810, and 1811*. Liverpool: Smith and Galway, 1817.

Bureman, Lina. "Kansas City Homecoming." *Kansas City Stories, Local History*. Missouri Valley Special Collections, Kansas City Public Library, July 26, 2008. http://www.kclibrary.org/kchistory/kansas-city-homecoming.

Bushnell Jr., David Ives. *Villages of the Algonquin, Siouan, and Caddoan Tribes West of the Mississippi*. Smithsonian Institution. Bureau of American Ethnology. Bulletin 77. Washington, DC: Government Printing Office, 1922.

Cher Oncle, Cher Papa: The Letters of Francois and Berenice Chouteau. Dorothy Brandt Marra, Marie Laure Dionne Pal, and David Boutros, eds. Kansas City: Western Historical Manuscript Collection, 2001.

Clarendon, Colin, and Sylvia Clarendon. *Clarendon Guide to Kansas City Restaurants*, Memphis: C & S Enterprises, 1982.

"Club Reno, aka the Reno Club." *Club Kaycee. Kansas City Jazz History*. 1996. University of Missouri. Kansas City Library Special Collections. http://library .umkc.edu/spec-col/clubkaycee/JAZZSPOT/clubreno.htm.

Company's Coming: Foods for Entertaining Friends and Family. Kansas City, MO: Junior League of Kansas City, Missouri, 1975.

Connell Jr., Evan S. *Mr. Bridge*. New York: Alfred A. Knopf, 1969.

David Ball interview. Johnson County Community College, Overland Park, Kansas. June 7, 2010. YouTube.

Dawson, John. "Public notice of Shannon's Hotel, *The Enterprise*, Oct. 27, 1855." *The Jarboes and Shannons in Early Kansas City*. August 27, 2013. http://pine countyherald.blogspot.com/2013/08/the-jarboes-and-shannons-in-early.html.

"Death to Popular Barbecue Man, 60: Illness Fatal to Charles L. Bryant." *Kansas City Call*, October 17, 1952.

DeSmet, Pierre-Jean. *Life, Letters and Travels of Father Pierre-Jean DeSmet, S.J. 1801–1873*. 4 vols. New York: Francis P. Harper, 1905.

DiCapo, Carl J., John David DiCapo, and Frank R. Hayde. *Italian Gardens: A History of Kansas City through Its Favorite Restaurant*. Kansas City: privately printed, 2010.

Donnelly, Bernard. *Scattered Sheets: Reminiscences of Father Bernard Donnelly, as Transcribed by Miss Mary Hunter, 1877*. St. Joseph: Two Trails Press, 2001.

"Fans Say There Are Few Rivals to Helen Stroud's Fried Chicken." *Kansas City Times*, June 16, 1972.

Federal Writers' Project, *Missouri: Guide to the 'Show-Me' State*. New York: Duell, Sloan and Pearce, 1941.

Ferris, Jacob. *The States and Territories of the Great West*. New York: Miller, Orton, and Mulligan, 1856.

"Flood Crest Nears Missouri Capital." *New York Times*, July 18, 1951.

Flynn, Jane. *A Taste of Kansas City: Then and Now*. Kansas City: Children's Center for the Visually Impaired, 2003.

Fowler, Richard B. *Leaders in Our Town*. Kansas City: Burd & Fletcher, 1952.

Garraghan, Gilbert J. *Catholic Beginnings in Kansas City: An Historical Sketch*. Chicago: Loyola University Press, 1920.

Harris, Nellie McCoy. "Memories of Old Westport." *Annals of Kansas City* 1, no. 4 (1947), 465–75.

"Henry Perry Has Cooked Good Barbecue for 50 Years." *Kansas City Call*, February 26, 1932.

"Henry Perry, The Barbecue King Is Dead." *Kansas City Call*, March 29, 1940. *International Cooking Library*, 1–5 (1913). *Google Books*. Available

at https://books.google.com/books?id=ljkyAQAAMAAJ&pg=PA10&dq=Fr
ench+Chef+Adrian+Delvaux&hl=en&sa=X&ei=PcAWVZzbJ4ecgwTv9oG
4AQ&ved=0CDEQ6AEwAA#v=onepage&q=Adrian%20Delvaux&f=true.
Accessed April 21, 2015.

James, Edwin. *Account of an Expedition from Pittsburgh to the Rocky Mountains.*
2 vols. London: Longman, Hurst, Rees, Orme and Brown, 1828.

Jason, Donald. "Kansas City Vote Widens Bias Law." *New York Times*, April 8,
1964.

Kaiser, Inez Yeargan. *Soul Food Cookery*, rev. ed. New York: Pitman Publishing,
1968.

"The Kansas City Banquet." *Michigan Argonaut* 8, no. 26 (May 17, 1890):
220.

Kasper, Shirl. "All in the Family: A Third Generation of Krizmans Is Making
Sausage in KCK." *Kansas City Star Magazine*, June 2, 1996.

Kingsley, Rose Georgina. *South by West, or Winter in the Rocky Mountains and
Spring in Mexico.* London: W. Isbister & Co., 1874.

Krizman's House of Sausage, 2014. http://www.krizmansausage.com/.

Lewis, Meriwether, and William Clark. *The Journals of Lewis and Clark.* Edited
by Bernard DeVoto. New York: Houghton Mifflin Company, 1997.

MacDonald, A. B. "A Home District Beautiful." *Ladies' Home Journal*, February
1921.

Manny's Mexican Restaurant of Kansas City, 2013. http://www.mannyskc.com.

McAlister, C. R. "Flying Mail." *Flying Magazine*, May 1992.

McGonigle's. June 16, 2015. https://www.mcgonigles.com/.

Memories Good Enough to Eat. Kansas City: Temple B'nai Jehudah, B'nai Sisterhood [1970].

Mirabile Jr., Jasper. *Jasper's Kitchen Cookbook: Italian Recipes and Memories
from Kansas City's Legendary Restaurant.* Kansas City: Andrews McMeel
Publishing, 2009.

"Moving a Great Crop." *The Roller Mill* 16 (September 1897): 146–47.

National Register of Historic Places. U.S. Department of the Interior, Multiple
Property Documentation Form. "Dr. James Compton Residence," January 23,
1979. http://dnr.mo.gov/shpo/nps-nr/79003677.pdf.

National Register of Historic Places. U.S. Department of the Interior, Multiple
Property Documentation Form. "Historic Resources of the 18th and Vine Area of
Kansas City, Missouri," July 22, 1991. http://dnr.mo.gov/shpo/nps-nr/84004142
.pdf.

National Register of Historic Places. U.S. Department of the Interior, Multiple
Property Documentation Form. "Quality Hill," September 1977. http://dnr
.mo.gov/shpo/nps-nr/78001657.pdf.

National Register of Historic Places. U.S. Department of the Interior, Multiple Property Documentation Form. "Residential Structures in Kansas City by Mary Rockwell Hook," August 9, 1983. http://dnr.mo.gov/shpo/nps-nr/64000399.pdf.

O'Neil, Buck, with Steve Wulf and David Conrads. *I Was Right On Time: My Journey from the Negro Leagues to the Majors*. New York: Simon & Schuster, 1996.

Our Own Cook Book, Woman's City Club of Kansas City Missouri. Mrs. James M. Coburn, compiler. Kansas City: Spencer Printing Co., 1920.

Parkman, Francis, Jr., *The Oregon Trail*. Penguin Classics edition. New York: Penguin Books, 1982 [1847].

Peck, John Mason. *Forty Years a Pioneer: Memoir of John Mason Peck, D.D.* Edited by Rufus Babcock. Philadelphia: American Baptist Publication Society, 1864.

Priscilla Art Cook Book of the First Lutheran Church. Kansas City: Spangler, 1948.

Roma Bakery, 2004. http://www.romabakerykc.com.

Silva, Jill Wendholt. "Peter May's House of Kielbasa Is a Family Affair." *Kansas City Star*, May 5, 2014.

Social Prospectus of Kansas City, Missouri. Kansas City: Research Bureau of the Board of Public Welfare, 1913.

Spalding, Charles Carroll. *Annals of the Kansas of Kansas*. Kansas City: Van Horn & Abeel's Printing House, 1858.

"Surprise Sit-In at Restaurant: Owner Closes for Day after Quiet Demonstration." *Kansas City Times*, June 21, 1963.

"Tea House by the Side of the Road—9 East 45th." *Swing*, January 1945.

Tolson, Melvin B. *Caviar and Cabbage: Selected Columns by Melvin B. Tolson from the* Washington Tribune, *1937–1944*. Edited by Robert M. Farnsworth. Columbia: University of Missouri Press, 1982.

Trillin, Calvin. *Messages from My Father*. New York: Farrar, Straus and Giroux, 1996.

Trillin, Calvin. "No! One of the World's Foremost Authorities on Ribs, Cheeseburger, French Fries and Frosty Malts Takes a Gourmet Tour of Kansas City." *Playboy Magazine*, April 1972.

United States Geological Survey. *Kansas-Missouri Floods of July 1951*: *Water Supply Paper 1139*, 1952. http://pubs.usgs.gov/wsp/1139/report.pdf.

Whitney, Carrie Westlake. *Kansas City, Missouri: Its History and Its People 1808–1908*. 3 vols. Chicago: S. J. Clarke Publishing Co., 1908.

Wright, John Livingston. *Down the Road with a Tramp Writer, Poems*. Boston: Black Lion Press, 1909.

Young, William H., and Nathan B. Young Jr. *Your Kansas City and Mine*, repr. ed. with added index. Kansas City: Midwest Afro-American Genealogy Interest Coalition, 1997.

SECONDARY SOURCES

"About KC Chefs." *American Culinary Federation Greater Kansas City Chefs Association*, 2014–2015. http://acf.kcchefs.org/about-kc-chefs/.

Adler, Eric. "Ruby McIntyre Remembered for Soul Food Café, Dies at 95." *Kansas City Star*, May 14, 2015.

Adler, Karen, and Judith M. Fertig. *The BBQ Queens' Big Book of BBQ*. Boston: Harvard Common Press, 2005.

"Advice from the Superfans: Tailgating at Arrowhead." *Visit Kansas City*. Kansas City Convention and Visitors Association, 2015. https://www.visitkc.com/.

"African-American Historic Sites of Independence, Walking/Driving Tour. Independence, Missouri." *City of Independence, Missouri*, 2015. http://www .ci.independence.mo.us.

Alfs, Matthew. *Edible and Medicinal Wild Plants of the Midwest*. New Brighton, MN: Old Theology Book House, 2013.

Almond, Steve. *Candyfreak: A Journey through the Chocolate Underbelly of America*. Chapel Hill, NC: Algonquin Books, 2004.

"Ancient Times." *City of Riverside, Missouri*. http://www.riversidemo.com/com munity/page/ancient-times. Accessed February 12, 2015.

"Arthur E. Stilwell." Pullman State Historic Site, October 2009. *Pullman Museum*. http://www.pullman-museum.org/theCompany/stillwell.html.

"Asian Community in Kansas City." *Visit KC* (*Kansas City Convention & Visitors Association*), 2015. https://www.visitkc.com/visitors/discover/diversity/ asian-community-kansascity.

"Best Home-Grown Product: Wishbone Salad Dressing." Best of Kansas City, 2000. *KC Pitch*, 2015. http://www.pitch.com/kansascity/best-home-grown product/BestOf?oid=2209963.

Blackmar, Jeannette M., and Jack L. Hofman. "The Paleoarchaic of Kansas." In *Kansas Archaeology*. Edited by Robert J. Hoard and William E. Banks, 2006, 46–75.

Boone, Dennis. "All in the Family." *Ingram's Magazine*, 2000–2015. www .ingrams.com/article/all-in-the-family/.

Braude, Michael. "Stroud's Remains a Fried Piece of Heaven." *Kansas City Business Journal*, November 29, 2009. http://www.bizjournals.com/kansascity/stories/2009/11/30/editorial3.html.

Broadway, Michael J. "Meatpacking." In *Encyclopedia of the Great Plains*. Edited by David J. Wishart. Lincoln: University of Nebraska Press, 2004, 246.

Brown, Theodore A. *Frontier Community: Kansas City to 1870*. Columbia: University of Missouri Press,1963.

Burnes, Brian, Dan Viets, and Robert W. Butler. *Walt Disney's Missouri: The Roots of a Creative Genius*. Kansas City: Kansas City Star Books, 2002.

Burns, Louis F. *A History of the Osage People*. Tuscaloosa: University of Alabama Press, 2004.

Burns, Louis F. *Osage Indian Customs and Myths*. Tuscaloosa: University of Alabama Press, 2005.

Caldwell, Dorothy J. "Christmas in Early Missouri." *Missouri Historical Review* 65, no. 2 (1971): 125–38.

Cannon, Poppy, and Patricia Brooks. *The President's Cookbook: Practical Recipes from George Washington to the Present*. New York: Funk and Wagnalls, 1968.

"Centenario de Union Station Celebra Famoso Camareo" ["Union Station Centennial Celebrating Famed Waiter"]. *Dos Mundos*, October 2014.

Chism, Lisa. "Stroud's: Legendary Chicken and More." *Herlife Magazine*, November 2014. http://herlifemagazine.com/kansascity/cravings/strouds-legendary-chicken-and-more/.

Coleman, Daniel. "Arthur E. Stilwell, Railroad President, 1859–1928." Missouri Valley Special Collections, Kansas City Public Library, 2008. http://www.kchistory.org/cdm4/item_viewer.php?CISOROOT=/Biographies&CISOPTR=198&CISOBOX=1&REC=13.

Coleman, Daniel. "Biography of Charles E. Kearney (1820–1898), Outfitter." Missouri Valley Special Collections, Kansas City Public Library, 2008. http://www.kchistory.org/cdm4/item_viewer.php?CISOROOT=/Biographies&CISOPTR=244&CISOBOX=1&REC=1.

Coleman, Daniel. "Clara and Russell Stover, Candy Makers." Missouri Valley Special Collections. Kansas City Public Library, 2008. http://www.kchistory.org/cdm4/item_viewer.php?CISOROOT=/Biographies&CISOPTR=128&CISOBOX=1&REC=1.

Coleman, Daniel. "Fred Wolferman, Owner, Wolferman's Gourmet Grocery, 1870–1955." Missouri Valley Special Collections. Kansas City Public Library, 2008. http://www.kchistory.org/cdm4/item_viewer.php?CISOROOT=/Biographies&CISOPTR=273&CISOBOX=1&REC=3.

Conrads, David. "Biography of Myron Green (1876–1953), Restaurateur." Missouri Valley Special Collections. Kansas City Public Library, 1999. http://www.kchistory.org/cdm4/item_viewer.php?CISOROOT=/Biographies&CISO PTR=71&CISOBOX=1&REC=1.

Coulter, Charles. *"Take Up the Black Man's Burden": Kansas City's African American Communities, 1865–1939.* Columbia: University of Missouri Press, 2006.

Crouch, Stanley. *Kansas City Lightning: The Rise and Times of Charlie Parker.* New York: HarperCollins, 2013.

Davis, Ardie A. "McGonigle's: A Chow Town Icon Known for Its Meat, Barbecue." *Kansas City Star*, June 19, 2014.

Diner, Hasia R. *Hungering for America: Italian, Irish, and Jewish Foodways in the Age of Migration.* Cambridge: Harvard University Press, 2001.

Driggs, Frank, and Chuck Haddix. *Kansas City Jazz: From Ragtime to Bebop.* Oxford: Oxford University Press, 2005.

Edge, John T. *Fried Chicken: An American Story.* New York: Penguin, 2004.

Edwards, Tai S. "The Osage Struggle to Survive in the Nineteenth-Century Trans Missouri West." *Kansas History* 36 (Winter 2013–2014): 219–33.

Elie, Lolis Eric. *Smokestack Lightning: Adventures in the Heart of Barbecue Country.* New York: Farrar, Straus, and Giroux, 1996.

"The Farmer's Wheat, the Baker's Flour." *Heartland Mill*, 2010. http://www.heartlandmill.com/.

Ferruzza, Charles. "The End of a Restaurant Dynasty: Bob Gaines, 1951–2010." *KC Pitch*, August 11, 2010. http://www.pitch.com/FastPitch/archives/2010/08/11/the-end-of-a-restaurant-dynasty-bob-gaines-1951-2010.

Ferruzza, Charles. "Global Grub. " *KC Pitch*, May 24, 2006. http://www.pitch.com/kansascity/globalgrub/Content?oid=2185403.

Ferruzza, Charles. "Kansas City Loved Polynesian Cuisine—It Still Does." *KC Pitch*, November 4, 2014. http://www.pitch.com/FastPitch/archives/2014/11/04/kansas-city-loved-polynesian-cuisine-it-still-does.

Ferruzza, Charles. "King of Tamale." *KC Pitch,* July 5, 2001. http://www.pitch.com/kansascity/king-of-tamale/Content?oid=2163635.

Ferruzza, Charles. "Roadhouse Blues." *KC Pitch*, December 19, 2002. http://www.pitch.com/kansascity/roadhouse-blues/Content?oid=2167742.

Ferruzza, Charles. "A Sugar Binge." *KC Pitch*. November 9, 2006. http://www.pitch.com/kansascity/a-sugar-binge/Content?oid=2183594.

Ferruzza, Charles, and Jonathan Bender. "KC's Bakeries Turn Up the Flour Power." *KC Pitch*, May 15, 2012. http://www.pitch.com/kansascity/kansas-city-bakeries-artisan bread/Content?oid=2881235&showFullText=true.

Foley, William E. *The Genesis of Missouri: From Wilderness Outpost to Statehood.* Columbia: University of Missouri Press, 1989.

Foster, George H., and Peter C. Weiglin. *Harvey House Cookbook: Memories of Dining along the Santa Fe Railroad.* Lanham: Taylor Trade Publishing, imprint of Rowman & Littlefield, 1992.

Frank, Thomas. "A Machine for Forgetting: Kansas City and the Declining Significance of Place." *Baffler*, no. 7, 1995. http://www.thebaffler.com/salvos/a -machine-for-forgetting .

"Fred Wolferman's Kansas City Coffers Are Filled with Dough Thanks to His Mega Muffins." *People* Archive. *People*, March 17, 1986. http://www.people .com/people/archive/article/0,,20093183,00.html.

Fried, Stephen. *Appetite for America: How Visionary Businessman, Fred Harvey Built Railroad Hospitality Empire.* New York: Random House, 2011.

Gibson, Sonny, editor. *Kansas City Early Negro History.* Kansas City: Mecca Enterprises, 2014.

Giffen, Jerena East. "'Add a Pinch and a Lump' Missouri Women in the 1820s." *Missouri Historical Review* 65, no. 4 (1971): 478–504.

Gilmore, Melvin. *Uses of Plants by the Indians of the Missouri River Region.* Washington, DC: U.S. Government Printing Office, 1919.

Gitlin, Jay. *The Bourgeois Frontier: French Towns, French Traders, and American Expansionism.* New Haven: Yale University Press, 2010.

Glaab, Charles Nelson. *Kansas City and the Railroads: Community Policy in the Growth of a Regional Metropolis.* Lawrence: University of Kansas Press, 1993.

Grant, William D. *Romantic Past of the Kansas City Region, 1540–1880.* Kansas City: Business Men's Assurance Company of America, 1987.

Grattan, Virginia L. *Mary Coulter: Builder Upon the Red Earth.* Flagstaff: Grand Canyon Association, 1992.

Guenther Jr., Keith J. "The Development of Mexican-American Cuisine." *National and Regional Styles of Cookery: Proceedings. Oxford Symposium.* Edited by Alan Davidson. Oxford: Oxford University Press, 1981, 262–85.

Hardeman, Nicholas Perkins. *Shucks, Shocks, and Hominy Blocks: Corn as a Way of Life in Pioneer America.* Baton Rouge: Louisiana State University Press, 1981.

Haward, Rosemary. "Candy from Kansas City." *Swing*, November 1947.

Herbst, John. "Green Parrot Inn Was 'The Place' to Eat Fried Chicken." *Jackson County Historical Society Journal* 39 (1999): 5.

"Hereford History." *American Hereford Association*, 2015. http://hereford.org/ node/47 .

"History of the Kansas City Barbecue Society." *Kansas City Barbecue Society*, 2015. http://www.kcbs.us/index.php.

Hoard, Robert J., and William E. Banks, editors. *Kansas Archaeology.* Lawrence: University of Kansas Press, 2006.

Hoedel, Cindy. "Remembering the Day 'Everything Changed.'" *Kansas City Star,* June 28, 2014. http://www.kansascity.com/news/special-reports/civil-rights-act -turns-50/article614480.html.

Hoffhaus, Charles E. *Chez les Canses: Three Centuries at Kawsmouth, the French Foundations of Metropolitan Kansas City.* Kansas City: Lowell Press, 1984.

Honig, Louis O. *Westport: Gateway to the Early West.* North Kansas City: Industrial Press, 1950.

Inness, Sherrie A. *Dinner Roles: American Women and Culinary Culture.* Ames: University of Iowa Press, 2001.

Johannessen, Sissel. "Farmers of the Late Woodland." In *Foraging and Farming in the Eastern Woodlands.* Edited by C. Margaret Scarry. Gainesville: University of Florida Press, 1993.

Johnson, Niel M. "Swedes in Kansas City: Selected Highlights of Their History." *Swedish-American Historical Quarterly* 43, no. 1 (1992): 19–39.

Kansas City: An Intimate Portrait of the Surprising City on the Missouri. Kansas City: Hallmark Cards, 1973.

Kansas City Memories . . . Vintage Photos, Places, and Things Remembered. Facebook Group.

LaMartina, Jerry. "Balls Food Stores Will Beef Up Hen House Website." *Kansas City Business Journal,* April 15, 2008.

Lanterman, Alice. "Development of Kansas City as a Grain and Milling Center." *Missouri Historical Review* 42, no. 1 (1947): 20–33.

Lee, Bonjwing. "The Burnt Ends of Kansas City: A Guided Tour." *Eater,* July 8, 2014. http://www.eater.com/2014/7/8/6194903/the-burnt-ends-of-kansas-city-a -guided-tour.

Lehatto, Jaquie. "Resolve, Refinement Central to Her: Dora Adelman, Owner of the Wishbone Restaurant." *Kansas City Star,* November 27, 2007.

Ling, Huping. *Chinese St. Louis: From Enclave to Cultural Community.* Philadelphia: Temple University Press, 2004.

Little, Leigh Ann, and John M. Olinskey. *Early Kansas City, Missouri.* Charleston, SC: Arcadia Press, 2013.

Ljungblad, Tammy. "Strawberry Hill Povitica Breads." *KansasCityStarVideo.* YouTube, May 4, 2014.

Logan, Brad. "Woodland Adaptations in Eastern Kansas." In *Kansas Archaeology.* Edited by Robert J. Hoard and William E. Banks, 76–92. Lawrence: University Press of Kansas, 2006.

Londré, Felicia Hardison. *The Enchanted Years of the Stage: Kansas City at the Crossroads of American Theater, 1870–1930.* Columbia: University of Missouri Press, 2007.

Lowie, Robert H. *Indians of the Plains*. Lincoln: University of Nebraska Press, 1982.

Mariani, John. *America Eats Out: An Illustrated History of Restaurants, Taverns, Coffee Shops, Speakeasies, and Other Establishments That Have Fed Us for 350 Years*. New York: William Morrow, 1991.

Mariani, John. *How Italian Food Conquered the World*. New York: Palgrave Macmillan, 2011.

Marshall, James. "The Kansa." In *Kansas Archaeology*. Edited by Robert J. Hoard and William E. Banks, 2006, 219–32.

Martin, Terrell L. "Prehistoric Settlement of Western Missouri during the Mississippian Period." *Missouri Archaeologist* 68 (2007): 1–28.

Maxwell, James H., and Bob Sullivan Jr. *Hometown Beer: A History of Kansas City Breweries*. Kansas City: Omega Innovative Marketing, 1999.

Miller, Patricia Cleary. *Westport: Missouri's Port of Many Returns*. Kansas City: Lowell Press, 1983.

Mirabile Jr., Jasper. "On the Apple Trail." *435: Kansas City's Magazine*, October 2012. http://www.435mag.com/October-2012/On-the-Apple-Trail/.

Miriani, Ronald. *Kansas City's City Market*. Kansas City: Kansas City Public Library, 2007.

Montgomery, Rick, and Shirl Kasper. *Kansas City: An American Story*. Kansas City: Kansas City Star Books, 1999.

Nolen, Rose M. *Hoecakes, Hambone, and All That Jazz: African American Traditions in Missouri*. Columbia: University of Missouri Press, 2003.

O'Brien, Michael J., and W. Raymond Wood. *Prehistory of Missouri*. Columbia: University of Missouri Press, 1998.

O'Brien, Patricia J., and Frances B. King. "The Yeo Site (23CL199): A Kansas City Hopewell Limited Activity Site in Northwestern Missouri and Some Theories." *Plains Anthropologist* 27 (1982): 37–56.

O'Connell, Joe. "Delmonico Steak: A Mystery Solved." November 30, 2003, updated 2011. *Steak Perfection*. http://www.steakperfection.com/delmonico/Steak.html.

O'Malley, Terence. "Black Hand Strawman: The History of Organized Crime in Kansas City." Lecture, Kansas City Public Library, Kansas City, MO, January 15, 2012.

One Hundred Years of Brewing: A Complete History of the Progress Made in the Art, Science and Industry of Brewing. Chicago: H. S. Rich & Company, 1901.

O'Neill, Patrick. *From the Bottom Up: The Story of the Irish in Kansas City*. Kansas City: Seat O'the Pants Publishing, 2000.

Past Patrons of Ruby's Soul Food Café. Facebook Group.

Paxton, Heather N. *The American Royal, 1899–1999*. Kansas City: BkMkPress/ University of Missouri–Kansas City, 1999.

Pearson Jr., Nathan W. *Goin' to Kansas City*. Urbana: University of Illinois Press, 1987.

Philips, Fred. "Back-In-The-Day Feature: Ruby's Soul Food Café." December 23, 2014. *KC Food Guys: Reviewing KC's Best Eats*. http://www.kcfoodguys .com/rubys/.

Pinney, Thomas. *A History of Wine in America: From Prohibition to the Present*. Berkeley: University of California Press, 1989.

Porter, Steve. "Hen House to Get on the Ball, Ball's Super Stores, That Is." *Kansas City Business Journal*, August 21, 1989.

Price, Pat. "Old Restaurants Never Die: Famous Flavors Capture Dining Pleasures of Bygone Restaurants." *Kansas City Star*, February 3, 1999, metropolitan edition.

Reddig, William R. *Tom's Town: Kansas City and the Pendergast Legend*. Columbia: University of Missouri Press, 1986.

Rhodes, Richard. "Cupcake Land. Requiem for the Midwest in the Key of Vanilla." *Harpers*, November 1986. *Harper's Archive*. http://harpers.org/archive/1987/11/ cupcake-land-requiem-for-the-midwestin-the-key-of-vanilla/.

Roe, Jason. "Muffin Man." *This Week in Kansas City History*. Kansas City Public Library. http://www.kclibrary.org/blog/week-kansas-city-history/muffin-man.

Roper, Donna C. "The Central Plains Tradition." In *Kansas Archaeology*. Edited by Robert J. Hoard and William E. Banks, 2006, 105–32.

Russell, Ross. *Bird Lives: The High Life and Hard Times of Charlie (Yardbird) Parker*. Reprt. ed. Jackson, TN: Da Capo Press, 1996.

Russell, Ross. *Jazz Style in Kansas City and the Southwest*. Berkeley: University of California Press, 1971.

Sax, David. *Save the Deli: In Search of Perfect Pastrami, Crusty Rye, and the Heart of Jewish Delicatessen*. Toronto: McClelland and Stewart, 2009.

Schauffler, Edward R. "Westport's No. 1 Romance." *Swing*, November 1945.

Schirmer, Sherry Lamb. *A City Divided: The Racial Landscape of Kansas City, 1900–1960*. Columbia: University of Missouri Press, 2002.

Serda, Daniel. "Finding Latin Roots: Hispanic Heritage in Kansas City." *Kansas Preservation* 33, no. 3 (2011): 8–15.

Shannon, William V. *The American Irish: A Political and Social Portrait*. Amherst: University of Massachusetts Press, 1989.

Sheraton, Mimi. "Kansas City's Pied Piper of Chickendom." *New York Times*, May 18, 1980.

Shortridge, James, *Kansas City and How It Grew, 1822–2011*. Lawrence: University of Kansas Press, 2012.

Siggillino, Margaret. "1960s." Edited by Sherri Liberman. *American Food by the Decades*, Santa Barbara: Greenwood/ABC-Clio, 2011: 146–71.

Skaggs, Jimmy M., *Prime Cut: Livestock Raising and Meatpacking in the United States, 1607–1983.* College Station: Texas A&M University Press, 1986.

Smith, Joyce. "Ball's Grocery Chain Plans Local Expansion." *Kansas City Star*, July 2, 1998.

Smith, Joyce. "Cascone's Remains a North Oak Landmark." *Kansas City Star*, 816 Business section, December 23, 2014.

Smith, Joyce. "Scimeca's Market Has a New Name." *Kansas City Star*, November 30, 2001.

Star Magazine Presents: The Best of Remember When: 100 Warm Tales of Life as We Lived It. Edited by Rhonda Cornelius. Kansas City: Kansas City Star Books, 2001.

Staten, Vince, and Greg Johnson. *Real Barbecue: The Classic Barbecue Guide to the Best Joints Across the USA.* Lanham, MD: Rowman & Littlefield, 2007.

"Stover, Clara (1893–1975); Stover, Russell (1888–1954)." *Dictionary of Missouri Biography*. Edited by Lawrence O. Christensen, et al. Columbia: University of Missouri Press, 1999, 728–29.

Things and Places We Loved in Greater KC When We Were Much Younger. Facebook Group.

"Thomas Joseph Pendergast (1872–1945)." *Historical Society of Missouri, Historic Missourians*. University of Missouri. http://shs.umsystem.edu/historic missourians/name/p/pendergast/.

Thorne, Tanis C. *The Many Hands of My Relations: French and Indians on the Lower Missouri.* Columbia: University of Missouri Press, 1996.

"Tours of Historic Westport." Westport Historical Society. http://westporthistorical.com/.

Unrau, William E. *The Kansa Indians: A History of the Wind People, 1673–1873.* Norman: University of Oklahoma Press, 1986.

Van Kirk, Sylvia. *Many Tender Ties: Women in Fur-Trade Society, 1670–1870.* Norman: Oklahoma University Press, 1983.

Van Ravenswaay, Charles. "Missouri Cookery." *Bulletin of the Missouri Historical Society* 3 (1946–1947): 53–59.

"Virtual Jewish World: Kansas City, Kansas/Missouri." *Jewish Virtual Library*, 2015. http://www.jewishvirtuallibrary.org/jsource/vjw/kansascity.html.

Wagner, Tricia Martineau. *It Happened on the Oregon Trail: Remarkable Events That Shape History,* 2nd ed. Guilford, CT: Globe Pequot Press, 2014.

Washington, Barbara A. "Ball's Tries New Hen House Concept in Johnson County." *Kansas City Business Journal*, September 24, 1990.

Wedel, Rudolph Waldo. *Prehistoric Man on the Great Plains*. Norman, OK: University of Oklahoma Press, 1961.

Whitaker, Jan. *Tea at the Blue Lantern Inn: A Social History of the Tea Room Craze in America*. New York: St. Martin's Press, 2002.

"The Wish-Bone Story." Wish-Bone, 2013–2015. http://www.wish-bone.com.

Wohleking, Walter. "From Research to Model: The Stilwell Oyster Car." *The Cannonball* 44, no. 3 (2014): 1–5.

Wolferman, Kristie C. *The Osage in Missouri*. Columbia: University of Missouri Press, 1997.

Worgul, Doug. *The Grand Barbecue: A Celebration of the History, Places, Personalities and Techniques of Kansas City Barbecue*. Kansas City: Kansas City Star Books, 2001.

Worgul, Doug. *A Table Full of Welcome: A Cookbook Celebrating Kansas City's Culinary Diversity*. Kansas City: Kansas City Star Books, 2002.

Yanovsky, Elias. *Food Plants of the North American Indians*. U.S. Department of Agriculture, Misc. Pub. no. 237. Washington, DC, July 1936.

Young, Kay. *Wild Seasons: Gathering and Cooking Wild Plants of the Great Plains*. Lincoln: University of Nebraska Press, 1993.

Index

Christmas, 58, 63, 73, 83, 107
City Beautiful Movement, 157
City Market, 72–73, 78, 108, 115. *See also* farmers' markets
Civil War, American, 10, 65, 86, 106. *See also* Border Wars
Clay County, Missouri, 108, 142, 153
Clarendon, Colin, 182, 184. *See also* restaurants, guidebooks
Clarendon, Sylvia, 182, 184. *See also* restaurants, guidebooks
Clark, William. *See* Corps of Discovery
Coates House Hotel, 123, 156
Coates, Kersey, 123–26, 156, 161
Coates Opera House, 124, 156
Coates, Sarah, 123–26, 156, 161
cold storage and refrigeration, 10, 109, 110. *See also* transportation
Colony Steak House. *See* Ralph Gaines Colony Steak House
Colorado, 50
Committee on the Practice of Democracy (COPOD), 100. *See also* African Americans
Compton, James, 142, 153. *See also* Sandy's Oak Ridge Manor Tea House; Stroud's North
Compton, Mary Ann, 142, 153
Connaught Town. *See* Irish
Connell, Evan S., 85–86
cookbooks, 34, 84–85, 86, 141, 162, 164, 210; *Above and Beyond Parsley*, 162; *Beyond Parsley*, 162; *Company's Coming*, 162; *Food Fit for the Gods*, 166; "Guadalupe Center" ms. cookbook, 164; *Harvey House Cookbook*, 206n22; *Memories Good Enough to Eat*, 163; *Our Favorite Recipes*,

157; *Our Own Cook Book*, 157; *Priscilla Art Cook Book*, 165; *Soul Food Cookery*, 89, 165; *A Table Full of Welcome*, 160
Coon-Sanders Original Nighthawk Orchestra, 128. *See also* Muehlebach Hotel
Corner Cafe, 178
Corps of Discovery, 81–82
Coulter, Mary, 134–35
Count Basie Orchestra, 94
Country Club Plaza, 78, 139, 140, 146–47, 158, 178. *See also* Nichols, J. C.
Creole. *See* French and French Creole
Crouch, Stanley, 95
Crossroads District, 19, 148

Dairy Farmers of America, 18
Deans of Swing, 93. *See also* Parker, Charlie "Yardbird"
delicatessens, 113, 171
department stores, 96, 100, 118, 139, 146
DiCapo, Carl J., 78, 130–32
Dillingham, Jay, 130
Diner, Hasia R., 73
dining: al fresco, 153, 161–65, 181; entertaining, 87, 99, 162, 161, 163–64, 167, 169, 170, 187; holidays, 83, 85, 89, 175; at home, 83–84, 86, 99, 153, 169, 175; picnics, 81, 162, 167; Saturday night/rent suppers, 94–95; tailgating, 167–68. *See also* hospitality
Dinner Horn Restaurant, 140
Directory of Colored Residents: Kansas City, Missouri, 1937–38, 98
Disney, Walt, 66

About the Author

Andrea Broomfield is a culinary historian and an English professor at Johnson County Community College. She is the author of *Food and Cooking in Victorian England: A History* (2007) and writes extensively about the Victorian era.